'NEW' INSTRUMENTS OF ENVIRONMENTAL GOVERNANCE?
National Experiences and Prospects

Of Related Interest

GREEN PARTIES IN NATIONAL GOVERNMENTS
edited by Ferdinand Müller-Rommel and Thomas Poguntke

ECOLOGICAL MODERNISATION AROUND THE WORLD
Perspectives and Critical Debates
edited by Arthur P.J. Mol and David A. Sonnenfeld

ENVIRONMENTAL MOVEMENTS
Local, National and Global
edited by Christopher Rootes

DILEMMAS OF TRANSITION
The Environment, Democracy and Economic Reform in
East Central Europe
edited by Susan Baker and Petr Jehlička

POLITICAL THEORY AND THE ENVIRONMENT
A Reassessment
edited by Mathew Humphrey

'NEW' INSTRUMENTS OF ENVIRONMENTAL GOVERNANCE?
National Experiences and Prospects

Editors

ANDREW JORDAN
RÜDIGER K.W. WURZEL
ANTHONY R. ZITO

FRANK CASS
LONDON • PORTLAND, OR

First published in 2003 in Great Britain by
FRANK CASS PUBLISHERS
Crown House, 47 Chase Side,
London, N14 5BP, England

and in the United States of America by
FRANK CASS PUBLISHERS
c/o ISBS
920 NE 58th Avenue, Suite 300
Portland, Oregon 97213-3786

Website: www.frankcass.com

British Library Cataloguing in Publication Data

New instruments of environmental governance: national
experiences and prospects. – (Environmental politics; v.
12, no. 1: Spring 2003)
1. Environmental policy
I. Jordan, Andrew, 1968– II. Wurzel, Rudiger III. Zito,
Anthony R., 1966– IV. Environmental politics
363.7'056

ISBN 0 7146 5366 7 (cloth)
ISBN 0 7146 8300 0 (paper)

Library of Congress Cataloging in Publication Data

'New' instruments of environmental governance : national experiences and
prospects / editors, Andrew Jordan, Ruediger K.W. Wurzel, Anthony R.
Zito.
     p. cm.
Includes bibliographical references and index.
   ISBN 0-7146-5366-7 — ISBN 0-7146-8300-0 (pbk.)
   1. Environmental policy. I. Jordan, Andrew, 1968- II. Wurzel,
Ruediger. III. Zito, Anthony R., 1966- IV. Title.
   GE170.N49 2003
   363.7'056—dc21

                                                            2003004134

This group of studies first appeared in a Special Issue: '"New" Instruments of Environmental
Governance? National Experiences and Prospects' of *Environmental Politics* (ISSN 0964-4016)
12/1 Spring 2003 published by Frank Cass.

Printed in Great Britain by
Antony Rowe Ltd., Chippenham, Wilts.

Contents

COMPARATIVE CONCLUSIONS

Acknowledgements

Earlier versions of most of the contributions in this volume were presented as papers at a European Consortium for Political Research (ECPR) workshop held at the annual joint sessions in Grenoble 2001. We are grateful to the ECPR for providing us with an opportunity to meet together over the course of a few days and discuss the themes raised in the papers. The joint sessions are a unique and hugely effective institution: long may they continue! By making some important changes to our original workshop proposal, Chris Rootes improved our chances of being selected by the ECPR. Mention should also be made of Brendan Flynn, who eagerly accepted our invitation to join the writing team at a later stage; we are grateful for his co-operation. Our own participation was generously funded by an Economic and Social Research Council (ESRC) Future Governance Programme grant (L216252013) under a project on 'Innovation in Environmental Governance: A Comparative Analysis of New Environmental Policy Instruments'.[1]

All the papers were extensively edited several times after the workshop to fit a standard template. In most cases the authors ended up writing completely new papers. We hope that our strong editorial hand and their hard work have lent the whole volume a level of internal coherence than is absent from many edited volumes. If we have succeeded in this endeavour, a large vote of thanks is owed to the authors, who responded to our editorial queries efficiently and, above all, graciously.

Finally, we owe a debt of gratitude to Neil Carter for endorsing the project at a very early stage and for commenting on several of the papers.

ANDREW JORDAN,
RÜDIGER K.W. WURZEL
ANTHONY R. ZITO

NOTE

1. For more information see: http://www.uea.ac.uk/env/cserge/research/fut_governance/Home.htm.

Acknowledgements

INTRODUCTION

'New' Instruments of Environmental Governance: Patterns and Pathways of Change

ANDREW JORDAN, RÜDIGER K.W.WURZEL and
ANTHONY R. ZITO

The deployment of 'new' environmental policy instruments (NEPIs), namely eco-taxes and other market-based instruments (MBIs), voluntary agreements (VAs) and informational devices such as eco-labels, has grown spectacularly in recent years. In 1987, the Organisation for Economic Cooperation and Development (OECD) [*OECD, 1994: 177*] reported that most national environmental policies still relied upon a regulatory or 'command and control' mode of action, but since then the number of MBIs has grown 'substantially' [*CEC, 2000: 2*]. Some estimates put the growth in use in OECD countries at over 50 per cent between 1989 and 1995 [*CEC,_2000: 2*]. Daugbjerg and Svendson [*2001: 3*] have estimated that the number of environmental taxes in OECD countries grew from just 30 in 1987 to over 110 in 1997. Environmental taxes are now a mainstay of the national budgeting process, accounting for around seven per cent of total government revenues in 2002.

VAs, too, are becoming much more popular. In 1997, the European Environment Agency (EEA) [*EEA, 1997*] put the total in the European Union (EU) 15 at around 300, with more and more being signed each year. Outside of France, the Netherlands and to a lesser degree Germany, there were virtually no VAs in use in the early 1970s; most countries relied upon issuing regulations to manage the relationship between society, the economy and the environment. Finally, within the EU 15, the number of industrial sites subject to eco-management and auditing systems(EMAS) has risen from zero to over 4,000 in just six years. EMAS, a set of voluntary environmental management standards which firms can choose to adopt, gives consumers more environmental information about how industry operates.

The research underpinning this study was undertaken for a project entitled 'Innovation in Environmental Governance: A Comparative Analysis of New Environmental Policy Instruments' which was generously funded by the Economic and Social Research Council's (ESRC) Future Governance Programme under grant number L216252013. For more details see: http://www.uea.ac.uk/env/cserge/research/fut_governance/Home.htm.

This shift is not, of course, confined to the EU Member States. Golub [*1998a, xiii*] suggests that the eagerness to extend the conventional toolbox of environmental management is producing a 'fundamental transition' in environmental policy the world over. In Japan, one (conservative) estimate put the total number of VAs at around 30,000 [*Andrews et al., 2001: 10*]. The US Environmental Protection Agency (USEPA) recently conducted an audit and discovered 'an enormous number' at the federal and state level, with 'literally thousands' at the sub-state level [*USEPA, 2001: 23, 85*]. The sheer diversity of instruments now employed in the USA, the report continued, is also 'remarkable' [*ibid.: ix*]. The USEPA [*ibid.: iv*] concluded that the growing popularity of NEPIs represents 'one of the most remarkable developments in environmental management over the past decade'.

New Instruments: A Revolution or an Evolution in Environmental Management?

Clearly, something is happening, but what is the long-term significance of the growing popularity of NEPIs? It is undeniably true that the total number and diversity of environmental policy instruments has grown, in some countries stunningly fast. However, there are still two aspects of the shift to using 'new' environmental policy instruments, which remain curiously under-researched. The first is how 'new' are they? The *Oxford English Dictionary* defines new as 'novel', 'not existing before', 'strange or unfamiliar', 'starting afresh', 'restored or renewed after decay'. 'New' is therefore a relative term; it has to be related in some way or another to what came before, which in our case, are regulatory instruments. However, we already know that regulatory instruments differ in the way they are calibrated and implemented from one country to the next, so what may be a 'new' environmental policy instrument in one country, may already be part of established practice in another. In other words, what is or is not 'new' is properly a matter for detailed empirical comparative and historical investigation, which traces current patterns back along their historical pathways of change.

The second relates to the comparative politics of their adoption and use. The existing literature tends to be dominated by three types of publication: (1) broad surveys of specific types of instruments (undertaken by international bodies such as the EEA and the OECD); (2) case studies of a specific type of instrument in a small selection of sectors and/or countries; and (3) broad surveys of countries. These publications tend to advocate one type of instrument (often using highly theoretical models), describe 'best practice' or simply classify NEPIs using different typologies. Of the studies that have tried to investigate the broader patterns of use for different sub-types of NEPIs, most bring together an inconsistent mix of instruments or sectors [*Andersen and Sprenger, 2000; Dente, 1995; Golub, 1998a; Knill and Lenschow, 2000*]. Obviously, this limits greatly the conclusions that can be drawn from such an exercise. Crucially, the prevailing literature has not directly addressed the apparently simple question of *why* do states appear to favour some policy instruments and not others? In short, 'why [do] some instruments appear in the repertoire of some [political] systems and not others' [*Anderson, 1971: 122*]?

This volume addresses these research needs by examining four interrelated questions. First, what are the most important drivers of (and barriers to) the continuing uptake of NEPIs in particular countries? Having undertaken a detailed empirical investigation of different country experiences, is it possible to make more informed assertions about what is motivating states to change, if indeed they are changing? Furthermore, are countries changing their national repertoires for similar reasons, or are they doing similar things for different reasons?

Second, what is the overall pattern of use? Who is adopting what, when and why? Unlike some other recent surveys, this collection examines the full range of NEPIs, rather than concentrating upon one, or perhaps two, sub-types in a small number of countries.

Third, how different (that is, 'new') are the NEPIs to the traditional style, structures and content of national environmental policy instruments? Does the appearance of NEPIs amount to a revolution in modern environmental policy, or a much slower and more conservative evolution of national environmental policies? Having examined NEPIs and their predecessors in considerable empirical detail, we should be in a better position to judge whether NEPIs are replacing or simply supplementing 'old' instruments, particularly regulation. There is an obvious inclination to label anything that is not regulation as a 'new' instrument, when a more detailed historical survey of their use could reveal that they were extensively employed a good deal earlier than the 1990s.

Finally, how well do popular theories of comparative politics and public policy explain the emerging pattern of instrument use in the environmental sector? There are two very broad schools of thought that speak to this question. At the risk of oversimplifying, the first regards the selection process as being highly instrumental, in which shifts in ideas and interests (that is, policy learning) are prominent. According to this view, a broad pattern of innovation across countries is capable of occurring if and only if the ideas and the political will to use them are present. The second emphasises the importance of deeply rooted national institutional legacies that give rise to distinctive and highly enduring 'national repertoires' of particular instruments [*Bennett, 1988: 439*]. Anderson [*ibid.: 122*] suggests that each national 'policy repertoire' is distinct from the broader, international repertoire of potentially applicable policy instruments. In contrast to the first school of thought, this second perspective predicts much more 'bounded' forms of innovation [*Weir, 1992*], with countries experimenting with what they know well, while shunning institutionally incompatible tools used elsewhere in the world. Each of these four questions is unpacked and explored at much greater length below.

The contributions in this volume focus on NEPI use in eight industrialised countries, namely Australia, Austria, Finland, France, Germany, Ireland, The Netherlands and the UK, which have historically different levels of environmental performance. Each analysis seeks to identify some of the underlying causes of NEPI use by situating the trends in instrument selection against the backdrop of broader developments in modern environmental politics, such as the internationalisation of policy-making and the emergence of ecological modernist ideas [*Weale, 1992*]. In order to make them generally comparable, each contribution concentrates upon three types of NEPI, namely MBIs, VAs and eco-labels. However, in order not to squeeze out national variation, where appropriate each study also includes a 'residual' category of NEPIs that are of particular national importance (for example, subsidies or informational devices such as EMAS), or which are 'new' to the country in question, although they are not conventionally defined as NEPIs. Finally, although the main purpose of this volume is to describe and explain the use made of NEPIs within and between different countries, for the reasons explained above each contribution also reviews recent trends in the use made of regulation to check whether it is also being applied in 'new' ways.

The remainder of this introduction proceeds as follows. Part III explains that our study not only illuminates the theory and praxis of modern environmental politics and policy making (and particular instrument selection and use), but also makes a much needed empirical contribution to the highly rarefied debate about the theoretical importance of governance in modern society. Many analysts believe that the use of instruments that do not rely upon the formal sanctions and authority of the state (that is, regulation) is the very essence of governance. So, by carefully documenting and comparing the use made of NEPIs in different national setting, we hope to assess how far environmental *governance* is supplanting or simply supplementing traditional forms of environmental *government*. Obviously, if NEPIs are not as important as some analysts have claimed, then perhaps the putative shift from government to governance may not be as significant as is often thought.

Part IV introduces and defines the main types of NEPI covered in this volume, while Parts V to VII draw upon the existing theoretical literature to begin answering the four questions outlined above. Thus, Part Five examines the most important drivers of NEPI use and the emerging patterns of use, Part VI examines how 'new' they are, and Part VII reviews two rival theoretical perspectives on instrument selection and use. Finally, Part VIII describes the analytical structure of the case study accounts, briefly describes the eight countries and introduces the rest of this collection.

'New' Environmental Policy Instruments: Government … or Governance?

Until now, NEPIs have tended to attract the attention of environmental social scientists, international agencies and think tanks. Economists, who like to extol the theoretical advantages of economic instruments in particular, dominated the early literature on NEPIs. The OECD and the EEA have emerged as important disseminators of best practice in the industrialised world, by cataloguing instruments, undertaking benchmarking exercises using large databases and measuring their effectiveness. Although immensely useful, this literature tends towards description and is also quite normative. Moreover, it also ignores (or downplays) the bureaucratic and institutional context in which instruments are selected and deployed, and the politics that surround their use [*Andersen and Sprenger, 2000*].

In some examples of work undertaken by economists, individual tools are subjected to detailed analysis in a way that suggests that regulation has never existed, or is inherently inferior. Not surprisingly, economists react with disappointment to the failure of political systems to adopt NEPIs as quickly or in the unadulterated manner that their models predict [*Siebert, 1976; Hanley et al., 1990; Pearce et al. 2000*]. Until relatively recently, the politics of NEPI selection and use have remained largely unexplored, which is a great pity because political science and policy analysis have a great deal to say about how and why tools are (or are not) adopted in the form that they are.

One of the main purposes of this volume is to shed new light on the comparative politics of instrument selection, adoption and implementation. However, it also speaks to a much more general debate about the structure and function of the state that spans the social sciences. The debate about 'governance' [*Czada and Schmidt, 1993; Marin, 1990; Pierre, 2000; Pierre and Peters, 2000*] seeks to understand contemporary changes in the way that society is governed. Put very simply, the claim is often made that although modern states continue to exist in society and remain important, their form has changed hugely [*Pierre, 2000, 5*]. According to many writers, state structures underwent a slow but nonetheless radical transformation in the latter part of the last century, as *government* metamorphosed into *governance*.

According to Stoker [*1998: 17*], the word 'government' refers to activities undertaken primarily or wholly by state bodies, particularly those 'which operate at the level of the nation state to maintain public order and facilitate collective action'. The term 'governance', on the other hand, refers to the emergence of new styles of governing in which the boundaries between the public and private sectors, and the national and international levels have blurred. For Stoker, then, 'the essence of governance is its focus on governing mechanisms *which do not rest on recourse to the authority and sanctions of government*' (emphasis added). Kooiman [*1993: 4*] summarises governance as follows:

> No single actor, public or private, has all knowledge and information required to solve complex, dynamic and diversified problems; no actor has sufficient overview to make the application of particular instruments effective; no single actor has sufficient action potential to dominate unilaterally in a particular governing model.

If we adopt these interpretations, then the increasing deployment of NEPIs is quite clearly a symptom of governance. It constitutes an attempt by states to share their steering capacity with other actors. According to this line of argument, hierarchical government structures are increasingly giving way to public–private partnerships and various forms of 'ecologicial self-organization' [*Teubner et al., 1994*]. We reflect below upon some of the factors that are stimulating the state to think and act in this way. The key point to make here though, is that a comparative empirical assessment of the way in which NEPIs are actually being deployed, should serve as an interesting test of when and how far governance has replaced government in the environmental sector. If the overall extent of innovation has been sudden and very strong, then perhaps we are witnessing the dawn of a new phase of environmental management characterised by governance. But if regulation remains important, then perhaps the shift from government to governance is more blurred and partial than the governance 'turn' in the social sciences suggest.

What Are 'New' Environmental Policy Instruments?

Policy instruments are the 'myriad techniques at the disposal of governments to implement their policy objectives' [*Howlett, 1991: 2*] (see also: Howlett and Ramesh, [*1993: 4*], and Schneider and Ingram [*1990: 527*]). Analysts have tried to flesh out this general definition by differentiating between three distinct though interrelated sub-types.

Bemelmans-Videc *et al.* [*1998: 50–2*] present such a typology focused on constrain, that is, regulation (*sticks*, that is, highly choice constraining); economic instruments (*carrots i.e.* moderately choice constraining); and information (*sermon*, that is, facilitates and informs free choice). This categorisation broadly matches the fourfold distinction we have used above, that is, (1) regulatory instruments, (2) MBIs, (3) VAs, and (4) informational devices. Some scholars suggest a fifth category, which involves some attempt to manipulate 'organisation', that is, the resources of government (such as the setting up of new – environmental – ministries or agencies [*Hood, 1983; Howlett, 1991: 81; Kern et al., 2000*]. However, we have decided to concentrate on a more narrowly defined concept of policy instruments.

Figure 1 provides a different, though equally simple typology of environmental policy instrument types according to how the ends and means of management are defined. In the top left-hand cell we find most types of regulation, which prescribe both the means and ends of environmental policy. Good examples are the bans that are sometimes imposed upon the use of particular substances, or the specification of emission limits for certain industrial processes. In the top right we also find many types of regulation, specifically those that require the use of a particular type of technology (for example, specifying the Best Available Technology (BAT) principle). In this cell, the operator of a particular process is simply required to use a particular type of technology, but may not be required to attain a given emission level. In the bottom left cell we find certain types of VA, but, interestingly, also types of regulation such as those that specify an environmental quality objective (EQO). Finally, the bottom right cell is where we normally find NEPIs such as MBIs, eco-labels and EMAS-type systems. This typology is especially revealing of the overlaps between the different instrument types. For instance, forms of regulation are found in three of the four cells.

FIGURE 1
A TYPOLOGY OF NEPIs

	Regulator SPECIFIES the goal to be achieved	Regulator does NOT SPECIFY the goal to be achieved
Regulator specifies HOW goal is to be achieved	Command and control (regulation)	Technology-based regulatory standards
Regulator does NOT SPECIFY HOW goal is to be achieved	Most negotiated VAs; some MBIs; some regulation (e.g. EQOs)	Most MBIs; some VAs; informational devices

Source: Based on Russell and Powell [*1996*].

These two typologies illuminate the relationship between different instruments types, but they do not explain the instruments themselves. The remainder of this section very briefly describes the different types of NEPI in the order that they appear in the national case studies.

Market-Based Instruments

A very broad definition of market-based instruments (MBIs) is that they are instruments that 'affect estimates of costs of alternative actions open to economic agents' [OECD, 1994, 17]. The total number of MBIs used in OECD countries has grown steadily since the early seventies, as has the range, which now extends from subsidies through to emission charges and tradable permits [OECD, 1998]. The OECD distinguishes between four main types of MBI: taxes (including charges and levies); subsidies; tradable emission permits; and deposit-refund schemes (see OECD [1998, 7–9] for a more extensive taxonomy). Charges and taxes are already quite well known, but tradable permit schemes are still relatively novel in most OECD countries outside the USA where they first originated. There are many sub-types of tradable permit schemes. Two key variables centre on (a) whether the authorities set an upper limit (that is, so-called caps) on the total amount of a substance (for example, carbon dioxide) that a particular sector or group of sectors can emit; and (b) how the permits to emit pollutants are initially allocated to the various firms involved (for example, for free (so-called 'grandfathering') or through an auction in which the highest bidder gets the permits). Once a tradable permit scheme is set up, firms are allowed to buy and sell the permits amongst themselves, which, at least in theory, should facilitate greater cost-effectiveness and allow greater scope for technological innovation (compared to traditional regulation).

Voluntary Agreements

The first VAs appeared in Japan in the 1960s and then later in France [Karamanos, 2001: 71]. There is, however, no commonly agreed definition of what they are. In some circles the term 'voluntary' is used interchangeably with 'environmental'. Other commonly used terms are 'codes of conduct', 'covenants' or 'negotiated agreements'. The EEA defines them as 'covering only those commitments undertaken by firms and sector associations, which are the result of *negotiations* with public authorities and/or explicitly recognised by the authorities' [EEA, 1997: 11] (emphasis added), but the EU Commission adopts a much more inclusive definition: 'agreements between industry and public authorities on the achievement of environmental objectives' [CEC, 1996: 5]. The OECD [1998: 4] also subscribes to this broader, more inclusive definition:

'voluntary commitments of the industry undertaken in order to pursue actions leading to the improvement of the environment'.

Börkey and Lévèque [*1998*] have helpfully provided a typology which differentiates between three different sub-types: unilateral commitments, public voluntary schemes, and negotiated agreements. *Unilateral commitments* consist of environmental improvement programmes instigated by individual companies or by industry associations. Strictly speaking, these are not really instruments of government, because they do not involve the state; they are instruments of governance because they offer industry a means to communicate its environmental commitment to the public. *Public voluntary schemes* (PVS) are established by public bodies, which define certain performance criteria and other conditions of membership. Individual companies are free to decide whether or not to join, although the scheme defines the criteria that have to be met. Most PVSs would qualify as an instrument of governance, although they still involve a great deal of government involvement in their design, adoption and monitoring. Finally, *negotiated agreements* are more formal ; 'contracts' between industry and public authorities aimed at addressing particular environmental problems. They may be legally binding. Usually, their content is negotiated between industry and public bodies. Consequently, they are much closer to the government end of the government-governance spectrum than the other two sub-types.

Eco-labels

Eco-labels are not very intrusive policy instruments in comparison to regulation (see Figure 1) and also some MBIs (such as tradable permits and eco-taxes). They mainly rely on moral suasion by providing consumers with information about the environmental impact of particular products and services [*Jordan et al., 2003*]. Eco-labels provide information to consumers in a standardised manner, allowing them to make more informed comparisons. Widely recognised and supported eco-labels may influence producers in a similar manner to traditional regulatory standards (especially if they stipulate the BAT principle) in markets where green consumerism is very strong [*OECD, 1999*]. Producers and service providers which cater for such markets (or market segments) have a strong incentive to apply for eco-labels to avoid possible competitive disadvantage *vis-à-vis* eco-labelled products/services provided by their competitors. However, eco-label schemes are largely ineffective (in terms of changing producer behaviour) in markets which are characterised by a low degree of environmental awareness, although they may help to raise public awareness about environmental issues.

Other Instruments

Each case study in this collection also contains a 'residual' category of NEPIs, which we define as instruments that are of national importance (for example, subsidies), or which are 'new' to the country in question. These include environmental impact assessment (for example, Finland) and subsidies (for example, France). There are other informational devices besides eco-labels, ranging from the softer tools such as information campaigns to EMAS.

'Old' Instruments: Regulation

Finally, each case study also investigates the contemporary form and function of regulation to gauge the extent to which it is also being applied in 'new' ways. A lot of the impetus for regulatory change is now coming from the EU simply because it is the pre-eminent source of national environmental policy in Europe [*Jordan, 2002; Wurzel, 2002; Zito, 2000*]. The EU affects national regulation both directly and indirectly. The EU has a direct effect by altering the nature of the regulation it adopts. For example, the Commission is making a concerted effort to employ framework Directives that set out a general framework of control, rather than highly prescriptive Regulations and Directives. The recent EU White Paper on governance [*CEC, 2001*] advocates 'co-regulation' – that is a blend of voluntary initiatives and binding legislative acts. The most high profile manifestations of co-regulation in the environmental sector are voluntary initiatives such as the Auto-Oil Programme which rely on so-called 'New Approach' Directives [*Friedrich et al., 2000*].

Under the 'New' Approach (it actually dates from the late 1980s), Directives set only the essential requirements to be achieved, leaving the technical conformance details to be negotiated between industry and the European standards body (CEN). So far, it has only been applied in the areas of packaging waste and integrated product policy. The EU also indirectly affects the operation of national regulation by adopting policies that differ from pre-existing national approaches. For example, national regulation in the UK has changed significantly since the 1970s through this slower and more diffuse process of Europeanisation [*Jordan, 1993; 2003*].

Why Are NEPIs Being Adopted?

Having defined NEPIs, we now turn to the first question outlined above i.e. what is driving the adoption of NEPIs? In his seminal account of state government innovation, Walker [*1969*] distinguishes between two main sources of change: those external and those internal to the state. These have since been developed into two distinct models: the external determinants model of change and the internal determinants model of change [*Berry and Berry, 1999: 170*]. Each of the eight case studies examines in considerable detail the most important external and internal drivers of NEPI adoption at the national level. However, it is perhaps worthwhile briefly identifying some of the most important external drivers beforehand, as the existing literature implies that they are common to most, if not all, the eight countries.

It is worth saying up front that the appearance of 'new' policy instruments is not an entirely new phenomenon. As long ago as the 1950s, Dahl and Lindblom [*1953: 8*] described it as 'perhaps the greatest political *revolution* of our times' (emphasis added). That said, a number of more specific factors combined in the 1980s and 1990s to fuel a search for 'new' instruments of environmental policy – a policy sector which of course barely existed in the 1950s.

Dissatisfaction with Regulation

The first driver was a growing dissatisfaction with regulation. For decades, standard economic accounts of environmental problems have underlined the extent to which policy-making by means of MBIs is more economically efficient and effective than regulation by administrative rules. In the late 1980s, this academic message began to attract a much wider and appreciative political audience. In particular, highly regulated industries such as those involved in the production of bulk chemicals began to advocate MBIs and also VAs as their preferred alternatives to regulation. Other actors, who were expressing dissatisfaction with regulation as the policy sector, paid more attention to the problems of implementation associated with the traditional forms of regulation. Policy-makers also began to appreciate that they would never achieve sustainable development – a new and increasingly important *leitmotif* of environmental policy giving equal weight to environmental, economic and social considerations – by regulation alone. Regulation might be well suited to dealing with point sources, but it simply could not be used to police diffuse sources and activities such as agriculture and global problems (such as greenhouse gas production) which occur at myriad locations.

The Perceived Strengths of NEPIs

Second, NEPIs were assumed to have a number of putative benefits over regulation. The European Commission claims that VAs: encourage industry to adopt a more proactive attitude to environmental protection; are more cost effective than regulation; allow a quicker and smoother achievement of policy goals [*COM (96) 560 final: 3, 6–7*]. The EEA [*1996: 15–19*] argues that MBIs also have a number of distinct advantages: they internalise externalities; they make the polluter pay; they are more cost effective than regulation and they provide a constant spur to innovate with new technologies. MBIs are a form of governance as they shift steering capacity from the state to non-state bodies. However, the precise extent of that shift depends upon how the MBIs are designed and implemented. In the 1990s, these and other advocates of NEPIs found they could push their case much more easily than before (see below).

The Governance 'Turn'

Third, the political attractiveness of NEPIs began to grow in most OECD countries starting in the 1980s. NEPIs fitted with the debate about governance – the idea that the state should not seek to interfere in every facet of social and economic life (see above). In an era of governance, the state is smaller, more networked and much less heavily reliant on binding legislation [*Marin and Mayntz, 1991*]. More recently, the allure of MBIs has grown even more rapidly, as politicians realised that they might offer a handy and politically less contentious source of revenue. Crucially, the concept of ecological tax reform – taxing economic 'bads' and recycling the revenue to promote economic 'goods' such as employment – fitted neatly with the emerging Third Way ideology of ruling (Social Democratic) parties in Germany and the UK.

Instrument Changes in the EU

Fourth, in the 1990s the EU began to experiment with NEPIs for a number of reasons [*Jordan et al., 2003*]. It was under political pressure from industry to simplify legislation and make it economically less burdensome (see the 1995 Molitor report on legislative simplification [*COM (95) 288, 21-6-95*]). NEPIs were an important means of promoting 'shared responsibility' – a theme of the 1992 Fifth Environmental Action Programme - to achieve sustainability. NEPIs also attracted new advocates in the early 1990s as the EU struggled to justify its involvement in national environmental affairs; they reflected the subsidiarity principle more than the preferred instrument of EU environmental policy since the 1970s – regulation [*Jordan, 2000*]. The Commission's environmental Directorate has also warmed to NEPIs, as they appear to offer sharper and more sensitive tools for cutting away at the knotty issue of sustainability.

Economic Pressures

Another contextual factor that made the idea of more flexible NEPIs more attractive was the economic conditions facing both the EU member states and other OECD countries such as Australia. The economic recession in the 1990s had a severe impact even in the wealthy Scandinavian countries. This pressure combined with the fears of increased global economic competition to focus governments more on the priorities of protecting firms and employment [*Golub, 1998b*]. Economic actors and their allies had a further weapon to argue against environmental regulation that imposed more costs and inflexibility from their perspective.

Growing Domestic Political Support

Finally, in recent years environmental groups and green parties have become much more supportive of NEPIs than they used to be. As with the EU, there are several motivations at work here. First, many regulations were never fully implemented; NEPIs appeared to remedy some of these failings [*Knill and Lenschow, 2000*]. And second, the tide of support behind NEPIs is now so great, that previously critical groups like Greenpeace and Friends of the Earth (FoE) have realised that they have to engage positively lest they are left behind by industry and regulators.

Barriers to Change

Pressing in the other direction are a number of obstacles to the widespread adoption of NEPIs [*Hanley et al., 1990; Pearce et al., 2000*]. The case study authors reflect upon these in much more detail, but it is probably worth identifying some of them beforehand. They include: the lack of economic expertise within national administrations; a cultural antipathy among bureaucrats, many of whom have a long training in the use of regulation; opposition from vested interests, including environmental pressure groups, but also sections of industry; legal constraints imposed *inter alia* by the EU; fears about competitiveness and the economic burden of NEPIs; and the potentially adverse distributional impacts of new MBIs. The case studies examine how these drivers and obstacles have interacted in particular national settings.

Concluding Comments

The case studies seek to describe the overall pattern of NEPI use in the eight countries (question two above). However, it is already abundantly clear from the very broad-brush comparative analyses that have been undertaken, that the overall pattern of NEPI use is quite strongly differentiated across countries and sectors. The remainder of this introduction explores and seeks to account for the overall pattern. Second, the use of instruments appears to be affected by the same leader-laggard dynamic that is said to drive other domains of environmental policy [e.g., *Héritier, 1995; Liefferink and Andersen, 1998*]. Often, one state or a small group of countries experiment with a particular policy tool and then experience disseminates outwards to other countries, often via international organisations such as the OECD and the European Commission. There is empirical evidence that policy diffusion and transfer may occur where other countries borrow the general principle (or specific elements) of policies and/or environmental policy instruments [*Kern et al., 2000*]. Third, the range of NEPIs used is also broadening, from a small number of MBIs and one or two VAs in the 1970s, to a veritable arsenal of different tools. One of the most urgent debates now taking place in some OECD countries, is how best to fit these different tools together into effective policy instrument mixes. Finally, there appears to be a pronounced North–South gradient which reflects the differences in economic development within the EU. Generally speaking, the wealthier Northern European states innovated earlier than the poorer Southern/peripheral EU member states (such as Ireland), and have also adopted many more NEPIs across a wider range of sub-types.

How 'New' Are NEPIs?

Innovation and Incrementalism in Public Policy

The third question outlined above was how 'new' are NEPIs? Does their apparently sudden and widespread appearance constitute a revolution in modern environmental policy, or a much slower and more conservative evolution of national environmental policies? The policy innovation literature defines innovation as the adoption of a policy that is new to the government that is adopting it [*Walker, 1969: 881*]. Consequently (but perhaps not very helpfully!), an innovative policy instrument could be defined as one that is 'new'. The distinction between old and new, and evolution and innovation (or revolution) bring us back to the hoary debate in policy analysis, which pitted the incrementalists against their critics. The former argue that most political change is highly incremental in nature, that is, it usually amounts to little more than a marginal alteration of existing policy goals and instruments [*Lindblom, 1965; Berry, 1990*]. According to this view, innovation is highly unusual; there is very little in modern political life that it entirely 'new'. The second, is much more optimistic about the possibility of innovation.

In this volume we have chosen to define the novelty (or otherwise) of a particular instrument by examining how far it departs from the traditional style, content and structure of national policy. These three are not hard and fast concepts, but they provide us with a fairly consistent typology for mapping out the historical and spatial distribution of change.

Policy Content, Structures and Style

Following Hall [*1993*], the content of policy refers to the way in which policy is expressed and the instruments used to implement it. He subdivides policy content into three different levels or parts. The first and highest level (in conceptual terms) is the goals of a policy. These operate within a policy *paradigm* or a framework of ideas that specifies not only the goals of policy and the kind of instruments that can be used to attain them, but also the very nature of the problems they are meant to be addressing. The second level equates to the instruments or techniques of policy, while the third and lowest level relates to the precise setting of those instruments. Traditionally, the dominant paradigm of environmental policy was curative, that is, how best to prevent pollution once waste matter had been created. The goals of policy were framed in such a way as to reduce the amount of waste entering the environment to a level that did, not impair human health and cause excessive environmental damage. The main tools were, as discussed above, regulatory. Very few governments had environmental ministries in the early 1970s. Those that did, tended not to be directly involved in the selection, calibration and implementation of instruments.

The style of policy normally describes the manner in which environmental policy decisions are made, although it also affects the way in which instruments are used. The most common, but fairly rough, categorisation of policy style is that offered by Richardson et al. [1982], which distinguishes between consensual vs. conflictual and reactive vs. proactive styles.

Finally, policy instruments do not exist in a bureaucratic and administrative vacuum. They have to be championed, designed, adopted and implemented by the administrative structures of government. These structures comprise the bureaucratic and procedural arrangements (for example, government departments, coordinating mechanisms, sub-national implementing agencies) that states establish either to make and/or implement policy. As explained above, most environmental policy instruments (in practice regulation) were the responsibility of environmental ministries.

Theories of Instrument Selection and Use

The fourth and final question posed above was how should we theorise the processes of instrument adoption and diffusion as described in the case study chapters? Or, to put it slightly differently, what factors are likely to influence the choice between different types of policy instrument, and how is that choice likely to be affected by a particular country's institutional and political characteristics (that is, the structure, style and content of its policies – see above)? Below, we concentrate upon two broad theoretical perspectives, which make very different predictions about the outcome of the selection process and the intervening influence of endogenous factors (for example, a country's institutional make-up and distinctive policy style) in shaping the form in which they are selected and deployed. The first emphasises the importance of policy learning in driving the selection of instruments. On this view, instruments are adopted to fit new policy requirements and policy paradigms. The overall pattern of use is likely to be uniform in those sectors and countries where the ideas driving change are in existence. Sudden bursts of innovation in instrument use may occur if and only if advocates manage to colonise key institutional niches.

The second emphasises the distorting effect of national institutional forms. An institutionally 'bounded' form of innovation produces distinctive and enduring national repertoires of particular instruments. According to this perspective (which has a great deal in common with incrementalist approaches) the same level of political pressure applied to different political systems is likely to generate a differentiated pattern of change, which follows the grain of existing national institutional forms.

Ideational Theories

Ideas are dominant in this body of literature: they drive the search for new instruments. Policy change is first and foremost a *cognitive* struggle between different groups to improve their understanding of the causes of policy problems or the suitability of particular instruments to act as solutions [*Hall, 1993: 278*]. According to these theories, policy instruments play an *instrumental* role in the policy process. Normally, existing instruments are simply recalibrated to reflect changing circumstances and political demands, but occasionally sudden, and unforeseen (external) events will completely de-stabilise a policy area, triggering a frantic search for new instruments and explanatory frameworks (paradigms).

Two very popular examples in this canon are Hall's study of social learning and Sabatier's Advocacy Coalition Framework (ACF). Hall [*1993: 292*] argues that policy-making occurs within the context of a particular set of ideas 'that recognise some social interests as more legitimate than others and privilege some lines of policy over others.' At any point in time, one set of ideas (a policy paradigm) prevails. This is 'a framework of ideas and standards that specifies not only the goals of policy and *the kind of instruments that can be used to attain them*, but also the very nature of the problems they are meant to be addressing' (emphasis added).

For Hall, policy change can occur at all three of the levels discussed above: (1) the precise calibrations of policy instruments (first order); (2) the particular techniques or policy instruments employed to provide policy solutions (second order); (3) the overarching goals that guide policy-making (third order). Shifts in the first two levels occur regularly and incrementally and are associated with 'normal' policy-making. They involve slight changes to the existing repertoire of instruments, for example, tightening an emission limit. A paradigm shift of substantial proportions is required to knock them from well-trodden paths, altering the underlying goals of a policy area (third order change). Such shifts take place periodically as new problems emerge, and anomalous or 'unexplainable' events accumulate.

The widening debate eventually spills over into the public sphere, drawing in a much broader array of pressure groups, journalists, intellectuals and academic analysts, who compete to alter the prevailing policy discourse.

Sabatier's [1998] advocacy coalition framework (ACF) conceives of the policy process in terms of discrete *sub-systems*. Within each subsystem are advocacy coalitions (ACs) comprising actors with similar core beliefs or values. The ACF divides beliefs into three hierarchical layers reflecting a decreasing resistance to change. Deep core beliefs define an individual's basic philosophy and are immune to empirical challenges. Near (policy) core beliefs relate to fundamental value priorities surrounding the policy area, such as perceptions of causation and strategies for realising deep core values. Finally, there is an outer band of secondary elements, which prescribe how policies should be implemented (that is, the choice of instruments).

At any one time, there is likely to be a dominant coalition which sets the intellectual framework (a paradigm?) within which individual policy decisions are made, and defines a series of minority coalitions. The struggle between these coalitions provides the primary motor of policy change. For ACs, learning is an instrumental process of achieving a priori beliefs. While changes at the secondary level emerge incrementally as different coalitions engage in a cognitive struggle, changes in the core aspects of a policy require an exogenous 'shock' outside the sub-system.

Institutional Theories

Institutional theories focus on 'the whole range of state and societal institutions that shape how political actors define their interests and that structure their relations of power to other groups' [*Thelen and Steinmo, 1992: 2*]. These theories assume that the choice of instruments is shaped by the historical-institutional context in which the act of selection takes place. This view characterises many of the 'new' institutional theories of politics, especially the historical and sociological variants. March and Olsen [*1998: 948*] define an 'institution' as 'a relatively stable collection of practices and rules defining appropriate behaviour for specific groups of actors in specific situations'. National institutions would therefore include each country's repertoire of policy instruments.

The fact that these repertoires provide appropriate solutions to national problems gives them an institutional embeddedness that is hard to dislodge unless the instrument in question is manifestly dysfunctional. Over the course of time, actors invest substantial time and resources adapting to particular policies and tools, locking them in place [*Pierson, 1993*]. Even then, any ensuing institutional change is likely to be incremental and path dependent (that is, shaped by what has already accumulated). Importantly, actor preferences are derived endogenously on the basis of what is appropriate (that is, politically acceptable and can be implemented on the ground) in a given institutional context. Consequently, they try to satisfice (that is, muddle through) within pre-existing institutional constraints rather than design new solutions or instruments.

Institutional theories suggest that institutions form and adapt slowly, in the process investing in certain norms, values and cultures. When these norms and procedures become institutionalised they are not changed easily unless there are sudden, external shocks. 'Revolutionary policy learning' [*Kitschelt, 1991*] is therefore extremely rare. In the environmental sphere typical triggers are sudden ecological catastrophe or a spectacular policy failure. However, when confronted with such challenges actors first refine what they have before searching for novel approaches. The tendency to cling to existing policy instruments that appear to work rather than innovate with new ones ensures that institutions endure long after they cease to be optimal ('competency traps') [*March and Olsen, 1989: 53–67*].

In other words, institutions are 'sticky' in that they persist beyond the historical moment and condition of their original design ('the stickiness of adaptation') [*ibid., 1989: 169*]. This arises because societies invest time and resources in adapting to tools, locking them in place. Economists argue that the increasing returns reaped from remaining with regulation may make a decisive shift to NEPIs highly unattractive to all those (including regulators and the regulated) involved in the regulatory process [*Arthur, 1994: 112*]. If we add in the bureaucratic costs of establishing, setting, reviewing and re-tuning NEPIs, the incentive to innovate appears to be very low indeed. To conclude, in sharp contrast to ideational theories, institutions powerfully refract external political pressures for change in ways that perpetuate existing arrangements. Thus the implementation of a common set of ideas on NEPIs is likely to produce 'widely divergent outcomes in societies with different institutional arrangements' [*North, 1990: 101*].

Theorising the Adoption of NEPIs

What predictions are these two literatures likely to make about the distribution of NEPIs in Europe? Ideational theories are more likely to account for the (seemingly) wholesale switch to NEPIs in Europe and other parts of the world in terms of networks of ideas and expertise. One possible explanation might be the emergence of a transnational community of experts imbued with a strong belief in the superiority of NEPIs as against traditional, regulatory policy instruments. However, ideational theories say little about what happens afterwards, that is, when the ideas are implemented in different national contexts. Do countries adopt the same set of new tools in one revolutionary wave or do they evolve what they already have to make it look as if they are implementing the new paradigm? Incrementalists such as Lindblom [*1959*] (see above) would presumably argue that incrementalism (or muddling through) is commonplace, whereas genuine innovation is rare. A second possibility is that actors apply NEPIs more strongly and uniformly in those countries where the coalition is dominant and more sporadically where it is not. Finally, ideational theories assume that policy makers are fairly unencumbered by institutional constraints and rationally oriented in their objectives. They do not, for example, cling to particular types of instrument because they 'appear' to work well or are supported by a particularly powerful constituency of interests (that is, policy drives instrument choice, not the other way round).

Institutional theories on the other hand make very different predictions. The first and most obvious point is that instruments will change only very slowly. The most oft-cited barriers to innovation are often broadly 'institutional', namely bureaucratic resistance, complexity (the difficulty of fitting them in alongside existing instruments) and political inertia (see Hanley *et al.* [*1990*]; Keohane *et al.* [*1998*]). Second, instruments that work with the grain of national institutions are more likely to be adopted than those that work against them. The EEA's [*1997: 39*] analysis of VAs in Europe does indeed confirm that national administrative structure decisively affects instrument selection (compare the UK and Netherlands – see above). Third, the structuring/filtering effect of national institutions may only become fully apparent after studying the transfer of policy instruments through into the implementation stage. If 'discordant' instruments are adopted (that is, ones which do not fit national institutional legacies) they will be eroded during the implementation phase to achieve a better goodness of fit. To conclude, institutional approaches predict fairly low levels of innovation unless and until there are sudden exogenous shocks to the system. Generally, the overall pattern of instrument use will be fairly heterogeneous, reflecting the resilience and longevity of national institutional traditions.

Conclusions

The remainder of this volume is devoted to the eight case studies. These are followed by a set of comparative conclusions that seek to answer the four questions identified above. The case studies have been written to fit a standard structural template which covers the main drivers and/or barriers to NEPI use, the traditional content, structure and style of national policy, the main trends in the use of NEPIs and a set of conclusions.

The countries, which are dealt with in alphabetical order, represent a broadly representative selection of EU states. The addition of Australia offers an insight into whether the same dynamics of change are present within a broadly comparable, non-EU state. The Netherlands and Germany are often portrayed as environmental 'lead' states, which forcefully advocate high environmental standards at home and in international settings [*Liefferink and Andersen, 1998*]. However, while the Netherlands has a long history of experimenting with different instrument types, Germany has struggled to overcome the long tradition of being a 'high regulatory' state [*Héritier et al., 1996*]. Austria and Finland also have strong environmental reputations, but whereas Finland pioneered the use of environmental taxes, adopting the world's first carbon dioxide tax in 1990, Austria has been a much slower developer. France, meanwhile, pioneered the use of certain types of VAs and MBIs as early as the 1970s, but these tools are only now being extensively adopted across French environmental policy. Australia and the UK could be placed in a middle position as far as their environmental reputations are concerned, though both began to experiment enthusiastically with NEPIs in the 1990s. Finally, Ireland is often characterised as a laggard state in the EU and even today, the extent of innovation with NEPIs has been very limited. The EU is obviously a common factor among almost all these countries, but because of insufficient space we have chosen to omit it from our case selection (but see Jordan *et al.* [*2003*] for an analysis of its role).

The contributors were asked to examine the broad trends and search for underlying explanations rather than identify and comment upon each and every NEPI. Therefore, this volume offers a broad, comparative political assessment of the state of play in the early part of the new millennium, not an exhaustive audit as this could easily replicate the EEA's and the OECD's work. Finally, space limitations restricted the accounts from detailed analysis of the effectiveness of the instruments. However, where relevant, some of the studies draw on secondary literature to comment upon the effectiveness of particular tools where assessments have been undertaken or when effectiveness has emerged as a political issue within a particular state.

REFERENCES

Andersen, M.S. and R.-U. Sprenger (eds.) (2000), *Market-based Instruments for Environmental Management: Politics and Institutions*, Cheltenham: Edward Elgar.
Anderson, C. (1971), 'Comparative Policy Analysis: The Design of Measures', *Comparative Politics*, Vol.4, No.1, pp.117–31.
Andrew, R. *et al.* (2001), *Voluntary Agreements in Environmental Policy*, Prague, Czech Republic: University of Economics Press.
Arthur, B. (1994), *Increasing Returns and Path Dependence in the Economy*, Ann Arbor, MI: University of Michigan Press.
Bemelmans-Videc, M., Rist, R. and E. Vedung (1998), *Carrots, Sticks and Sermons: Policy Instruments and Their Evaluation*, New York: Transaction Publishers.
Bennett, C.J. (1988), 'Regulating the Computer: Comparing Policy Instruments in Europe and the US', *European Journal of Political Science*, Vol.16, No.2, pp.437–66.
Berry, F. and W. Berry (1999), 'Innovation and Diffusion Models in Policy Research', in P.

Sabatier (ed.), *Theories of the Policy Process*, Boulder, CO: Westview Press.

Berry, W. (1990), 'The Confusing Case of Budgetary Incrementalism: Too Many Meanings For a Single Concept?' *Journal of Politics*, Vol.52, No.1, pp.167–96.

Börkey, P. and F. Lévèque (1998), *Voluntary Approaches for Environmental Protection in the EU*, ENV/EPOC/GEEI(98)29/final. Paris: OECD.

CEC (Commission of the European Communities) (1996), *Communication from the Commission on Environmental Agreements (COM (96) 561 final)*, Brussels: CEC.

CEC, (Commission of the European Communities) (2000), *Database on Environmental Taxes in the EU Member States*, consultancy prepared by Forum for the Future, July 2001, Brussels: CEC.

CEC, Commission of the European Communities (2001), *European Governance. A White Paper, COM(2001) 428 final*, Brussels: CEC.

Czada, R. and M. G. Schmidt (eds), 1993, *Verhandlungsdemokratie, Interessenvermittlung, Regierbarkeit*, Opladen: Westdeutscher Verlag.

Dahl, R. and C. Lindblom (1953), *Politics, Economics and Welfare*, New York: Harper & Bros.

Daugbjerg, C. and G. Svendsen (2001), *Green Taxation in Question*, Basingstoke: Palgrave.

Dente, B. (ed.) (1995), *Environmental Policy in Search of New Instruments*, Dordrecht: Kluwer.

EEA (European Environment Agency), (1996), *Environmental Taxes: Implementation and Environmental Effectiveness*, Copenhagen: EEA

EEA, (European Environment Agency) (1997), *Environmental Agreements: Environmental Effectiveness*, Copenhagen: EEA.

EEA, (European Environment Agency) (2000), *Environmental Taxes: Recent Developments in Tools for Integration*, Copenhagen: EEA.

Friedrich, A., Tappe, M. and R.K.W. Wurzel (2000), 'A New Approach to EU Environmental Policy-Making? The Auto-Oil I Programme', *Journal of European Public Policy*, Vol.7, No.4, pp.593-612.

Golub, J. (ed.) (1998a), *New Instruments of Environmental Policy*, London: Routledge.

Golub, J. (ed.) (1998b), *Global Competition and EU Environmental Policy*, London: Routledge.

Hall, P. (1993), 'Policy Paradigms, Social Learning and the State', *Comparative Politics*, Vol.25, No.3, pp.275–96

Hanley, N. *et al.* (1990), 'Why Is More Notice Not Taken of Economists' Prescriptions For the Control of Pollution?' *Environment and Planning A*, Vol.22, pp.1421–39.

Héritier, A. (1995), '"Leaders" and "Laggards" in European Clean Air Policy', in B. Unger and F. van Waarden (eds.), *Convergence or Diversity?*, Aldershot: Avebury.

Héritier, A., C. Knill and S. Mingers (1996), *Ringing the Changes in Europe. Regulatory Competition and the Redefinition of the State. Britain, France and Germany*, Berlin: de Gruyter.

Hood, C. (1983), *The Tools of Government*, London: Macmillan.

Howlett, M. (1991), 'Policy Instruments, Policy Styles and Policy Implementation', *Policy Studies Journal*, Vol.19, No.2, pp.1–21.

Howlett, M. and M. Ramesh (1993), 'Patterns of Policy Instrument Choice', *Policy Studies Review*, Vol.12, No.1/2, pp.3–24.

Jordan, A.J. (1993), 'Integrated Pollution Control and the Evolving Style and Structure of Environmental Regulation in the UK', *Environmental Politics*, Vol.2, No.3, pp.405–27.

Jordan, A.J. (2000), 'The Politics of Multilevel Environmental Governance: Subsidiarity and Environmental Policy in the European Union', *Environment and Planning A*, Vol.32, No.7, pp.1307–24.

Jordan, A. (2002), *The Europeanization of British Environmental Policy*, London: Palgrave.

Jordan, A.J. (2003), 'The Europeanisation of National Government and Policy: A Departmental Perspective. *British Journal of Political Science* (in press).

Jordan, A. Wurzel, R.K.W. and A. Zito (2003), 'European Governance and the Transfer of 'New' Environmental Policy Instruments', *Public Administration* (in press).

Karamanos, P. (2001), 'Voluntary Environmental Agreements', *Journal of Environmental Planning and Management*, Vol.44, No.1, pp. 67–84.

Keohane, N., Revetz, R. and R. Stavins (1998), 'The Choice of Regulatory Instruments in Environmental Policy', *Harvard Environmental Law Review*, Vol.22, No.2, pp.317–67.

Kern, K., Jörgens, H. and M. Jänicke (2000), 'Die Diffusion umweltpolitischer Innovationen. Ein Beitrag zur Globalisierung von Umweltpolitik', *Zeitschrift für Umweltpolitik*, 23, pp.507–46.

Kitschelt, H. (1991), 'Industrial Governance Structures, Innovation Strategies and the Case of

Japan', *International Organization*, Vol.45, No.4, pp.453–93.

Knill, C. and A. Lenschow (eds.) (2000), *Implementing EU Environmental Policy*, Manchester: Manchester University Press.

Kooiman, J. (ed.) (1993), *Modern Governance: New Government-Society Interactions*, London: Sage.

Liefferink, D. and M. Skou Andersen (eds.) (1998), *European Environmental Policy: The Pioneers*, Manchester: Manchester University Press.

Lindblom, C. (1959), 'The Science of Muddling Through', *Public Administration Review*, Vol.19, No.6, pp.78–88.

Lindblom, C. (1965), *The Intelligence of Democracy*, New York: Free Press.

March, J. and J. Olsen (1989), *Rediscovering Institutions*, New York: Free Press.

March, J. and J. Olsen (1998), 'The Institutional Dynamics of International Political Orders', *International Organisation*, Vol.52, No.4, pp.943–69.

Marin, B. (ed.) (1990), *Governance and Generalized Exchange: Self-Organizing Policy Networks in Action*, Frankfurt: Campus.

Marin, B and R. Mayntz (1991), *Policy Networks: Empirical Evidence and Theoretical Conclusions*, Frankfurt: Campus.

North, D. (1990), *Institutions, Institutional Change and Economic Performance*, Cambridge: Cambridge University Press.

OECD, (1994), *Managing the Environment: The Role of Economic Instruments*, Paris: OECD.

OECD (1998), *Evaluating Economic Instruments*, Paris: OECD.

OECD, (1999), *Voluntary Approaches for Environmental Policy*, Paris: OECD.

Pearce, D. *et al.* (2000), *Market-based Instruments in the UK*, report for the UK Round Table on Sustainable Development, EFTEC/CSERGE: London and Norwich. Available at: http://www.uea.ac.uk/env/cserge/research/fut_governance/papers.htm.

Pierre, J. (2000), *Debating Governance*, Oxford: Oxford University Press.

Pierre, J. and B.G. Peters (2000), *Governance, Politics and the State*, Basingstoke: Macmillan.

Pierson, P. (1993), 'When Effect Becomes Cause', *World Politics*, Vol.45, No.4, pp.598–628.

Richardson, J. Gustafsson, G. and G. Jordan (1982), 'The Concept of Policy Style', in J.J. Richardson (ed.), *Policy Styles in Western Europe*, London: Allen & Unwin.

Russell, C. and R. Powell, (1996), 'Practical Considerations and Comparison of Instruments of Environmental Policy', in J. Van der Bergh (ed.), *Handbook of Environment and Resource Economics*, Cheltenham: Edward Elgar.

Sabatier, Paul (1998), 'The Advocacy Coalition Framework', *Journal of European Public Policy*, Vol.5, No.1, pp.98–130.

Schneider, A. and H. Ingram (1990), 'Behavioural Assumptions of Policy Tools', *Journal of Politics*, Vol.52, No.2, pp.510–29.

Siebert, H. (1976), *Analyse der Instrumente der Umweltpolitik*, Göttingen: Schwartz.

Stoker, G. (1998), 'Governance As Theory', *International Social Science Journal*, Vol.155, pp.17–28.

Teubner, G, L. Farmer and D. Murphy (eds.) (1994), *Environmental Law and Ecological Responsibility: The Concept and Practice of Ecological Self-Organization*, Chichester: John Wiley.

Thelen, K. and S. Steinmo (1992), 'Historical Institutionalism in Comparative Politics', in S. Steinmo *et al.* (eds.), *Structuring Politics*, Cambridge: Cambridge University Press.

USEPA (United States Environmental Protection Agency) (2001), *The United States Experience with Economic Incentives for Protecting the Environment*, EPA 240-R-01-001, USEPA, Washington, DC. USA.

Walker, J. (1969), 'The Diffusion of Innovations Among the American States', *American Political Science Review*, Vol.63, pp.880–99.

Weale, A. (1992), *The New Politics of Pollution*, Manchester: Manchester University Press.

Weir, M. (1992), 'Ideas and the Politics of Bounded Innovation', in S. Steinmo *et al.* (eds.) *Structuring Politics*, Cambridge: Cambridge University Press.

Wurzel, R.K.W. (2002), *Environmental Policy-Making in Britain, Germany and the European Union: The Europeanisation of Air and Water Pollution Control*, Manchester: Manchester University Press.

Zito, A. (2000), *Creating Environmental Policy in the European Union*, London: Macmillan.

NATIONAL EXPERIENCES

The Politics of 'Light-Handed Regulation': 'New' Environmental Policy Instruments in Australia

ELIM PAPADAKIS and RICHARD GRANT

Introduction

Institutional emphasis on direct regulation in Australia reflects the country's geography, climate and exploitation of resources. Although Australia covers a vast territory, most people live in a small number of coastal cities in the eastern region. Concerns about the environment relate to dumping partially treated effluents into the sea with impacts on human health and biodiversity [*Mercer, 1999*] and unsustainable European patterns of agricultural development [*Commonwealth of Australia, 1989: 46*], exacerbated by land clearing for agriculture and urban development and by poor management (including damage of seedlings by livestock and use of fertilizers, herbicides and pesticides). Agriculture is often unsustainable due to such constraints as low rainfall, infertile soils, flat topography, large distances from markets and lack of large navigable rivers linking the inland to the coast [*Carden, 1999: 84*].

To address these issues Australia has relied on command and control systems, with the state playing a crucial role in 'nation-building', developing agriculture by creating transportation and communication infrastructure [*Loudon, 2000: 11*]. The original institutions of a penal colony were crucial in establishing patterns for government involvement in economic development [*Aitkin, 1983: 176*], resulting in a state 'stronger, more intrusive, legitimately interventionist instrument than Victoria's Britain' [*Collins, 1985: 151*]. In the 1980s, as the environment entered the political agenda, environmentalists backed policies which reflected utilitarian traditions of state intervention and legalism.

Although most interventions in Australia still entail regulatory approaches, key drivers of environmental policy have proposed a mix of instruments and voluntary or market based approaches, heralding an opportunity to adopt a different paradigm. Is Australia therefore becoming a pioneer in adopting 'light handed' regulatory approaches, combining intervention with market based and voluntary approaches?

Older reviews of market based instruments, such as those conducted by the OECD, indicate that 'pollution charges, user charges, differential taxes, levies and fees, deposit refunds, tradable permits, eco-taxes and tax incentives are not extensively used in Australia for environmental purposes' [*1998: 140*]. However, more recent changes in the content and discourse of policy have included significant initiatives to incorporate economic, voluntary and regulatory approaches. Furthermore, as acknowledged by the OECD, the distinctive contribution by Australian policy-makers since the late 1980s is implementation of such microeconomic reform as reductions in tariffs and industry assistance, deregulation of financial markets and increased efficiency of government enterprises: 'The removal of artificial barriers to competition is expected to encourage *more efficient pricing* of goods and services, and an attendant improvement in resource use' [*OECD, 1998: 134*].

There is argument over the impact of such measures on the environment, in such areas as increasing competition in electricity markets and subsidies to such natural resource intensive businesses as the aluminium industry [*Hamilton, 2001: 36, 63–7*]. Yet, in its overall approach to microeconomic reform, Australia has pursued an agenda distinct from the EU (and hence many OECD countries), rendering it increasingly receptive to market based instruments in addressing environmental problems. These approaches are linked to an enduring reliance on regulatory frameworks, albeit ones that hugely de-emphasise traditional command and control approaches.

In comparing Australia to EU or OECD countries one needs to differentiate between levels of commitment to new notions of state involvement in environmental protection, notably sustainable development. Australia (like Canada, Germany, Japan and the UK) is categorised as 'cautiously supportive' of sustainable development [*Lafferty and Meadowcroft, 2000a: 412*]. At either end of the spectrum one finds such 'enthusiastic' countries as the Netherlands, Norway and Sweden and a 'disinterested' United States. Yet, the metaphor of sustainable development is limited in encapsulating shifts to NEPIs. As with any analysis of policy paradigms, one needs to register changes in enthusiasm to integrating sustainable development into discursive practices of central governments. In Australia there was a waning in intensity of sustainable development related initiatives in the 1990s (compared to the Netherlands, Norway and Sweden) [*Lafferty and Meadowcroft, 2000a: 346, Table 12.2a and 12.2b*].

More fundamentally, the metaphor of sustainable development is not aimed at capturing commitment to NEPIs. Instead, if we focus on microeconomic reform in Australia, coupled with traditions of intervention in economic policy, we appreciate the conduit for a distinctive approach to NEPIs – one that entails state interest in setting policy instruments combined with efforts to stimulate market mechanisms. In sum, NEPIs are adopted in ways that reflect traditional concerns about nation-building along with innovative microeconomic reform. Though critics of government from the Right and Left argue the government has either been too lax or too rigorous in pursuing microeconomic reform and reducing commitment by the state to steering society, the re-election in November 2001 of a Liberal–National Coalition government for a third term is likely to ensure further emphasis on NEPIs.

Australian Environmental Policy

Policy Structures

Possibilities for introducing NEPIs need to be seen in the context of challenges to traditional roles of the state in welfare and economic development. An important aspect of the Australian state, derived from the Constitution, is the three-tiered shape of the federal political system: the Commonwealth (or Federal government), governments of the States and Territories and Local government. States and Territories hold extensive powers to legislate, and to manage and regulate the environment. Local government is responsible for land use planning and aspects of development. Yet, recent shifts in power towards the Commonwealth, due partly to signing international conventions like the UN World Heritage Convention, have reshaped relations between state and federal governments, and *de facto* redefined the powers of the states. Another consideration is pressure applied by social movements on Federal governments to override the states.

Although structures of environmental policy still reflect the division of powers denoted by the Constitution, in the 1970s interest groups and changes in elite attitudes were pivotal in creating new institutional arrangements. The Federal Office of the Environment was established in 1971 and the Australia Environment Council a year later. State governments established their own laws and agencies. The Whitlam Labor government (1972–75): formed a separate department to deal with environmental issues; created the Australian National Parks and Wildlife Service and the Australian Heritage Commission; signed international treaties on the environment; and provided a legislative basis for the Environmental Impact Statement in 1974 with the *Environmental Protection (Impact of Proposals) Act*.

The 1980s saw the creation of institutions aimed at integrating economic and environmental concerns at all government levels such as the Resource Assessment Commission (RAC), established in 1989 to identify a range of values involved in using resources, and the Ecologically Sustainable Development (ESD) Working Groups. The 1998 Environment Protection and Biodiversity Conservation Bill enshrined in legislation for the first time the promotion of Ecologically Sustainable Development. There remained barriers in institutional structures, such as potentially conflicting roles of various levels of government and lack of effective coordination [*Productivity Commission, 1999*]. Yet, a 'whole of government' approach was introduced in principle and there were improvements in knowledge about the state of the environment [*State of the Environment Advisory Council, 1996*] and economic costs and benefits of different policies.

The RAC broadened and intensified capacity to integrate various considerations into policy. Similarly, ESD working groups attempted to combine sustainable development with Prime Minister Hawke's unique style of 'consensus' politics [*Economou, 1996*]. Promises to accommodate environmental and economic goals became central pillars of policy. The National Strategy for Ecologically Sustainable Development (NSESD) focused on coordination of environmental policies among public institutions, and this was backed by a November 1991 agreement among Heads of Government to create an intergovernmental ESD Steering Committee and a December 1992 meeting of the Council of Australian Governments (COAG) (comprising the leaders of Commonwealth, State and Territory governments and the President of the Local Government Association). Recommendations by ESD working groups and the Intergovernmental Agreement on the Environment (IGAE) (May 1992) became the basis for developing policy. Involvement by COAG, the highest-ranking association for intergovernmental cooperation, was vital in realising ESD principles at all levels of government.

These institutional structures promised much but delivered less than expected, thereby creating a greater opening for NEPIs. The partial realisation of ESD and persistent fragmentation of government departments and tiers of administration were acknowledged in official reports [*State of the Environment Advisory Council, 1996: 11, 15; Productivity Commission, 1999*]. The advent of a Coalition government in 1996 challenged perceptions of the leadership role played by the Labor Party when the new administration created a $1.15 billion Natural Heritage Trust, funded through partial privatisation of the national telephone carrier, Telstra. This supported plans for national vegetation, rehabilitation of the Murray-Darling River Basin, a national land and water resources audit, a national reserve system and tackling pollution of the coast and seas. Although the initial impetus for ESD diminished, the government supported linkages between the NSESD and other initiatives (IGAE, National Greenhouse Response Strategy, Australian Greenhouse Office and National

Strategy for the Conservation of Australia's Biological Diversity). The ESD strategy also ensured recognition of the co-existence of environmental and economic objectives, thereby diminishing conflicts between Departments focusing on either industry or the economy.

Yet, the advent of a Coalition government signalled a shift towards attitudes more receptive to NEPIs than traditional forms of statutory intervention. The focus on trade liberalisation was such that 'most decision makers' believed 'the wealth created by economic activities will overcome environmental effects' [*OECD, 1998: 8*]. Re-assessment of direct intervention entailed refinement of economic and regulatory instruments (through greater use of product charges, deposit refunds and emission trading and the adoption of the user pays principle in waste management and waste water treatment) [*OECD, 1998: 2*]. It also led to greater interest in the role of business and free markets along the lines specified by writers on 'natural capitalism' [*Hawken et al., 2000*]. Commonwealth and state governments have therefore promoted such notions as 'light-handed regulation' [*Andrews, 2000a*], emissions trading [*Hillman, 2000*] and sustainable industries [*Commonwealth of Australia, 2000a: 43*].

Policy Style

Although Australian politics is often characterised as adversarial, there are numerous examples of consensual approaches, especially by Labor from 1983 to 1996 in addressing some environment issues. The proactive, consensual style was premised on governments retaining control over processes of intermediation. The arrangements for environmental policy assumed neo-corporatist characteristics [*Economou, 1993: 407; Downes, 1996: 175*], and attempted to address shortcomings of reactive policies, which had inflamed conflicts.

However, the deterioration of these arrangements preceded the advent of the Coalition government in 1996. The Hawke Labor government, though interventionist in environmental policy, had already – through deregulation, reducing public capital expenditure as a proportion of total outlays, dismantling tariff barriers, and decreasing public sector staffing levels – sparked vigorous debate over whether or not it any longer represented the 'Labor tradition' [*Maddox, 1989*]. From 1992 the Keating Labor government unleashed 'devolution' by dismantling the RAC, delaying implementation of most recommendations of the ESD working groups, providing a 'regional' focus to activities of the Australian Heritage Commission and endorsing the IGAE [*Economou, 1999: 71*].

Furthermore, despite trenchant criticism by some of Coalition policies on issues like climate change, the environment has diminished as a source of division among the major parties. There is widespread agreement on the need to balance environment and economy. Efforts to introduce NEPIs complement this consensus. However, in our overall assessment, the tendency towards consensus is not as ingrained as a style of making decisions in Australia as in some northern European nations. The proactive approach is also less developed than in some countries.

The Content of Policy

Ever since the environment became a salient issue, the overall goals guiding policy have tended to be pragmatic and eclectic. In the 1970s Australian governments were wary of radical proposals. There was tacit acknowledgement of problems and the need for regulation. The approach can be characterised as accepting the tenets of 'administrative rationalism' [*Dryzek, 1997*], of using existing bureaucratic expertise and mechanisms and viewing environmental issues as 'minor, technical, soluble and politically uncontentious' [*Jacobs, 1997: 3*].

It is only with greater federal intervention in the 1980s that efforts were undertaken to develop comprehensive and proactive approaches reaching far beyond the confines of the established bureaucracy. The focus on federal intervention was indicative of the politicisation of the environment and an appreciation that decisions were not purely technical. One indicator was the elevation of the Environment portfolio in the Federal Cabinet. Furthermore, increases in federal power coincided with a period when the traditional role of governments, to own directly and/or manage natural resources in order to procure socially acceptable outcomes and correct market failure, shifted to providing incentives for business to devise their own solutions and for markets to self-regulate the use of natural resources.

This reflects a shift that occurred by the 1990s as policy makers questioned the state's role in national economic development, reflected in such trends as the decline in public capital expenditure as a proportion of total outlays since the mid-1960s, in the state's capacity to shape the sectoral structure of the economy through reducing tariffs, and in public sector employment. Furthermore, the notion of sustainable development signalled a move away from a conflict between environmental and economic values, and towards deregulation and support for industries seeking to gain competitive advantage through eco-efficiency and other measures. Thus, traditional instruments available to government, notably direct regulation (for example, legislation permitting fixed amounts of emissions), are being supplemented (rather than replaced) by three other categories of instruments: economic instruments (for example, taxes and subsidies) within existing markets, economic instruments defining new markets (via property rights) and voluntary measures [*Byron, 2001*].

This did not mean an end to regulation and bureaucratic legalism. First, there is resistance in sectors of the community to any such reversal. Although some writers acknowledge the value of new measures like voluntary agreements, taxes and incentives – to augment rather than supplant traditional regulatory approaches – they are sceptical about any moves to dilute the role of federal agencies [*Hamilton, 2001*]. In other words, efforts to change the setting of policy instruments are contested, particularly regarding the devolution of responsibilities to regional and local levels. Hence, some writers portray the 1980s, when the Labor government began to embrace environmentalists' concerns and establish such institutional structures as the RAC and ESD Working Groups, as a 'golden age of Commonwealth activity' [*Economou, 1999: 80*]. Initiatives by Labor are represented as proactive and long-term rather than reactive, with the aim of incorporating peak interest groups [*Economou, 1993: 399–400*]. Second, many practices of the 'golden age' were founded on traditions of intervention. In other words, despite moves towards 'devolution' and the use of NEPIs, there is *a strong focus on coordinating policies at the federal level*. This is evident in the creation of such frameworks for sustainable development as the NSESD and the Australian Greenhouse Office (AGO). Third, although many writers assume the state plays a diminished role in environmental protection [*Crowley, 1999: 48*], some commitments by the Coalition (IGAE, NSESD, Natural Heritage Trust, enhancing co-operation between agencies and developing measures for and monitoring sustainable development) do not fit this characterisation.

Although there is criticism of failure or reluctance to implement Agenda 21 and Australia's position at Kyoto [*Crowley, 1999: 47*], the reality is Labor initiated some of these trends. Coalition governments have, however, been more assertive than Labor in distancing themselves from statist traditions. The Coalition is also sceptical about multilateral agreements (on greenhouse emissions), has taken a strong line on defining the 'national interest' largely in economic terms and has affinity with critiques of 'big government'. This has made the Coalition receptive to NEPIs and involving business in finding solutions.

Overall, the kinds of policy tools adopted in Australia could best be characterised as a form of flexible regulation, responsive to political conditions (especially due to the short electoral cycle and the crucial importance of a small number of marginal electorates to who controls government) and to financial constraints. A representative example of this kind of approach is the December 1992 endorsement of the NSESD by the Council of Australian Government, which was subject to (1) adequate funds being available and (2) specific circumstances prevailing in particular states. These represent a significant potential limitation on realisation of the

NSESD. This is perhaps one reason why NEPIs represent an alternative or complementary approach to the neo-corporatist character of many policies. A likely future scenario, based on goals framed by traditions of pragmatism and eclecticism, and under a Coalition regime, is of an increasing focus on NEPIs. Furthermore, even if Labor were in government, experimentation with NEPIs would continue. The ESD strategies introduced by Labor in the 1990s already contained elements that rendered the state more receptive to NEPIs, though to a lesser degree than under the Coalition. The Coalition, despite espousing free market values, has been cautious in introducing NEPIs. It also contains factions with differing views about the extent of statutory intervention to protect certain social groups and how far to cede power to market forces.

Given this history and set of traditions, one would expect NEPIs to be adopted at all levels of government, with the Federal government setting targets or overall objectives and the states being allowed to choose their own path in terms of both innovation and the precise mix of policy instruments. One would also expect the three levels to play a lead role in experimentation and innovation at different times, depending on the variability of who holds power at the Federal and State levels. However, one would expect the style and approach to vary little among jurisdictions given traditions of co-operative federalism, structures set in place in the 1980s for a more proactive approach to environmental policy and the need to appear to co-operate in the face of public opinion. The public is unlikely to be swayed by radical statist or free-market prescriptions, preferring a pragmatic approach that supports some experimentation with NEPIs. This makes it unlikely that NEPIs will rapidly supplant flexible forms of regulation.

Why are NEPIs Being Adopted?

The metaphor of sustainable development is not designed to reflect commitment to such NEPIs as market based incentives or voluntary agreements. A more revealing driver of commitment to NEPIs in Australia is the agenda for microeconomic reform. Prior to its re-election in 2001, and since then, the Liberal–National Coalition has been criticised for failing to live up to its own rhetoric of implementing a microeconomic reform agenda. Nonetheless, the relevance of this agenda to introducing NEPIs remains salient and a key driver to their adoption.

Another important driver of NEPIs is the argument, aired over the past decade, that markets may play a positive role in environmental protection. The early proponents of this argument did not consciously support NEPIs. They were not environmentalists but advocates of the market and its efficiencies. However, translation of their arguments into environmental policy was a key driver for NEPIs. Such organisations as the Australian Chamber of Commerce, the Commonwealth Treasury, the Institute of Public Affairs and the Tasman Institute recognised the need to protect natural resources, and the flexibility of markets in providing incentives to this end. Fogarty [*1991*] argued several factors were traditionally overlooked in efforts to blame markets for environmental degradation – the most important being the specification of property rights. Hence, in the nineteenth century inadequate specification meant open access to resources like the ocean for fishing, large-scale destruction of some species and the collapse of industries for whaling and sealing. For Fogarty and others [*Moran et al., 1991*] governments play a crucial role in defining and monitoring property rights. Although critical of government interference in general, they emphasised its role in regulating the market.

Another important driver was the Commonwealth government. In the early 1990s, the Labor government devised the NSESD, in line with ideas about NEPIs. This signalled a 'whole of government approach', aimed at integrating concerns about the economy, environment and social equity. The strategy resolved to 'develop, improve and enhance the effective use of pricing and economic instruments as a means for achieving better management of our natural resources' [*Commonwealth of Australia, 1992, Objective 20.1*]. Specifically, it argued the usefulness of tradable rights in managing resources, assessment of economic instruments, and testing the effectiveness of mixes between market and regulatory mechanisms. The testing of economic incentives within a quasi-regulatory approach included consideration of social and environmental costs. To this end, there was concern about issues of generational equity arising from changes to pricing and taxation policy. Proposals to explore market instruments were not viewed as a constraint on development. Rather, the objective was to 'pursue opportunities to achieve greater diversity in our economic and industrial structure, while ensuring that environmental objectives were not compromised' [*Commonwealth of Australia, 1992: Objective 21.1*]. Crucially, tax reform, microeconomic reform and trade liberalisation were viewed as consistent with rapid adoption of best environmental technologies. This argument followed the initial advocates of market-based incentives in right-wing think tanks. The NSESD recommended ecologically sustainable development through free markets and productivity reforms.

Furthermore, environmentalists pressured Australian governments and some industry sectors to pay unprecedented attention to allocation of property rights, focusing on the cost to business of polluting resources and ensuring users have an incentive to improve their efficiency and environmental performance. The aim, even if this is yet to be achieved, is for markets to allocate to the highest value user and for business to devise cleaner technologies.

Another driver of NEPIs is the pressure to 'shift the boundary' between public and private sectors, a process encouraged by Coalition governments. As Loudon points out, the underpinning for these changes can be found in new legislation and initiatives [2000: 8–10], including outsourcing public sector corporate and information management and technology services, 'strategic alliances' with the private sector (for instance, for the latter to manage government properties), awarding government contracts to small and medium enterprises, and competitive tendering and contracting.

None of these drivers is unique to Australia. The high level of exchange between officials in and through organisations like the OECD and the requirements by nation states at least to respond to such challenges as the Rio Summit and Agenda 21, mean that some pressures are similar across countries. Other nations have demonstrated a commitment to microeconomic reform, the contrast between regulatory and free market economy approaches has been challenged throughout Europe, and advocates of the market and its efficiencies have enjoyed considerable influence around western democracies. Furthermore, governments in Europe and many OECD countries have developed strategies for sustainable development in response to the World Commission on Environment and Development and international agreements which require reporting back to the United Nations. They have also responded to pressures by environmentalists and industry to focus on allocation of property rights.

Although none of these drivers is peculiar to Australia, their application is unique and tailored to national traditions. This can be an advantage in creating opportunities for successful experimentation with NEPIs. However, it may also be a function of barriers to implementation in a country like Australia. These barriers include overriding expectations that the state intervene to create and guarantee the success of a 'voluntary' agreement, wanting the state to provide subsidies either to render a new initiative competitive or protect certain industries from competition. There is strong reliance on intervention or subsidy to buttress the introduction of new instruments. The state is also expected by others, say the aluminium industry, to protect it from 'unfair competition'. On the question of 'voluntary agreements', these entail, both in Australia and elsewhere, significant levels of government intervention. The OECD [2000] differentiates between three approaches: 'public voluntary programmes' designed by environmental agencies and open to individual firms to participate, 'negotiated agreements' (bargains struck between government and industry) and 'unilateral commitments' by industry without any government involvement. The Greenhouse Challenge (see below) and many other initiatives in Australia (for instance in relation to environmental labelling) certainly fall largely into the first category and to a lesser degree into the second category.

One barrier to implementation is lack of agreement as to the appropriate mix – between voluntary, interventionist, free market, proactive and reactive approaches. There is inadequate information about the efficiency of different instruments. The level of integration and coordination of environmental policy across different areas of government responsibility leaves much to be desired [*Productivity Commission, 1999*]. The most encouraging development, at least from the perspective of proponents of NEPIs, is the combination of realism about what is feasible in the Australian context and willingness fairly rapidly to take on board new ideas whether they emerge from Europe or the United States.

Hence the approach to policy does make concessions to traditional structures, particularly the role of the states and territories in environmental policy-making, and to the prevailing view about the need for regulation. However, this approach also entails experimentation with new ideas such as environmental labelling, market-based incentives and new partnerships or voluntary agreements. The notion of 'light-handed' regulation captures this effort to experiment in a manner that does not conflict fundamentally with state traditions. These traditions should not, however, be regarded as static. Australia certainly has a history of state regulation and intervention. Yet, it has embraced ideas that challenge the traditional consensus – be it in rolling back the welfare state in the 1970s, introducing microeconomic reform in the 1980s, or shifting the boundaries between the state and private sectors in the 1990s. Furthermore, Australian governments have demonstrated versatility in adopting ideas from apparently competing traditions. For instance, in environmental policy there is engagement with sustainable development, which reflects European ideas about combining economic progress and state intervention to protect the environment, and with ideas from the United States about natural capitalism.

One way of understanding the drivers to supplement or move away from regulatory traditions, at least as conceived by the current regime, is to analyse statements by policy-makers. According to former Minister for the Environment, Senator Robert Hill, although outcomes of international negotiations were uncertain, the government could 'endeavour to make the framework in which policy is formulated as clear as possible, and encourage businesses to plan for the possibility of change' and by assisting them 'to develop voluntary agreements' [*Commonwealth of Australia, 2000b: 3*]. Elsewhere, Hill noted how the Pew Centre for Global Climate Change 'represents 22 of the largest corporations in the United States ... that have accepted the basic science of climate change' and should serve as a role model for Australian companies 'to take advantage of the economic opportunities that could arise from the implementation of the Kyoto Protocol' [*2000a: 2–3*].

Another objective is to 'encourage private sector investment in revegetation or programs aimed at promoting farm forestry and the establishment of new plantations' which reduce carbon in the atmosphere and 'restore degraded land, reduce salinity and provide habitat for our endangered species' [*Hill, 2000b: 4*]. One of the principal measures to realise this plan is a National Carbon Accounting Scheme which aims 'to provide a sound basis for future reporting for the national greenhouse inventory, particularly the agriculture and land-use change and forestry sectors' [*2000b: 4*]. However, Hill immediately added that regulatory measures supported by about $1 billion of public expenditure were part of the government's strategy [*2000b: 5*]. In another speech the Minister expressed commitment to a 'mix of measures' [*Hill, 2000c: 4*], a theme echoed by the Chief Executive Officer of the AGO: 'The current mix of current programs includes voluntary, regulatory and market based approaches' [*Andrews, 2000b*].

NEPIs in Australia

Market-Based Instruments

Economic instruments are used across Australia to address a wide range of problems. Though an OECD report found economic instruments were not widely used, it drew attention to several initiatives by the Commonwealth or the States (see Box 1).

The enhancement since then of such instruments results from recognition by policy makers of the economic costs of environmental damage, of market failure and of how market based instruments may be 'ideally suited' to tackle such failure [*Gordon and Hatfield Dodds, 2000*].

Among recent innovations are a 'load based licensing system' and a 'load based pollutant charge' introduced in July 1999 by the New South Wales Environment Protection Authority: 'Under the scheme, discharges are controlled by absolute maximum load, or volume, limits accompanied by a new license fee structure. Pollution charges are levied on the annual pollutant load discharged by a firm to provide an ongoing incentive to reduce loads' [*Gordon and Hatfield Dodds, 2000*]. The authors noted it was premature to assess the effectiveness of the scheme in providing incentives for improving environmental performance and the adoption of cleaner technology.

BOX 1

Taxes, charges, fees and levies on emissions	
COM	motor fuel tax; tax on leaded gasoline; and noise levy
NSW	special environment levy on waste water; trade waste quality charges; and waste disposal levy.

Licence fees	
COM	licences for ozone-depleting substances
NSW	licence fee for discharges to rivers
QLD	visits to national parks and conservation reserves (like the Great Barrier Reef); and bushland acquisition levy
SA	licence fee for emissions to air and for discharges to the marine environment
VIC	licence fee for emissions to air and for discharges to rivers; and landfill levy (based on volume and type of trade waste)

Deposit refunds	
SA	beverage containers (beer, soft drinks and mineral water)
	Tradable discharge permits
NSW	Hunter River Salinity Trading Scheme; South Creek Bubble Licensing Scheme (phosphorous levels)
NSW, SA, VIC	Murray Darling Basin Salinity Scheme (credits tradable between states)

Tradable resource use rights	
COM	transferable quotas in fisheries management
NSW, QLD, SA, VIC	transferable water entitlements
NSW QLD, SA, TAS, VIC	log pricing and allocation

Performance bonds	
VIC	lender liability for contaminated site clean-up

COM: Commonwealth; NSW: New South Wales; QLD: Queensland; SA: South Australia; TAS: Tasmania; VIC: Victoria

Based on OECD [*1998: 141, Table 6.4*].

Another attempt to introduce market instruments is the New South Wales Carbon Rights Legislation Amendment Act (1998), which recognised 'ownership of, and trade in, carbon sequestration rights from State forests in New South Wales'. The Act was designed to support the 1999 launch 'of the world's first exchange-traded market for carbon sequestration credits by the Sydney Futures Exchange and State Forests of New South Wales', and thus enable 'buyers to purchase credits (denominated in one metric ton of CO_2 equivalent) as a hedge in a future emissions trading market or bundle them with a product sales to create emission-free products' [*Gordon and Hatfield*

Dodds, 2000]. Although the demutualisation of the Sydney Futures Exchange was apparently a factor which led it to withdraw from this initiative, it is indicative of links established between 'light-handed' regulatory approaches and the private sector.

Another initiative, demonstrating the intention of policy makers, is the effort by the Commonwealth government to develop emissions trading systems. These systems represent what Byron [*2001*] refers to as 'economic instruments defining new markets'. Detailed consideration of such systems and what sectors might be covered by them has been conducted by the AGO [*1999a, 1999b, 1999c, 1999d*]. One outcome was the declaration by the Federal government that 'it would only implement a mandatory national emissions trading system if the Kyoto protocol is ratified by Australia and enters into force, and if there is an established international emissions trading regime' [*Commonwealth of Australia, 2000a: 42*]. The notion of trading systems remains an integral part of the agenda and is focused on developing domestic emissions trading schemes and systems to credit early greenhouse abatement action.

Crucially, Hill privileges market-based over administrative strategies: 'Research carried out by ABARE (Australian Bureau of Resource and Agricultural Economics) indicates the cost to countries of achieving greenhouse targets is much less through an emissions trading system – particularly one that operates internationally – than through administrative policies and measures' [*2000a: 5;* also *James, 1997*]. Australia understandably regards itself as 'one of the strongest proponents of the use of an uncapped international emissions trading system to meet greenhouse gas abatement targets' and 'has put considerable effort into the development of a possible national trading system, using the Kyoto Protocol as a template for the rules, eligibility, and design procedures' [*Gordon and Hatfield Dodds, 2000*].

Voluntary Agreements

The most widely publicised Federal program for reducing greenhouse gas emissions is Greenhouse Challenge, introduced by Labor 1995. Unlike incentive-based structures of other programs, this is a voluntary scheme to raise industry awareness of its polluting activities and cost-effective ways to reduce emissions. The scheme provides access to experts who advise on technical, financial and cultural issues affecting performance and devise action plans. Greenhouse Challenge involved 558 companies and industry associations as at 15 November 2001, with the aim of reducing CO_2 emissions by 20 Mt per annum. The scheme is marketed to business on the strength of potential efficiency gains, corresponding incentives to adopt leading technology, and community recognition of environmental performance. Significantly, participants include key industry sectors: '100 per cent of aluminium production; 98 per cent of electricity generators, distributors and transmitter emissions; 78 per cent of emissions generated by mining; and increasing numbers in the agricultural and transport sectors' [*Commonwealth of Australia, 2000a: 42*]. The scheme does not attempt to ensure compliance through regulation and only includes a limited proportion of potential emissions. Companies agree to random independent verification of their actions.

Total funding for the scheme between 1995 and 2003 is $36 million. Organisations sign a Cooperative Agreement with the Commonwealth to reduce emissions. Each agreement typically comprises a greenhouse gas inventory, an action plan for greenhouse gas abatement and a forecast of future emissions. An evaluation of the programme showed it had achieved significant reductions in emissions (23.5 Mt) and was enhancing the capacity 'to identify, monitor, manage and report' emissions [*Commonwealth of Australia, 1999*]. The aim is to double the number of participants to 1,000 by 2005, with emphasis on recruiting large emitters. The programme is seen as pivotal in capacity building in industry by securing commitment of CEOs, changing workplace cultures, effective management of data (to prepare companies for an emissions trading regime), reducing impacts on the environment and creating opportunities 'to demonstrate environmental credentials to the community' [*Andrews, 2000a*]. Performance verification was taken a step further by involving 35 of the largest firms that had signed up to the programme. A separate analysis described the programme as 'an excellent first step', and argued it will become even more effective if 'requirements for audit and verification' included testing the 'incorporation of environmental concerns into internal decision making, processes and culture' [*Parker, 1999: 74*].

Another initiative, presented as part of the National Greenhouse Strategy (NGS) under the heading 'greenhouse best practice in industrial processes and waste management', is the $3 million 'Eco-efficiency programme' launched by the Federal Environment Ministry, Environment Australia. The program has led to agreements with the Housing Industry Association and the Australian Food and Grocery Council 'to promote, demonstrate and monitor improved eco-efficiency practices' [*Commonwealth of Australia, 2000a: 66*]. An 'Eco-Efficiency Agreement' is a three-year, voluntary accord between the Commonwealth and an industry association. The aim is for both parties to promote eco-efficient practices among members of the association. The tools to implement and monitor eco-efficiency include environmental audits, environment management systems, environmental reporting, environmental accounting and life cycle assessment [*Commonwealth of Australia, 2002a*].

Finally, a major voluntary initiative, launched in August 1999, was the National Packaging Covenant. This aimed 'to minimise the environmental impacts of consumer packaging and paper waste, close the recycling loop and develop economically viable and sustainable recycling collection systems' [*Commonwealth of Australia, 2000c: 3*]. The central concept in the Covenant is 'product stewardship', implemented through collaboration between industry and government. The Covenant is 'a self-regulatory and voluntary measure', backed by the National Environment Protection (Used Packaging Materials) Measure (NEPM), which 'requires jurisdictions to impose recovery activities on non-Covenant brand owners, and seeks to create a level playing field that protects Covenant signatories from market disadvantage' [*Commonwealth of Australia, 2000c: 3*]. There are formal obligations to report on progress, particularly to the National Environment Protection Council. Eight Commonwealth, State and Territory Ministers, two local governments, nine industry associations and 13 industry organisations or companies initially signed the Covenant.

By October 2000 there were 131 signatories, including eight governments, five local governments or regional organisations, 12 industry organisations and 106 companies. Although the scheme has faced opposition by the Australian Local Government Association, two of the local government signatories to the Covenant represent nearly one third of all local governments in Australia – the one in Queensland, which represents 125 local governments and the one in Victoria, which represents 78 councils. Another factor in the early stages of this initiative is that 'Many organisations also indicated they were waiting to analyse the implications of the NEPM legislative requirements on their operations' [*Commonwealth of Australia, 2000c: 5*]. Furthermore, many signatories have not yet submitted Action Plans and there is much to be done in ensuring independent verification of actions by participants, accountability and penalty for non-compliance and quantifiable performance indicators [*Commonwealth of Australia, 2000c: 14*].

None the less, it is a significant voluntary initiative in terms of the initial engagement. In July 2000 the national shopping retailer Coles Myer, which represented about 20 per cent of the entire retail market, became a signatory. Overall, notwithstanding the challenges of implementation, the Covenant attracted 'substantially more signatories than any previous ANZECC [*Australian and New Zealand Environment and Conservation Council*] Agreement concerning the management of packaging waste' [*Commonwealth of Australia, 2000c: 1*].

Eco-labels

The Federal government promotes labelling to enable consumers to ascertain the environmental impact of products and 'make responsible product choices' [*Commonwealth of Australia, 2002b*]. There have been several initiatives. Mandatory Fuel Consumption Labelling requires business (in this case the car industry) to advertise the environmental liability of products in terms of fuel consumption. From 1978 to 1987 a voluntary agreement between the government and the Federated Chamber of Automotive Industries ensured the trend of national average fuel consumption in new cars continued to decline. New legislation, effective from January 2001, made it mandatory for fuel consumption labels to be placed on car windscreens at point of sale. These model-specific labels show the fuel consumption in numerical terms, such as litres/100 km.

There are several joint initiatives between the Federal government and the States and Territories to promote environmental labelling. An early experiment, 'Environmental Choice Australia' (1992–94), was aborted after failing to gain industry support. A more successful scheme, the *Energy Rating* label scheme for major appliances, is a mandatory scheme covering such appliances as refrigerators, air conditioners, dish and clothes washers and clothes dryers. A system of star rating labels enables direct comparisons of the energy efficiency of appliances. This highly successful scheme, introduced in 1986, has gained widespread support from industry.

Another voluntary initiative, the Australian Energy Star Program, involves industry and covers office equipment (including computers, printers, fax machines and photocopiers) and will be extended to home entertainment equipment (such as television sets, video recorders, DVD players and audio equipment). Office equipment under this scheme is designed to switch to 'sleep' mode when not in use, and home entertainment goods are designed to reduce the power consumption when in 'standby' mode. The potential energy savings from this scheme are considerable. GHG emissions could be reduced by 2.28 million tonnes (CO_2 equivalent) 'If the energy-saving features were activated on all Energy Star compliant computers in Australia' [*Commonwealth of Australia, 2002c*]. Equipment in this scheme has to meet specified energy efficiency standards. The scheme is based on international benchmarks, originally created by the US EPA in 1992. Another aspect of this initiative is involvement as 'Energy Star Partners' of such corporations as Compaq, Sony, Apple, IBM, Sharp, Intel, Microsoft, Acter, Epson, Minolta, Fuji Xerox, Hewlett Packard, Brother, Harvey Norman, Ricoh, Hitachi, Wyse, Canon, Philips, TEAC, Lexmark, Samsung, Ipex, Toshiba, LG and Pioneer [*Commonwealth of Australia, 2002d*].

In all these initiatives, even when the evolution of the instrument is indigenous, there is keen awareness about programmes in other countries – such as *Environmental Choice Canada, Blue Angel* in Germany and the European Union Eco-Label Scheme. Evidence from OECD reports on labelling is cited to back local labelling schemes as are the ISO standards. [*Commonwealth of Australia, 2002b*].

Other Instruments

Several schemes entail incentive funding to generate commercial interest in reducing greenhouse gas emissions through alternative energy sources. The Photovoltaic Rebate Program, the Renewable Energy Commercialisation Program, the Renewable Energy Showcase Program and the Renewable Equity Energy Fund offer funds on a competitive basis, promoting adoption of equipment and processes for renewable energy. Where technology is already available, a cash rebate for consumers applies. In other cases, the government funds industry investment in new technology. The requirement is the venture be a good prospect commercially and of significant environmental benefit. The Renewable Energy Equity Fund is based on decisions of an investment manager according to strict guidelines, rather than a government regulator.

The Greenhouse Gas Abatement Program (GGAP) and the Alternative Fuel Conversion Programme allocate funds to those projects designed to reduce emissions. As with renewable energy programmes, projects need to be commercially viable and result in quantifiable and additional abatement of greenhouse gases. The GGAP was allocated $400 million between 2000–1 and 2003–4. It supports projects that result in *quantifiable* and *additional* abatement not expected to occur in the absence of GGAP funding. The objective is to reduce net greenhouse gas emissions by supporting activities likely to result in substantial emission reductions or sink enhancement. Projects that will deliver abatement exceeding 250,000 tonnes of CO2 equivalents per annum are given priority.

The Alternative Fuel Conversion Programme, a four-year program which began in 2000, was allocated $75 million to assist operators of heavy commercial vehicles and buses weighing 3.5 tonnes gross vehicle mass or more, to convert their vehicles to operate on either CNG or LPG, or purchase new vehicles running on these fuels. Applications are assessed competitively according to relative performance against expected greenhouse gas emission reductions resulting from the proposals, the degree to which proposals promote community awareness of issues, the financial viability of applicants and the need to substantiate conversion or fuel system upgrade costs through a process in which at least two competitive quotes are sought. The scheme is one of direct funding with market-based incentives.

Finally, the Emissions Reduction Incentive Program, funded through a commitment of $13 million over five years, provides supplementary funding for councils towards project costs designed at reducing greenhouse gas emissions across a wide range of areas. The first round of applications closed in February 2001.

According to Gwen Andrews, the main criterion for evaluating projects is cost effectiveness in reducing emissions, for example by using new technologies or supporting sustainable land management 'through better integration of greenhouse considerations into agricultural and forestry practices' or 'promoting the development and uptake of sustainable energy in regional Australia, including bio-fuel and biomass for energy' [*2000a*]. The GGAP will also provide government and industry 'experience in assessing abatement projects against baselines, and in rigorous financial assessment of potential abatement activities' and 'provide some evidence from across the economy of the cost of abating emissions, which will be a useful pointer to the value of carbon in the economy' [*Andrews, 2000a*].

The strategic objectives of the GGAP are to encourage technological development and highlight advantages to business of 'early movers' in emission abatement. For Andrews the current mix of government programmes emphasises 'cost minimisation' and encourages 'low cost abatement opportunities from all sectors of the economy' [*2000b*]. She also adds: 'But in spite of the large government investment, the truth of the matter is that in the near to medium term, the paradigm will have to shift from a government investment model to one that involves the entire economy. And it is for this reason that the government has asked the AGO to look at emissions trading as a possible policy response.'

'Old' Instruments: Regulation

The mix of approaches to environmental policy is reflected in initiatives like the *Renewable Energy Action Agenda* – part of an effort to create an industry with annual sales of $4 billion by 2010 – and the *Renewable Energy (Electricity) Act* 2000 which sets *mandatory* (two per cent) targets for energy from this source. In other words, this legislation compels industry to develop renewable energy. Even ardent critics of the government acknowledge the Mandatory Renewable Energy Program 'is expected to give a significant boost to the renewable energy industries and place Australia in a better position to meet emission reduction targets' [*Hamilton, 2001: 127*].

The Renewable Energy Certificate (REC) legislation, created the world's first mandatory environmental instrument. The subsidy of $30 or $40 per megawatt hour is a small addition to consumers' power bills. But the incentives for the market have proved beyond government expectations. Take the plan by the firm *Enviromission*, which aims to combine solar energy with turbine power to create the world's tallest man-made structure – a five-kilometre wide, one-kilometre high solar chimney [*ABC Television 7:30 Report, 5 Sept. 2001*]. There is strong interest in RECs among wind power engineers, with the industry calling for more ambitious government targets. One indicator of the success of market-based instruments is where firms pressure regulators to increase their requirements.

Programmes for greenhouse gas abatement depend on a mix of market, voluntary and regulatory instruments. Many initiatives form part of the NGS, a $1 billion undertaking by the Commonwealth (endorsed by State and Territory governments) to tackle climate change and meet international commitments to reduce emissions. The NGS aims to limit emissions through partnerships with governments, industry and the community. One partnership is the Cities for Climate Protection campaign, developed by the International Council for Local Environmental Initiatives to assist local governments in reducing greenhouse emissions. The involvement in this scheme, from 1998, by 99 Australian local governments (covering 47.5 per cent of the country's population) represents, according to the Federal government, 'the fastest uptake and largest number of participating local governments in the world' [*Commonwealth of Australia, 2000a: 41*].

The NGS includes measures to promote efficient and sustainable energy use and supply. Though the initial impact of some reforms ran counter to the policy objective of reducing greenhouse emissions, measures like the deregulation of the natural gas industry are expected to reduce emissions [*Commonwealth of Australia, 2000a: 47*]. Many initiatives in energy use highlight a range of regulatory approaches, including efforts to 'fine-tune' or target certain areas in a strategic manner. For instance, in July 2000, the government applied new standards to generators used in power stations, which should reduce greenhouse gas emissions by 4 Mt per annum by 2012. Another form of regulation relates to setting energy efficiency standards for residential and commercial buildings as well as energy performance codes and standards for domestic appliances and commercial and industrial equipment.

The initial impression conveyed by key initiatives such as the NGS is one of continuity in traditional regulatory approaches, with several qualifications: growing emphasis on voluntary arrangements, targeting of resources to encourage the creation of competitive eco-efficient industries, the importance of strategic (rather than operational) interventions by the Commonwealth and other agencies and research on economic or market-based systems (such as emissions trading).

Conclusion

The current pattern points to genuine interest in and experimentation with 'new' tools. In terms of structures, there is willingness to supplement traditional arrangements with NEPIs, and experiment with 'light-handed' regulation. With regard to policy styles, there remains a mixture of adversarialism and consensus. Despite significant efforts to achieve consensus and growing interest across the political divide in NEPIs, adversarial policy styles are unlikely to disappear. Above all, pragmatism and eclecticism in policy making and content are enduring features. NEPIs are unlikely suddenly to supplant traditional regulation. The Federal Government will strive to play a coordinating role, and although NEPIs are being adopted in theory and practice by state governments, the latter are likely to implement distinctive strategies and mixes of policy instruments. Experimentation with NEPIs will be subject to scrutiny in terms of whether or not they are achieving stated objectives.

There will be continuing support for regulation, albeit in a more flexible more. When the Chief Executive of the AGO, Gwen Andrews, told an audience of business people that 'we are aiming for a light-handed regulatory approach, with only minimal government intervention where essential' [2000a], she was backing arrangements that combine traditional approaches with the introduction of NEPIs. The current regime has wanted to minimise statutory interventions [Loudon, 2000], a way of thinking that flows partly from the decline in confidence in established institutions [Papadakis, 1999], and a concomitant belief that markets are better providers of economic and social incentives than government.

The shape of NEPIs in Australia none the less remains largely a process steered by the state. Their success depends on government setting incentives and penalties. As James argues, 'governments can influence usage patterns by controlling the quantities of environmental or natural resource attributes that are traded, or by controlling their prices, either directly where there is a mandate to set prices or indirectly through charges, taxes, subsidies and other economic incentives' [1997: 13]. Statutory traditions are used to bolster these initiatives, hence the claim that Australia's state-sponsored NGS is, on a per capita basis, 'the highest investment by a national government to reduce emissions' [Hill, 2000d]. This seems to support arguments that even 'voluntary' agreements 'appear to herald a dramatic extension of the role of the state, rather than a withdrawal' [Lafferty and Meadowcroft, 2000b: 452].

However, this impression can only be sustained if one insists on analysing state interventions, in other words, on examining solely the role of the state in changing processes of consumption and production. A more complete account would examine the role of 'wealth-generating industries' that operate in accord 'with bio-physical realities' [Carden, 1999: 102]. This would, in effect, entail acknowledgement of some tenets of natural capitalism [Hawken et al., 2000]. The new mix of policy instruments reflects scepticism (among some political and business leaders) about direct regulation. Emissions trading systems are regarded as potentially far more effective than administrative and regulatory measures in tackling climate change. Furthermore, the new initiatives imply a critique of cost-benefit approaches that assume incompatibility between environmental protection and the costs of running a business. They suggest that sustainable development (which posits a central role for government in steering society) needs to be supplemented NEPIs.

Although proponents of NEPIs challenge the notion that industry's role is necessarily destructive, they face several hurdles. First, parts of industry resist the argument that they are operating unsustainably. Second, there are adversarial relations and lack of trust between government, industry and environmental groups about the compatibility of environment and development. Third, there is the complication of redesigning government institutions that have long played a central role in creating and enforcing regulations. Finally, it will take more time to evaluate whether or not the introduction of NEPIs, even on a modest scale, has been successful in changing behaviour. Overall, NEPIs in Australia are not so much replacing regulation but introducing an element of deregulation, and exist alongside modified regulatory structures, providing complementary means for addressing environmental problems.

REFERENCES

Australian Greenhouse Office (AGO) (1999a), *Emissions Trading: Establishing the Boundaries*, Canberra: Commonwealth of Australia.
Australian Greenhouse Office (1999b), *Emissions Trading: Issuing the Permits*, Canberra: Commonwealth of Australia.
Australian Greenhouse Office (1999c), *Emissions Trading: Crediting the Carbon*, Canberra: Commonwealth of Australia.
Australian Greenhouse Office (1999d), *Emissions Trading: Designing the Market*, Canberra: Commonwealth of Australia.
Aitkin, Don (1983), 'Big Government: the Australian Experience', *Australian Quarterly*, Vol.55, No.2, pp. 168–83.
Andrews, Gwen (2000a), Speech to *The Financial Review Conference on Emissions Trading* by the Chief Executive of the Australian Greenhouse Office, Sydney, March 2000 (http://www.greenhouse.gov.au/communications/presentations/afr.pdf) (6 February 2001).
Andrews, Gwen (2000b), 'Everybody Likes a Sure Bet but How Often do They Come Along?' Presentation to the Sydney Mining Club by the Chief Executive of the Australian Greenhouse Office, Sydney 6 July 2000 (http://www.greenhouse.gov.au/communications/presentations/sydney_mining.pdf) (6 Feb. 2001).
Byron, Neil (2001), 'Economic Instruments and Taxation Measures for Natural Resource Management. The Role of Government, the Private Sector and the Community', *Second Environmental Economics Round Table Proceedings*, Research Paper No.7. Commonwealth of Australia, (http://www.erin.gov.au/pcd/economics/round2/byron.html) (8 November 2001).
Carden, Matthew (1999), 'Unsustainable Development in Queensland', in Walker and Crowley [*1999*].
Collins, Hugh (1985), 'Political Ideology in Australia: The Distinctiveness of a Benthamite Society', *Australia: The Daedalus Symposium*, Sydney: Angus & Robertson.
Commonwealth of Australia (1989), *Our Country, Our Future, Statement on the Environment*,

Canberra: AGPS, July.

Commonwealth of Australia (1992), *National Strategy For Ecologically Sustainable Development* (www.ea.gov.au/esd/national/strategy/index.html) (7 Nov. 2001).

Commonwealth of Australia (1999), *Greenhouse Challenge Program Evaluation Report.* Canberra: Australia Greenhouse Office.

Commonwealth of Australia (2000a), *National Greenhouse Strategy. 2000 Progress Report,* Canberra: Australian Greenhouse Office.

Commonwealth of Australia (2000b), *Encouraging Early Greenhouse Abatement Action,* Canberra: Australian Greenhouse Office.

Commonwealth of Australia (2000c), *National Packaging Covenant. First Annual Report* (http://www.ea.gov.au/industyr/waste/covenant/annualreport) (23 May 2002).

Commonwealth of Australia (2002a), *Eco-Efficiency Agreements* (http://www.ea.gov.au/industry/eecp/agreements/involved.html) (23 May 2002).

Commonwealth of Australia (2002b), *Environmental Labelling,* (http://www.ea.gov.au/industry/eecp/tools/tools8.html) (21 May 2002).

Commonwealth of Australia (2002c), *Energy Star* (23 May 2002).

Commonwealth of Australia (2002d), *Who are the Energy Star Partners?* http://www.energystar.gov.au/estarpartners.html (21 May 2002).

Crowley, Kate (1999), 'Explaining Environmental Policy: Challenges, Constraints and Capacity', in K.J. Walker and K. Crowley (eds.) *Australian Environmental Policy 2,* Sydney: UNSW Press.

Downes, David (1996), 'Neo-Corporatism and Environmental Policy' *Australian Journal of Political Science,* Vol.31, No.2, pp.175–90.

Dryzek, John (1997), *The Politics of the Earth. Environmental Discourses,* Oxford: Oxford University Press.

Economou, Nick (1993), 'Accordism and the Environment: The Resource Assessment Commission and National Environmental Policy-Making', *Australian Journal of Political Science,* Vol.28, No.3 pp.399–412.

Economou, Nick (1996), 'Australian Environmental Policy-Making in Transition: The Rise and Fall of the Resource Assessment Commission', *Australian Journal of Public Administration,* Vol.55, No.1, pp. 12–22.

Economou, Nick (1999), 'Backwards into the Future: National Policy Making, Devolution and the Rise and Fall of the Environment', in Walker and Crowley [*1999*].

Fogarty, John (1991), 'Managing the Environment: an Historical Perspective', in Alan Moran, Andrew Chisholm and Michael Porter (eds.), *Markets, Resources and the Environment,* Sydney: Allen & Unwin.

Gordon, Simon and Steve Hatfield Dodds (2000), 'Development in the Design and Use of Economic Instruments since 1987', *Second Environmental Economics Round Table Proceedings* Convened by Senator Robert Hill, Minister for the Environment and Heritage, Canberra, 5 July 2000 Environmental Economics Research Paper No.7, Commonwealth of Australia (http://www.ea.gov.au/pcd/economics/round2/gordon.html) (23 May 2002).

Hamilton, Clive (2001), *Running from the Storm,* Sydney: University of New South Wales Press.

Hawken, Paul, Lovins, Amory B. and Lovins, L. Hunter (2000), *Natural Capitalism: The Next Industrial Revolution,* London: Earthscan.

Hill, Robert (2000a), Speech to 'The Financial Review Conference on Emissions Trading' by the Federal Minister for the Environment and Heritage, Sydney, 30 March 2000 (http://www.greenhouse.gov.au/communications/presentations/afr.pdf) (6 Feb.2001).

Hill, Robert (2000b), 'Beyond Kyoto – Australia's Efforts to Combat Global Warming', A speech to the Pew Centre on Global Climate Change, Washington, 25 April 2000.

Hill, Robert (2000c), 'Warming to the challenge. The role of Australian Business in Combating Global Warming' World Business Council on Sustainable Development and the Australian Business Council Forum, Melbourne, 5 May 2000 (http://www.greenhouse.gov.au/communications/presentations/worldbc.pdf).

Hill, Robert (2000d), 'Working it Out: Australia's Approach to the Hague Climate Change Conference,' An address to the Queensland Chamber of Commerce and Industry, Brisbane 14 Nov. 2000.

Hillman, Ralph (2000), Statement by Mr Ralph Hillman, Australian Ambassador for the Environment, to the Senate Environment, Communications, Information Technology and the Arts Reference Committee: Climate Change, 9 March (http://www.dfat.gov.au/media/speeches/department/000309_climate_change.html) (5 Dec. 2001).

Jacobs, Michael (1997), 'Introduction: the New Politics of the Environment' in Michael Jacobs (ed.), *Greening the Millennium? The New Politics of the Environment*, Oxford: Blackwell.

James, David (1997), *Environmental Incentives: Australian Experience with Economic Instruments for Environmental Management*, Environmental Economics Research Paper No.5, Environment Australia, Canberra.

Lafferty, William and Meadowcroft, James (2000a), 'Patterns of Government Engagement', in Lafferty and Meadowcroft (eds.) [*2000*].

Lafferty, William and James Meadowcroft (2000b), 'Concluding Perspectives', in Lafferty and Meadowcroft (eds.) [*2000*].

Laffert, William and James Meadowcroft (eds.) (2000), *Implementing Sustainable Development: Strategies and Initiatives in High Consumption Societies*, Oxford: Oxford University Press.

Loudon, Michael (2000), 'Public and Private: The Shifting Boundary', *Canberra Bulletin of Public Administration*, Vol.96, pp.8–12.

Maddox, Graham (1989), *The Hawke Government and Labor Tradition*, Melbourne: Penguin Books.

Mercer, David (1999), 'Tourism and Coastal Zone Management: The Uneasy Partnership', in Walker and Crowley [*1999*].

Moran, Alan, Chisholm, Andrew and Michael Porter (eds.) (1991), *Markets, Resources and the Environment*, Sydney: Allen & Unwin.

OECD (1998), *Environmental Performance Reviews: Australia. Conclusions and Recommendations*, Paris: OECD.

OECD (2000), *Voluntary Approaches for Environmental Policy: An Assessment*, Paris: OECD.

Papadakis, Elim (1999), 'Constituents of Confidence and Mistrust in Governmental and Nongovernmental institutions', *Australian Journal of Political Science*, Vol.34, No.1, pp.75–93.

Parker, Christine (1999), 'The Greenhouse Challenge: Trivial Pursuit?' *Environmental and Planning Law Journal*, Vol.16, No.1, pp.63-74.

Productivity Commission (1999), *Implementation of Ecologically Sustainable Development by Commonwealth Departments and Agencies*, Canberra: Commonwealth of Australia.

State of the Environment Advisory Council (SEAC) (1996), *Australia: State of the Environment 1996*, Canberra: AGPS.

Walker, K.J. and K. Crowley (eds.) (1999), *Australian Environmental Policy 2*, Sydney: UNSW Press.

Struggling to Leave Behind a Highly Regulatory Past? 'New' Environmental Policy Instruments in Austria

RÜDIGER K.W. WURZEL, LARS BRÜCKNER,
ANDREW JORDAN and ANTHONY R. ZITO

Introduction

Since the 1980s, Austria has achieved a formidable environmental policy record. It has adopted a wide range of relatively stringent environmental laws (leading to a significant reduction in classic mass pollutants such as sulphur dioxide and nitrogen oxides), opted for fairly ambitious climate change reduction targets and reached one of the highest levels of renewable energy use in Europe [*Lauber, 1997a, 1997b, 2000, 2003; Liefferink and Andersen, 1998; OECD, 1995a, 2001a; UBA, 2001*]. However, Austria's belated environmental leader status has been achieved by relying primarily on traditional 'command-and-control' regulation and subsidies for environmentally less harmful products, services and production processes [*Lauber, 1997a: 83; 1997b; Mol et al., 2000; OECD, 1995a, 2001a*]. The Austrian uptake of 'new' environmental policy instruments (NEPIs), namely market-based instruments (that is, eco-taxes and tradable permits), voluntary agreements (VAs) and informational devices (for example, eco-labels) has remained low when compared to other environmental leader states such as Denmark, the Netherlands, Sweden and, to a lesser degree, Finland and Germany [*EEA, 1997, 2001; Lauber, 1997b: 612–18; Mol et al., 2000; OECD, 1995a, 1995b, 2001a, 2001b*].

Austria benefited economically from the adoption of relatively stringent environmental laws and generous subsidies for pollution abatement technologies as can be seen from the development of a highly successful export-oriented environmental technology industry [*Lauber, 1997b; OECD, 1995a, 2001a*]. However, since the mid-1990s, Austria's enthusiasm for adopting unilaterally stringent environmental policy measures has waned.

The research underpinning this account was undertaken for a project entitled 'Innovation in Environmental Governance: A Comparative Analysis of New Environmental Policy Instruments' which has been generously funded by the Economic and Social Research Council (ESRC) under its Future Governance Programme (grant number L216252013). The authors would like to thank all interviewees as well as Volkmar Lauber and Dieter Pesendorfer for their helpful comments. All factual errors and normative judgements remain solely the responsibility of the authors.

Austria has made overall slow progress as regards the adoption of 'new' environmental policy instruments despite increasing demands for more flexible and cost-efficient approaches to environmental policy. Austria's use of market-based instruments is moderate when compared to most Northern European states although it is significantly higher than in most Southern European states [*CEC, 1996; EEA, 1997, 2001; Öko-Institut, 1998*]. Austria has adopted, for example, a waste tax (1989), energy taxes (1996 and 2000) and a relatively wide range of tax measures in the transport sector. However, it has refrained from carrying out a comprehensive ecological tax reform and most of its environmental taxes were at least initially adopted primarily for fiscal reasons.

There is only a low number of VAs in Austria which has not yet made use of tradable permits. By early 2002, the number of VAs stood at about 30 [*Wirtschaftskammer, 2002*]. In 1991, Austria set up an eco-label scheme which, however, has been only moderately successful [*Jordan et al., 2002*]. The Austrian eco-label scheme was founded 13 years after the German and two years after the Nordic Council's eco-label schemes. However, it predates the Australian (1992), Dutch (1992), French (1992) and Spanish (1993) eco-label schemes and was set up in the early phase of a global diffusion of national and multi-national eco-label schemes which occurred in the early 1990s [*Kern et al., 2000; Jordan et al., 2002*].

As can be seen from Table 1, which gives an overview of the use of NEPIs in Austria, traditional regulation and subsidies have remained the most important policy instrument in the environmental policy field [*Lauber, 1997a, 1997b, 1997c, 2003; OECD, 1995a, 2001a*]. Since the late 1990s, the adoption of environmental laws has slowed down although Austria still remains a 'high regulatory state' [*Héritier et al., 1996; Lauber, 2003*].

The remainder of this analysis assesses when and why Austria has innovated with NEPIs. The second section analyses Austria's environmental policy structures, style and content while paying particular attention to the role of policy instruments. The third section identifies the most important drivers and obstacles to NEPI innovation in Austria. The fourth and fifth

TABLE 1
ENVIRONMENTAL POLICY INSTRUMENTS IN AUSTRIA

Type of policy instrument	Extent of usage
Eco-taxes	Moderate use of eco-taxes. Energy taxes in 1996 and 2000
Tradable permits	Not yet adopted.
Eco-label scheme	Set up in 1991. Moderate uptake. Awarded for 505 products and 182 tourism service providers.
Voluntary agreements	Moderate use: About 30 by early 2002.
Traditional regulation	High although moderate decline since the late 1990s.
Subsidies	High although moderate decline since the late 1990s.

sections assess the development of the different types of NEPIs and their relationship with traditional regulatory tools. The final section examines the overall pattern of NEPI use while assessing the relationship between 'new' and 'old' policy instruments.

Austrian Environmental Policy

Structures

The core institutional structures of the Austrian environmental policy system are characterised by a relatively high degree of fragmentation. This is largely a reflection of the fact that important environmental competences are split between several ministries but also relates to the federal system. The Ministries for Environment, Transport, Agriculture, and Economics have been the most important environmental policy actors within the federal government – though often in reversed order as regards their political influence. The Economics Ministry has significant competences on environmental issues which relate to industry, tourism and energy while the Agriculture Ministry, which was merged with the Environmental Ministry in 2000, holds most of the water management competences.

The Environmental Ministry has undergone several major organisational changes (as well as name changes)[1] during the last three decades. In 1972, it was set up as the Ministry for Health and Environment (BMGU). However, this was largely an act of symbolic politics because the BMGU was allocated only very few competences and suffered from a lack of staff resources [Lauber, 1997a, 1997b]. In 1987, the BMGU was transformed into the Ministry for Environment, Youth and Family (BMUJF) while being granted important political competences and greater staff resources [interviews, 2001; Lauber, 1997a, 2000]. In 2000, the BMUJF was merged with the Agricultural Ministry to form the Ministry for Agriculture, Forestry, Environment and Water Management (BMLFUW). The latest organisational change, which triggered the merger between the Environmental and the Agriculture Ministry, has been interpreted by some observers as a merger of unequal ministries that symbolised the downgrading of the importance of environmental policy under a newly elected Conservative–Right Wing (ÖVP/FPÖ) coalition government [interviews, 2001; ENDS Daily, 7 March 2000]. The Minister in charge of the BMLFUW, Wilhelm Molterer (ÖVP), who under the previous Social Democratic–Conservative (SPÖ–ÖVP) coalition government had already been in charge of the agricultural portfolio, devoted relatively little political attention to environmental issues although this was mainly due to the neoliberal agenda of the new coalition.

EU membership (since 1995) has overall increased the political importance of the bureaucracy (including the role of the Environmental Ministry) and individual ministers *vis-à-vis* other stakeholders [*Falkner and Müller, 1998; Lauber, 2003*]. The relative political importance of the Environmental Ministry therefore has increased over time although the overall importance of environmental issues has declined since the mid-1990s.

Austria traditionally has one of Europe's highest ratios of law graduates amongst its civil servants [*Lauber 1997a: 96*]. This generally also holds true for the Environmental Ministry although, in the 1990s, it established a small administrative unit for economic instruments which is staffed with environmental economists, several of whom also work within the specialist units (such as climate change, transport and waste) (interviews, Environmental Ministry officials, 2001). During much of the 1990s, the Minister in charge of the Environmental Ministry was Martin Bartenstein (ÖVP), an industrialist who moved into politics. In speeches he formally promoted the selective use of market-based instruments although in practice only slow progress was made by the Environmental Ministry as regards the adoption of NEPIs (Interviews, Environmental Ministry officials and Business Chamber representatives, in 2001 and 2002). As will be explained below, one important explanatory factor for the reluctance to adopt NEPIs is the lack of support from the most important societal stakeholders (that is, the social partners).

In 1985, the Environmental Agency (UBA) was set up to provide the government with scientific expertise. The UBA is answerable to the Environmental Ministry and is mainly staffed with scientifically trained officials. Unlike, for example, the German Environmental Agency, the Austrian UBA has remained primarily a scientific agency which rarely takes on a political role by, for example, making comprehensive policy proposals or by advocating policy measures that are more stringent than those proposed by the Environmental Ministry [interview, UBA official, 2002; *Wurzel, 2002*]. This explains why the UBA has hardly been involved in the domestic debate about the pros and cons of NEPI use in Austrian environmental policy (interviews, UBA officials, 2001 and 2002).

In 2000, the UBA was privatised and transformed into a limited company which operates like a semi-independent research institute. This reorganisation was in line with general privatisation efforts and the outsourcing of government agencies by the coalition government of the day. It has been condemned by environmental groups (interviews, 2000). However, its impact on the daily work of UBA staff has been limited. The same is true for the relationship between the UBA and the Environmental Ministry apart from the fact that cost-effectiveness considerations now have to be undertaken before the ministry can request scientific studies from the agency (interviews, UBA officials, 2002).

Federal system: Austria is a federal state in which the provinces *(Länder)* are granted important environmental policy competences particularly with regard to nature conservation, wildlife protection, air emissions from heating systems and non-hazardous waste [*Lauber, 1997a, 1997b; OECD, 1995a*]. The municipalities also have significant competences on environmental issues such as non-hazardous waste and sewage treatment. However, compared to, for example, American, German and Swiss federalism, the Austrian federal system has allocated its nine provinces only relatively limited environmental competences. Moreover, the Austrian political system has become more centralised during the last two decades. Constitutional amendments in 1983, 1988 and 1993 all increased the powers of the federal government *vis-à-vis* the provinces in the environmental policy field [*Lauber, 1997a: 84; OECD, 1995a*]. A constitutional amendment raised the importance of environmental protection which has become a general constitutional aim to be respected by the state *(Staatsziel)*, although environmental groups had demanded that the protection of the environment be made a right which citizens could invoke in the courts [*Lauber, 1997b; OECD, 1995a: 23*].

Environmental Regulatory Style

Austria has often been characterised as a corporatist state in which a close tripartite relationship between the government, employers and unions is an essential feature of policy-making [*Schmitter, 1974; Scruggs, 1999, 2001*]. However, there is strong empirical evidence that Austrian corporatism has waned and given way to more pluralistic forms of policy-making during the last three decades [*Crepaz, 1995; Dachs et al., 1997; Gehrlich, 1992; Lauber, 2000; Luther and Müller, 1992a, 1992b*]. Austrian politics has nevertheless retained a strong emphasis on consensus amongst the core interest groups. For historical reasons the social partnership *(Sozialpartnerschaft)* between the unions and employers has played a central role in post-Second World War Austrian politics. During the interwar period (that is, between the First and Second World War) there were bitter conflicts between competing 'political-ideological communities' [*Lauber, 2000: 33*] or political camps *(Lager)* which even led to civil war in Austria before it was taken over by Nazi Germany [*Dachs et al., 1997; Lauber, 1997b, 2000: 33–4; Luther and Müller, 1992a*]. Since the end of the Second World War, consensus and political accommodation among the social partners and government actors have therefore become central macro-political action guiding norms within the new Austrian state. The waning of corporatism at first did not erode this fundamental rule of Austrian politics. However, the Conservative–Right Wing goverment tended to ignore the social partnership.

The Chamber of Business (*Wirtschaftskammer*) and the Chamber of Labour (*Arbeiterkammer*) are important veto players within the Austrian policy-making process. The Business Chamber has close links with the conservative People's Party (ÖVP) while the Labour Chamber is closely associated with the Social Democratic Party (SPÖ). The SPÖ, which since 1970 has been the largest political party in parliament, and the ÖVP have formed grand coalition governments for much of the last five decades. The Freedom Party (FPÖ) once contained a strong liberal element but was transformed into an extreme right-wing party under its populist leader, Jörg Haider, during the 1990s. The Freedom Party has participated in coalition governments in 1983–86 and 2000–2002.

In 1999, the ÖVP and Freedom Party formed a coalition government in spite of international protests and EU sanctions. It collapsed in September 2002. The Conservative–Right Wing coalition government exhibited a general dislike of traditional (environmental) regulation without making greater use of NEPIs. Eco-taxes even became a taboo subject within the Environmental Ministry (Interviews, Environmental Ministry officials, 2001 and 2002). The impact of the Conservative–Right Wing coalition government on Austrian environmental policy was less pronounced than feared by many environmental groups for two main reasons (interviews, 2001 and 2002). First, there has been a considerable degree of continuity in Austrian environmental policy because the conservative ÖVP has fielded the Environmental (as well as the Economics and Agriculture) Ministers under various coalition governments since the 1980s. Second, a gradual down-grading of the importance of environmental policy issues had already set in by the mid-1990s [*Lauber, 1997a, 2003*]. To a large degree it was triggered by economic recession, a spiralling budget deficit, increased international competition, EU membership and a moderate decline in public environmental awareness.

Social Democratic Party-led Austrian coalition governments in particular traditionally adopted a pro-active policy stance which relied on selective state intervention within the market place and emphasised the need for consensus amongst the social partners. During the 1960s and 1970s, Austrian economic policy-making became widely know as 'Austro-Keynesianism' [*Lauber, 1997d; Luther and Müller, 1992a*]. The Austrian governments' active policy stance towards economic policy-making in particular and public policy problem-solving in general greatly facilitated Austria's rapid transformation from a largely agrarian state into a highly developed industrialised country which relies heavily on tourism for its economy. In the 1970s, economic growth rates were amongst the highest in Europe while unemployment rates were amongst the lowest. However, Austro-Keynesianism, which relied heavily on deficit spending, began to run into economic and political difficulties in the 1980s. First, unemployment started to rise despite state interventionist measures which triggered increasingly severe budget deficits. Second, competitiveness started to suffer in several key sectors. Finally, new values (for example, postmaterialist values) and political actors (such as environmental groups and the Green Party) emerged which remained largely excluded from the traditional social partnership that gave clear preference to economic growth.

Environmental groups, which challenged the economic growth paradigm, lacked close links to the traditional political parties and the social partners. They used unconventional methods in order to get their demands heard by the political establishment. Mass demonstrations against Austira's first nuclear power station at Zwentendorf in the 1970s and a large hydraulic dam at Hainberg in the 1980s led the government to abandon both projects. The upsurge in environmental groups and the rise of postmaterialist values benefited the Green Party which was elected into the national parliament for the first time in 1986. The electoral success of the Green Party also led to a 'greening' of the traditional parties and the social partners although to varying degrees.

In the late 1980s, the SPÖ propagated the 'ecological restructuring of industrial society' while the ÖVP pleaded for the introduction of an 'eco-social market economy' [Lauber, 1997b: 613]. Even the Freedom Party under its populist right-wing leader, Jörg Haider, has not been immune to environmental policy considerations. However, the traditional mainstream parties (SPÖ and ÖVP) and social partners found it difficult to overcome the conventional wisdom that there is a trade off between economic prosperity and a high level of environmental protection. The dichotomy between economy and ecology dominated Austrian politics until the mid-1980s [Lauber, 1997a, 1997b]. It was bridged by mainstream parties temporarily in the late 1980s. However, the harsher economic climate since the early 1990s has made Austrian governments again reluctant to adopt stringent environmental policy measures unilaterally. Especially the ÖVP and Business Chamber have warned that Austria will suffer economically if it fails to adopt more flexible and cost-effective environmental policy measures.

The SPÖ and Labour Chamber have become considerably 'greener' than the ÖVP and Business Chamber. The Labour Chamber has called for the adoption of an ecological tax reform since the early 1990s while the SPÖ favoured for some time the Greens as coalition partner during the 2002 election campaign. The electoral success of the Green Party and its status as a potential coalition partner is further evidence that Austrian politics has become more pluralistic in recent decades.

Policy Content

Laws for the protection of natural resources can be traced to the nineteenth century as can be seen from the 1811 Civil Code which stipulated a provision for the protection of forests against excessive felling [*Lauber,* *1997a: 81*]. However, the first modern day environmental regulations date back to the early 1970s although the precautionary principle *(Vorsorgeprinzip)* was mentioned for the first time only in the 1980 steam boiler emission law [*Lauber, 1997b: 610*]. Austrian environmental policy has relied heavily on 'command-and-control' regulations and subsidies [*Lauber, 1997a: 87; 1997b; 2000; 2003; OECD, 1995a, 2001a*]. The precautionary principle legitimises government action even in the absence of scientific proof where there is thought to be a significant risk that (irreversible) environmental damage would otherwise occur. It facilitated the adoption of relatively stringent environmental regulations that stipulate the best available technology (BAT). During the 1980s, Austria adopted a wide range of detailed and relatively ambitious environmental laws which earned it a reputation as an (belated) environmental leader state [*Lauber,* *1997a*]. Austria's strong reliance on a wide range of 'command-and-control' regulations has not been without critics. For example, one OECD [*1995a: 97*] report stated that 'a flurry of legislative activities ... has led to a dense regulatory framework with a large number of laws and regulations ... The interdependence of the various laws and their complexity make it more and more difficult to understand the whole body of legislation, let alone control it.'

Before it joined the European Union (EU) in 1995, Austria fought hard for a clause in the accession treaty which left in force (initially for a period of five years) several national environmental laws that were more stringent than EU legislation [*BMUJF, 1998; Lauber, 1997a, 1997b; Liefferink and Andersen, 1998; Trattnigg, 1997*]. However, in early 2001, a deregulation law was passed by parliament which explicitly stated that Austria would in future no longer seek to adopt an environmental leader role within the EU. Parliament later adopted a declaration which again watered down the essence of this so-called 'no golden plating' statement which was adopted by a Conservative–Right Wing (ÖVP–FPÖ) coalition government that was keen to be seen as paving the way for economic reform and deregulation (interviews, Environmental Ministry officials, 2002). However, for many observers this statement merely made explicit what had gradually become the implicit Austrian policy stance since the late 1990s (interviews, Environmental Ministry officials and NGO representatives, 2001 and 2002). Despite its recent reluctance unilaterally to adopt more stringent environmental standards, Austria often still finds itself in the camp of the environmental leader states on the international level and within the EU on a relatively wide range of environmental issues (such as car emission regulations and climate change protection) [*Lauber, 2003*].

Why Are NEPIs Being Adopted?

Demands for greater NEPI innovation has grown in Austria in recent years. However, there are significant obstacles to the wider use of NEPIs.

Drivers

In its review of Austrian environmental policy, the OECD [*1995a: 97*] identified the following three 'compelling reasons' for the wider use of NEPIs. First, rising marginal costs of pollution abatement as overall environmental quality improves; second, the serious deficit in the national budget; and, third, the growing exposure of the Austrian economy to international competition. All three reasons constitute important drivers. Especially during the 1980s, Austria has adopted a wide range of relatively stringent environmental laws. According to some policy actors (such as the Business Chamber) adding new environmental regulations to deal with the remaining pollution would produce rapidly diminishing returns. The spiralling budget deficit put the Austrian government, which was determined to fulfill the criteria for joining European Monetary Union (EMU), under considerable pressure to adopt austerity measures, cut subsidies (including environmental subsidies) and to ensure that regulation (including environmental regulation) would not hamper economic growth and foreign investment. Austria is a small state with a relatively open market economy. It is therefore strongly exposed to global competition which has increased since the 1990s. Many Central and Eastern European countries are in close geographic proximity and offer wages and environmental regulations which are below Austrian standards.

There are at least four additional important drivers for NEPIs use in Austria. They include EU membership, the role of international organisations (such as the OECD and United Nations (UN)) for the transfer of NEPIs to new national constituencies, the demands for certain NEPIs put forward by influential domestic political actors and the arrival of environmental economists within the Environmental Ministry.

EU membership has led to the introduction of a new generation of policy measures into Austrian environmental policy which until recently made little use of procedural measures such as environmental impact assessment (EIA) and the eco-audit and management systems (EMAS), that is, a voluntary self-declaratory scheme that turned out to be very popular with Austrian companies [*Lauber, 2003*]. Austria would not (yet) have considered the adoption of tradable permits without the EU Commission's proposal for an EU-wide scheme which itself is a reaction to the Kyoto Protocol. However, as will be explained below, the EU has also acted as a barrier to NEPIs innovation especially with regard to eco-taxes.

International organisations such as the OECD and World Bank have long campaigned for the wider use of NEPIs. The OECD's reviews on Austrian environmental policy [*1995a*] and economic policy [*2001a*] as well as its publications on environmental taxes [*1995b, 2001b*] have triggered a major political debate on the domestic level about the use of market-based instruments. Claims that Austrian environmental policy relies on high standards but is not cost-efficient have led to the commissioning of domestic studies on the impact of environmental regulation on Austrian water management [*Arbeiterkammer, 2001; PricewaterhouseCoopers, 2001*]

Influential domestic political actors (such as the social partners) started to demand the wider use of NEPIs since the 1990s. The Business Chamber has championed deregulation and the use of VAs while the Labour Chamber has supported a major ecological tax reform which should be used to reduce non-wage labour cost. In the early 1990s, the government set up tax commissions which considered the ecological tax reform although such plans were later abandoned.

The setting up of a small unit for environmental economic instruments as well as the placing of environmental economists within the specialist units of the Environmental Ministry has softened the opposition against NEPIs from ministry staff which otherwise predominantly consists of law graduates who are often sceptical about the usefulness of non-regulatory tools.

Barriers

However, there are also formidable obstacles which have prevented the rapid and wide take up of NEPIs in Austria. First, environmental regulation is still considered an effective policy tool by many Austrian policy makers. Even the OECD [*1995a, 2001a*], which has repeatedly criticised Austria for failing to adopt the most cost-effective measures, has in the past consistently emphasised that it has achieved a high level of environmental protection. Austria has significantly reduced mass pollutants (such as sulphur dioxide and nitrogen oxides), opted for ambitious climate change reduction targets (despite the fact that its carbon dioxide emissions are well below the OECD average both per capita and in terms of GDP), reached one of the highest levels of renewable energy use in Europe and outperforms the EU average by 150 per cent as regards rail transport [*Lauber, 1997a: 104; Lauber, 2003*].

Second, legally trained officials, who are often doubtful about the feasibility of non-regulatory tools, still dominate staff resources within the Environmental Ministry. Third, important policy actors are opposed to the use of market-based instruments. Industry and the Business Chamber are opposed to environmental taxes while environmental groups for long denounced tradable permits as unethical 'rights to pollute'. The Business Chamber and Workers Chamber were initially opposed to tradable permits. More recently they have both softened their opposition and now even appear to favour this type of NEPI although they still disagree about the exact design of tradable permits (interviews, 2002).

Fourth, the corporatist Austrian policy style which puts great emphasis on consensus and political accommodation has militated against the rapid uptake of market-based policy instruments. The social partners are closely involved in the domestic law-making process which is characterised by consensus and political accommodation. Subsidies further eased the acceptance of relatively stringent environmental regulations while a considerable degree of distrust seems to exist within Austrian political culture as regards compliance with non-regulatory policy tools such as VAs [interviews, 2001 and 2002; also *Lauber, 2000; Liefferink and Mol, 2000: 199*].

NEPI Use in Austria

Austria has only recently begun to innovate with a wider range of NEPIs although traditional regulation and subsidies are still the dominant environmental policy instruments.

Market-Based Instruments

Tradable permits and eco-taxes are generally the most widely used market-based instruments.

Eco-taxes: Some of the earliest Austrian eco-taxes were levied on motor vehicles and petrol and diesel fuels although the main purpose was to generate revenue for the state. As in most OECD countries, the transport sector accounts for the lion's share of the revenue generated from eco-taxes [*OECD, 2001b*]. In 1994 and 1995, mineral oil taxes were raised by between 50 and 150 per cent although these tax increases were mainly driven by fiscal considerations. In the late 1990s, Austrian mineral oil taxes were amongst the highest in Western Europe. This led to high petrol prices compared to European countries and encouraged 'petrol tourism' ('*Tanktourismus*') in areas close to the border (interviews, 2000 and 2001). However, this kind of 'tourism' has largely disappeared (and partly been reversed) since the introduction of the German ecological tax reform in

1999 [*Wurzel et al., 2003*] and the steep rise in mineral oil taxes in many Central and Eastern European countries. The high mineral oil taxes had the unintended effect that a limited number of companies switched from oil to coal firing because coal was not levied with higher taxes. This switch was not beneficial environmentally because coal has a higher carbon content compared to oil. Coal firing therefore releases a higher amount of the climate change gas carbon dioxide compared to the burning of oil or gas (interview, Environmental Ministry official, 2002).

When public concerns about acidification and dying forests rose steeply in the early 1980s, Austria adopted fiscal incentives in order to promote the speedy uptake of unleaded petrol and cars equipped with catalytic converters. Fiscal incentives generally fail to internalise the external pollution cost. Instead they act as subsidies for less polluting products and/or technologies. However, Austria has used fiscal incentives in combination with tax rises on, for example, leaded petrol in order to implement the polluter pays principle. It was not until the 1990s that Austria linked its car registration and annual vehicle taxes explicitly to environmental criteria (such as the engine size of vehicles which is a reasonably good measure for fuel consumption and thus also carbon dioxide output).

Energy is another important sector within which (relatively moderate) eco-taxes have been used relatively widely. Major energy tax rises were introduced in 1996 and 2000. The 1996 tax was levied on electricity and gas while the energy tax rise in 2000 concerned only electricity. However, out of fears that energy tax rises might damage Austrian industry's international competitiveness, a ceiling was set for energy-intensive industries which were entitled to a rebate under the Energy Levy Reimbursement Act. Initially this rebate was granted only to the manufacturing industry. However, after a legal challenge by an Austrian service provider, the Administrative Court and the European Court of Justice (ECJ) ruled illegal the law which restricted the rebate to the manufacturing industry. Households have therefore arguably become the main target of the energy taxes.

There are also eco-taxes outside the transport and energy sector. For example, Austria had already adopted a waste tax in 1989. It has contributed to the introduction of the BAT for landfill sites [*OECD, 2001b*]. A limited number of eco-taxes also exists in the agricultural sector. Austria adopted a fertiliser tax which, however, was scrapped shortly before it joined the EU because it was deemed to be incompatible with internal market rules although the farming lobby was not unhappy to see this tax go [*Glatz, 1995: 8*].

In 1997, the Environmental Ministry estimated that approximately eight per cent of the total tax revenue was linked to environmental objectives

[*BMUJF, 1997: 1*]. However, the Environmental Ministry also concluded that only 12 out of 74 measures (that is, approximately 17 per cent) adopted under the national climate change strategy could be categorised as market instruments [*BMUJF, 1997*]. Over time, the use of eco-taxes has been widened incrementally and largely on an *ad hoc* basis. Until recently, the Austrian government's fiscal priorities were the main driver for most eco-taxes although environmental objectives have become more important since the 1990s as can be seen from the above mentioned fuel and motor vehicle taxes.

In the 1990s, a major political debate took place about a large scale ecological tax reform although its origins can be traced to the 1980s. Eco-taxes had initially been championed mainly by environmental groups and the Green Party. However, the Labour Chamber and the SPÖ gradually also warmed to the idea of an ecological tax reform being used to lower non-wage labour costs and thus creating additional jobs by making Austrian industry more competitive. In the late 1980s, the ÖVP demanded a move towards an 'eco-social market economy' which included the use of market-based instruments and even the Freedom Party moved towards supporting more effective environmental policy instruments [*Lauber, 1997b: 613*]. In the early 1990s, the political debate seemed to have been won by the proponents of an ecological tax reform although it was still fiercely opposed by the Business Chamber and industrial actors. However, rising unemployment and increased competition within the EU's internal market as well as from Eastern Europe and the global markets prevented Austrian (SPÖ–FPÖ and FPÖ–Right Wing coalition) governments from adopting unilaterally an ecological tax reform.

Because of the difficult economic situation a tax reform commission was set up in 1997–98. It considered the use of eco-taxes but failed to endorse the unilateral adoption of a full-scale ecological tax reform. It rejected arguments put forward in studies from the highly regarded Austrian Institute for Economic Research which had come to the conclusion that a national ecological tax reform would create additional jobs rather than endanger the competitiveness of Austria's industry [*WIFO, 1995, 1998*]. The Environmental Ministry felt only insufficiently consulted by the tax reform commission while environmental groups were not invited to give evidence at all (interviews, 2001 and 2002). Chancellor Victor Klima (SPÖ) and Vice-Chancellor Wolfgang Schüssel (ÖVP) finally put an end to the debate within the government about the adoption of national ecological tax reform by ruling it out, although the (SPÖ–ÖVP coalition) government continued to support the introduction of an EU-wide carbon dioxide/energy tax. During the Conservative-Right Wing (ÖVP–FPÖ) coalition government in 1999–2002, the issue of an ecological tax reform became a 'taboo subject' even for the Environmental Ministry officials, many of whom privately still favour such a reform (interviews, 2001 and 2002). However, the Austrian government has recently adopted an electronic road pricing system for lorries which will come into operation in 2004 [*BMLFUW, 2002*].

The domestic political debate about an ecological tax reform has subsided although it has been kept alive by environmental groups, the Green Party, the Labour Chamber and parts of the SPÖ and ÖVP as well as by international organisations such as the OECD. The OECD [*1995a, 2001a*] has repeatedly urged Austria to make wider use of market-based instruments (including environmental taxes and tradable permits) as well as VAs.

Tradable permits: Tradable permits have not yet been used in Austria. Until recently tradable permits were strongly opposed by the social partners and other stakeholders (such as environmental groups). Tradable permits still suffer from a lack of wide societal acceptability. However, since the EU Commission has put forward its proposals for an EU-wide tradable permits scheme [*CEC, 2000, 2001*] a remarkable change of attitude has taken place within the Business Chamber and the Labour Chamber who both now appear broadly to welcome the use of tradable permits (interviews, 2000–2002).

Austria has very limited domestic experience with tradable permits. The Clean Air Act allows for so-called bubble solutions (which exhibit some of the characteristics of tradable permit schemes) although their use has remained highly restricted [*Glatz, 1995: 5*]. Tradable permits were listed as one possible policy instrument in the 1996 National Environmental Plan which, however, has failed to make a significant impact on domestic environmental policy [*Bundesregierung, 1996: 22*]. Austria introduced an eco-point system, which relates to air emissions, in order to restrict the number of heavy good vehicles that are allowed to use certain Alpine roads. The Austrian eco-point system does not amount to a tradable permit scheme although it helped to curb transalpine road freight traffic. The system had to be reviewed when Austria joined the EU and has since been watered down considerably [*Lauber, 1997a, 2003*]. Between 2000 and 2002 the Electricity Management Act, which liberalised the domestic electricity market in line with wider EU developments, allowed for a tradable permit quota system for small hydro-power stations [*BMLFUW, 2001*].

However, the main driver for the adoption of tradable permits in Austria has been the EU Commission's proposal for an EU-wide tradable permit scheme [*CEC, 2000, 2001*] which itself is a reaction to the Kyoto Climate Change Protocol which lists tradable permits as one possible policy instrument for complying with climate change gas reduction targets. Initially the Austrian government adopted mainly a 'wait-and-see' approach with regard to the EU's tradable permit scheme although it actively participated in Commission and

Environmental Council tradable permit working groups (interviews, Environmental Ministry and Commission officials, 2001 and 2002).

The Environmental Ministry has recently taken on a more active policy stance with regard to tradable permits. It commissioned a feasibility study for a national tradable permit scheme from the Austrian Institute for Economic Research [*WIFO, 2000*]. The Economics Ministry, which was initially sceptical about tradable permits has now also warmed to the idea of their use (interviews, 2001). There are two main reasons why tradable permits have become more accceptable to governmental and corporate actors in Austria. First, Austria has committed itself to a relatively ambitious climate change reduction target (that is, a 13 per cent reduction target for carbon dioxide emissions between 2008–2012 based on 1990 emission levels). As the deadline has moved closer, the Austrian government and stakeholders increasingly realised that such an ambitious target cannot be achieved without major additional reduction measures. However, eco-taxes and/or additional regulatory measures were ruled out as counter-productive to economic growth by the Conservative-Right Wing coalition government which was acutely aware of industry's strong opposition to such measures.

Second, opposition from the Business and Labour Chamber against tradable permits has waned since the publication of the Commission's proposal for an EU-wide tradable permits scheme [*CEC, 2000, 2001*]. The social partners still hold differing views about the best design of tradable permit schemes. For example, the Business Chamber prefers voluntary participation and the initial allocation of permits for free (so-called 'grandfathering') while the Labour Chamber supports a mandatory system which allocates tradable permits through an auction process and imposes challenging emission limits (so-called 'caps'). Similar differences exist between the Economics Ministry and the Environmental Ministry. However, the social partners' principled opposition against tradable permit schemes has given way to a desire to influence the actual design of the EU's tradable permit scheme which seems inevitable as its adoption falls under qualified majority voting (interviews, 2001 and 2002). Most of Austria's largest companies are organised in the Association of Industrialists which has been considerably more open-minded about the use of tradable permits than the Business Chamber which represents mainly small and medium sized companies. Environmental groups, on the other hand, have remained largely unconvinced about the merits of tradable permits and instead demand the adoption of an ecological tax reform (that is, domestic action).

Voluntary Agreements

Austria has made only moderate use of VAs [*CEC, 1996; EEA, 1997; Lauber, 1997c; Lauber and Ingram, 2000; Mol et al., 2000; Öko-Institut,*

1998]. By 2002, there have been approximately 30 VAs, the majority of which was adopted already in the early 1990s [*Wirtschaftskammer, 2002*]. The 1996 National Environmental Plan nevertheless labeled VAs as a 'new' tool for Austrian environmental policy [*Bundesregierung, 1996*]. Since the late 1990s, the Business Chamber and the Economics Ministry have tried to encourage the use of VAs within a wider deregulations strategy although to little effect [also *Lauber, 1997c; Mol et al., 2000*]. The Conservative–Right Wing coalition government (1999–2002) formally promoted the use of non-regulatory policy tools and stressed the need for deregulation. However, it also failed to increase the uptake of VAs. Compared to Germany and the Netherlands, which have both adopted more than 100 VAs [*Wurzel et al., 2003*], Austria's use of VAs is low. However, in a recent VA league table by the European Environmental Agency (EEA), Austria finished in third place out of the 15 EU member states [*EEA, 1997*].

The Business Chamber and industry prefers a wide definition of VAs which includes negotiated agreements (that is, VAs which have been negotiated between industry and governmental actors) as well as unilateral statements from industry. The majority of Austrian VAs have been put forward by industry in order to pre-empt government legislation [*Wirtschaftskammer, 2002*]. For constitutional reasons all Austrian VAs have to be legally non-binding. Because VAs lack legally binding sanctions, transparency and third party representation (during the negotiation process), the Labour Chamber and environmental groups are opposed to the use of this type of NEPI while the Environmental Ministry has remained divided (interviews, 2001 and 2002). However, even industrial actors are often concerned that VAs do not provide for sanctions against free-riders. For many domestic environmental policy actors, Austrian political culture exhibits a deep-seated distrust of VAs [interviews with Environmental Ministry officials and Labour Chamber representatives, 2001 and 2002; also *Liefferink and Mol, 2000; Lauber, 1997c*].

Most Austrian VAs can be found in the waste sector and tackle issues such as recycling (for example, tyres and batteries) and the phasing out of environmentally harmful substances [*EEA, 1997; Lauber and Ingram, 2000; Mol et al., 2000; Wirtschaftskammer, 2002*]. The 1990 Waste Management Act triggered a range of VAs because industry was keen to pre-empt legally binding implementation decrees. There are very few VAs outside the waste sector. Unlike Germany and the Netherlands, Austria has not made use of VAs in the energy sector and/or in fulfilling its climate change reduction targets. An inter-ministerial working group which deals with the national climate change strategy has considered the use of VAs but received little support from industry (interview, Environmental Ministry official, 2002).

Eco-labels

After several unsuccessful attempts, Austria finally set up its own national eco-label scheme in 1991. Its adoption was largely due to the personal initiative of the Environmental Minister, Marilies Flemming, an upsurge in public environmental awareness, the entry of the Green Party into parliament in the late 1980s and the global diffusion of this type of NEPI in the early 1990s (interviews, 2000; *Jordan et al., 2002; Kern et al., 2000; Schuster, not dated; Schwar, 1999*).

The German eco-label scheme, which had been set up already in 1978, acted as a model for the Austrian scheme. Austrian consumers were already familiar with the German eco-label scheme because German products are widely sold on the Austrian market which is not separated by a language barrier from the German market. However, the creators of the Austrian eco-label scheme tried to avoid some of the shortcomings of the German scheme (interview, Environmental Ministry official, 2001). Compared to the German eco-label scheme, the Austrian eco-label puts greater emphasis on life-cycle analysis which takes into account a cradle-to-grave approach for products and services. Austria acted as a pioneer when it adopted an eco-label for tourism which plays a very important role for the domestic economy. In 2002, the Environmental Ministry extended the national eco-label scheme to schools which constitutes another innovation (interview, Environmental Ministry official, 2002).

The Austrian eco-label is awarded by the Environmental Ministry (rather than an independent third party as is the case for the German eco-label scheme) although the Economics Ministry, the Association of Consumer Information, the Eco-Label Committee and various technical agencies and working groups are all also involved in the selection process. Anyone can apply for the Austrian eco-label although foreign companies must have an office within the EU or an European Free Trade Association (EFTA) state.

The uptake of the national eco-label has remained moderate despite government public relations campaigns and innovations such as the eco-label for tourism services (that is, hotels and farms which offer holidays). After a difficult start, the interest in the national eco-label has been growing in recent years. By the end of 2001, 114 companies were awarded eco-labels for 505 products in addition to 183 eco-labels for tourist services such as hotels [*BMLFUW, 2002*]. The uptake of the national eco-label is therefore considerably higher than in the Netherlands which adopted its national eco-label in 1992. However, the Austrian eco-label cannot match the national German and multinational Nordic Council eco-label schemes in terms of the number of awarded products and services. The Austrian eco-label scheme is based on relatively stringent criteria and was not designed as a mass label.

It consequently suffers from low consumer recognition and is not widely sought after by producers. The main objective of the Austrian eco-label scheme is to provide consumers with more product transparency and to raise environmental awareness. However, it also aims to bring about behavioural changes amongst consumers (who are encouraged to buy environmentally less harmful products and services) *and* producers (for whom the eco-label is meant to act as a market incentive which encourages the production of environmentally less harmful products and services).

The EU eco-label, which was set up in 1992, is little known in Austria. It took ten years before the first Austrian companies applied for the EU eco-label whose criteria are widely perceived as less stringent in comparison to the national eco-label scheme although this is no longer the case for several products and services. Environmental Ministry officials have recognised that better cooperation is needed between the national and the EU eco-label schemes (interviews, 2001 and 2002). However, no government funding has been made available to promote the EU label scheme.

Other Instruments

The Austrian government and industry were initially sceptical about the EU's environmental management and eco-audit system (EMAS) which is a voluntary informational tool. It constitutes a new policy instrument for Austrian environmental policy which has relied heavily on traditional regulatory tools [*Lauber, 1997a, 1997b, 2003*]. However, Austrian companies have made wide use of EMAS.

Despite considerable NEPIs innovation, Austria has found it difficult to overcome its high regulatory past. Traditional (command-and-control) regulatory instruments still dominate Austrian environmental policy. Industry demands a reduction in (environmental) regulation but half-hearted privatisation and deregulation attempts by various government coalitions have not led to a large scale substitution of traditional regulatory tools with NEPIs. Instead NEPIs are mainly used as supplementary tools within the national environmental policy instrument repertoire which is heavily tilted towards the use of traditional regulation and subsidies. Austria's environmental performance in the late 1980s and early 1990s, which earnt it a status as a belated environmental leader state, seemed to justify the emphasis on regulation and subsidies. Moreover, Austria benefited economically from the adoption of relatively stringent environmental laws and generous subsidies for pollution abatement technologies as can be seen from the development of a highly successful export-oriented environmental technology industry [*Lauber, 1997b; OECD, 1995a, 2001a*].

Austria has made wide use of subsidies in the environmental policy field [*BMLFUW, 2000; Komunalkredit, 2000; Lauber, 1997a, 1997b; OECD, 1995a*]. This partly explains the high percentage of renewable energy in Austria. Subsidies, which fit in well with the consensus oriented policy style that seeks to accommodate the central demands of the core policy actors (that is, mainly the social partners), have eased considerably industry's acceptance of relatively stringent environmental laws. However, rising unemployment, a spiralling budget deficit and increased international competition have led increasingly to demands for more cost-efficient policy instruments. Moreover, ever more stringent regulation at some point in time will lead to diminishing margins of return (that is, it becomes ever more expensive to reduce the remaining pollution).

The water sector is a good example of such a development. Austria has adopted relatively stringent water regulations during the last two decades. The quality of water in Austria is generally seen as very good (although there are some problems areas). The OECD [*1995a, 2001a*] has repeatedly stressed the environmental success of water management in Austria while also pointing out that the generally high water quality has been achieved at a high cost because market-based instruments have not been used. A recent study by PricewaterhouseCoopers [*2001*], which was commissioned by the Environmental Ministry, has been even more critical about the lack of market forces and market-based instruments within the Austrian water management sector. Its findings have been broadly welcomed by the Business Chamber. However, the claims put forward in this study were quickly rejected by the Labour Chamber which commissioned a counter study that stressed the environmental success and value-for-money of the current regulatory regime as well as the dangers of greater reliance on market forces for the quality of water in Austria [*Arbeiterkammer, 2001*]. Clearly, there are still major political differences between the social partners as regards the appropriate mix of traditional regulatory tools and NEPIs [interviews, Business and Labour Chamber representatives, 2000–2002; *Arbeiterkammer, 1993, 2001; Wirtschaftskammer, 1999*].

Conclusion

Austria has made only moderate use of NEPI innovation although demands for greater use of NEPIs have increased considerably in recent years. The use of NEPIs has remained uneven. Some types of NEPIs have not yet been used, such as tradable permits) while others are mainly adopted within one particular sector. For example, VAs are primarily used in the waste sector while tradable permit schemes have only been seriously considered since the EU Commission has tabled proposals for an EU-wide tradable permit scheme. Austria has adopted a waste tax (1989), energy taxes (1996 and 2000) and a relatively wide range of transport sector taxes although it has refrained from carrying out a comprehensive ecological tax reform largely out of fears that it may harm industry's international competitiveness. The Austrian eco-label scheme, which was adopted in 1991, has been moderately successful in terms of the number of products and services labeled. The adoption of eco-labels for tourist services and schools shows that Austria has not simply relied on a transfer of certain types of NEPIs from abroad but undertaken some genuine domestic NEPI innovations.

However, traditional regulatory tools and subsidies still dominate Austrian environmental policy. There has been no full scale substitution of traditional regulation (and subsidies) with NEPIs in Austria. This is not to deny the fact that NEPIs are now used much more frequently than only a decade ago. However, NEPIs are used largely as a supplementary tool alongside traditional regulation and are adapted in such a way that they fit in well with the traditional domestic structures, policy style and content. For example, all Austrian VAs are legally non-binding and fail to impose sanctions if breached.

Austrian corporatism has waned considerably during the last few decades and given way to a more pluralistic policy-making process and a stronger reliance on market forces. Rising unemployment, serious budget deficits, EU membership and increased international global competition have led to increased demands for a reconsideration of traditional policy-making procedures and policy instrument preferences. However, in Austria there is still a need to establish a basic consensus amongst the social partners on fundamental policy changes or paradigm shifts such as a full-scale substitution of traditional policy instruments with NEPIs. The traditional Austrian policy structures and style as well as Austria's relatively strong past environmental performance and thus the lack of major policy disasters have left in place strong path-dependencies which help to explain why an incremental policy instrument adaptation has taken place rather than a policy instrument revolution.

NOTE

1.   Because of the numerous name changes and in order to avoid confusion, the term Environmental Ministry is used throughout this contribution.

REFERENCES

Arbeiterkammer ((1993), *Ökologische Perspektiven für Österreich. 20 Jahre Umweltpolitik der AK*, Vienna: Bundeskammer für Arbeiter und Angestellte.
Arbeiterkammer (2001), *A Critique of the 2001 PricewaterhouseCoopers Report on Water Services in Austria*, Vienna: Bundeskammer für Arbeiter und Angestellte.
BMLFUW (2000), *Klimarelevanz des österreichischen Förderungssystems*,Vienna: Bundesministerium für Land- und Forstwirtschaft, Umwelt und Wasserwirtschaft.

BMLFUW (2001), *Third National Climate Report of the Austrian Federal Government*, Vienna: Bundesministerium für Land- und Forstwirtschaft, Umwelt und Wasserwirtschaft.

BMLFUW (2002), *Das Österreichische Umweltzeichen. Jahresbericht 2001*, Vienna: Bundesministerium für Land- und Forstwirtschaft, Umwelt und Wasserwirtschaft.

BMUJF (1997), *Überblick über die bestehenden umweltökonomischen Instrumente in Österreich. Stand Jänner 1997*, Wien: Bundesministerium für Umwelt, Jugend und Familie.

BMUJF (1998), *Environmental Policy in Austria*, Vienna: Bundesministerium für Umwelt, Jugend und Familie.

Bundesregierung (1996), *Nationaler Umweltplan*, Wien: Österreichische Bundesregierung.

CEC (1996), *Communication from the Commission on Environmental Agreements*, COM(96) 561 final, Brussels: Commission of the European Communites.

CEC (2000), *Green Paper on Greenhouse Gas Emission Trading Within the European Union, COM(2000)87 final of 8 March*, Brussels: Commission of the European Communities.

CEC (2001), Proposal for a Directive of the European Parliament and of the Council Establishing a Scheme for Greenhouse Gas Emission Allowance Trading Within the Community and Amending Council Directive 96/61/EC, COM(2001)581 final, Oct. 2001, Brussels: Commission of the European Communities.

Crepaz, M. (1995), 'An Institutional Dinosaur: Austrian Corporatism in the Post-Industrial Age', *West European Politics*, Vol.18, No.4, pp.64–88.

Dachs, H. *et al.* (eds) (1997), *Handbuch des politischen Systems Österreichs. Die zweite Republik*, Vienna: Manzsche Verlags- und Universitätsbuchhandlung (third edition).

ENDS Daily (various years), Daily e-mail service, Environmental Data Services, London.

EEA (1997), *Environmental Agreements*, Copenhagen: European Environment Agency.

EEA (2001), *Environmental Taxes: Recent Developments in Tools for Integration and Sustainable Development*, Copenhagen: European Environment Agency.

Falkner, G. and W.C. Müller (eds.) (1998), *Österreich im europäischen Mehrebenensystem. Konsequenzen der EU-Mitgliedschaft für Politiknetzwerke und Entscheidungsprozess*, Vienna: Signum Verlag.

Gehrlich, P. (1992), 'A Farewell to Corporatism', *West European Politics*, Vol.15, No.1, pp.132–46.

Glatz, H. (1995), *Österreichische Umweltpolitik*, Vienna: Bundeskammer für Arbeiter und Angestellte.

Héritier, A., Knill, C. and S. Mingers (1996), 'Ringing the Changes in Europe: Regulatory Competition and the Redefinition of the State: Britain, France and Germany', Berlin: de Gruyter.

Jordan, A., Wurzel, R., Zito, A. and L. Brückner (2003), 'Consumer Responsibility-taking and Eco-labeling Schemes in Europe', in M. Micheletti, A. Føllesdal and D. Stolle (eds.), *The Politics Behind Products. Using the Market as a Site for Ethics and Action*, New Brunswick, NJ: Transaction Press (in press).

Kern, K., Jörgens, H. and M. Jänicke (2000), 'Die Diffusion umweltpolitischer Innovationen. Ein Beitrag zur Globalisierung der Umweltpolitik', *Zeitschrift für Umweltpolitik und –recht*, Vol.4, pp.507–46.

Kommunalkredit (2000), *Umweltförderungen des Bundes. 2000*, Vienna: Kommunalkredit Austria AG.

Lauber, V. (1997a), 'Austria: A Latecomer Which Became a Pioneer', in M. Andersen and D. Liefferink (eds.), *European Environmental Policy: The Pioneers*, Manchester: Manchester University Press, pp.81–118.

Lauber, V. (1997b), 'Umweltpolitik', in Dachs *et al.* [*1997: 608–27*].

Lauber, V. (1997c), 'Freiwillige Umweltvereinbarungen in der Europäischen Union und in Österreich: Bestandsaufnahme und Perspektiven', *Recht der Umwelt*, pp.107-11.

Lauber, V. (1997d), Wirtschafts- und Finanzpolitik', in Dachs *et al.* [*1997: 545–56*].

Lauber, V. (2000), 'The Political and Institutional Setting', in Mol *et al.* [*2000: 32-61*].

Lauber, V. (2003), 'The Europeanisation of Austrian Environmental Policy', in A. Jordan and D. Liefferink (eds.), *The Europeanisation of National Environmental Policy* (forthcoming).

Lauber, V. and V. Ingram (2000), 'Packaging Waste', in A. Mol *et al.* [*2000: 105–55*].

Liefferink, D. and M.S. Andersen (1998), 'Strategies of the 'Green' Member States in EU

Environmental Policy-Making', *Journal of European Public Policy*, Vol.5, No.2, pp.254–70.

Liefferink, D. and Mol. A. (2000), 'A Comparative Analysis of Joint Environmental Policy-Making', in Mol *et al.* [*2000: 192–216*].

Luther, K. and W. Müller (1992a), 'Consociationalism and the Austrian Political System', *West European Politics*, Vol.15, No.1, pp.1–15.

Luther, K. and W. Müller, (1992b), 'Austrian Consociationalism: Victim of its Own Success?' *West European Politics*, Vol.15, No.1, pp.201–23.

Mol, A., Lauber, V. and D. Liefferink (eds.) (2000), *The Voluntary Approach to Environmental Policy*, Oxford: Oxford University Press.

OECD (1995a), *Environmental Performance Reviews. Austria*, Paris: Organisation for Economic Co-operation and Development.

OECD (1995b), *Environmental Taxes in OECD Countries*, Paris: Organisation for Economic Co-operation and Development.

OECD, (2001a), *OECD Wirtschaftsberichte 2000–2001: Österreich*, Paris: Organisation for Economic Cooperation and Development.

OECD, (2001b), *Environmentally Related Taxes in OECD Countries. Issues and Strategies*, Paris: Organisation for Economic Cooperation and Development

Öko-Institut (1998), *New Instruments for Sustainability – The New Contribution of Voluntary Agreements to Environmental Policy*, Freiburg: Öko-Institut.

PricewaterhouseCoopers (2001), Optimisation of Municipal Water Supply and Sewerage as Part of a Sustainable Water Policy, http://staedtebund.wienat/service/pwc_endbericht.pdf

Schmitter, P. (1974), 'Still the Century of Corporatism?' *The Review of Politics*, Vol.35, No.2, pp.85–131.

Schuster, G. (not dated), *Das österreichische Umweltzeichen*, Vienna: Verlag Österreich.

Schwar, B. (1999), *Umweltzeichen und betrieblicher Umweltschutz*, Vienna: Verlag Österreich.

Scruggs, L. (1999), 'Institutions and Environmental Performance in Seventeen Western Democracies', *British Journal of Political Science*, Vol. 29, pp.1–31.

Scruggs, L. (2001), 'Is There Really a Link Between Neo-Corporatism and Environmental Performance? Updated Evidence and New Data for the 1980s and 1990s', *British Journal of Political Science*, Vol.31, pp.686–92.

Trattnigg, R. (1997), 'Veränderungen des österreichischen Netzwerks der umweltpolitischen Akteure nach dem EU-Beitritt', Vienna: University of Vienna (unpublished diploma).

UBA (2001), *Umweltsituation in Österreich: Sechster Umweltkontrollbericht*, Vienna: Umweltbundesamt.

WIFO (1995), *Makroökonomische und sektorale Auswirkungen einer umweltorientierten Energiebesteuerung in Österreich*, Vienna: Österreichisches Institut für Wirtschaftsforschung.

WIFO (1998), *Energieverbrauch, CO$_2$-Emissionen und Energiebesteuerung. Simulation mir dem Energiemodell Daedalus*, Vienna: Österreichisches Institut für Wirtschaftsforschung.

WIFO (2000), *Ein Erstansatz für ein nationales CO$_2$-Emissions-Trading System*, Vienna: Österreichisches Institut für Wirtschaftsforschung.

Wirtschaftskammar (1999), *Anatomie von freiwilligen Vereinbarungen*, Vienna: Wirtschaftskammar Österreich.

Wirtschaftskammar (2002), 'Freiwillige Vereinbarungen', Vienna: Wirtschaftskammar Österreich (unpublished memo).

Wurzel, R.K.W. (2002), *Environmental Policy-Making in Britain, Germany and the European Union: The Europeanisation of Air and Water Pollution Control*, Manchester: Manchester University Press.

The Politics of Regulatory Reform: 'New' Environmental Policy Instruments in Finland

RAUNO SAIRINEN

Introduction

Finland has often been described as an active country in the field of environmental policy. The level of environmental protection in Finland has been high by European standards since the 1980s. Finland joined the EU in 1995, since when its environmental policy agenda has influenced the Finnish one in many ways [*Lindholm, 2002*]. Since the early 1990s, environmental policy has been considerably extended and updated in Finland. The main emphasis has been on legal regulation, planning and economic instruments.

In addition to advancing new legislation, various 'new' policy instruments (NEPIs) have been developed [*ME 1997*]. The trend has been so significant that the period since 1987 could be characterised as having witnessed a wholesale regulatory reform of Finnish environmental policy [*Sairinen, 2000, 2002*]. The term 'regulatory reform' comes from Francois Leveque [*1996a, 1996, 1996c*] who argues that a large international shift from regulatory control models towards economic and more negotiative and persuasive models has occurred. The limitations and regulatory failures of the traditional command and control approach have sparked a search for a second generation of instruments which promises greater flexibility, efficiency, effectiveness and legitimacy. Changes in the modes of governance as well as new forms of socio-political interaction can be seen behind the regulatory reform (see also Kooiman [*1993*]).

What have been the concrete changes in Finnish environmental governing? First of all, many new environmental taxes were introduced in the 1990s [*OECD, 1997*]. Finland has been one of the forerunner-countries in this matter. There have been several eco-tax models in different policy fields under test and also in longer use. The total revenue of environmental taxation was 2.07 billion euros (FIM 12.3 billion) in 1993, 3.11 billion euros (18.5 billion in 1996) and 4.12 billion euros (24.5 billion) in 2000 (includes all energy taxes) [Statistics Finland, *1996, 2001*]. Thus, we can state that the amount of environmental taxes increased significantly during the 1990s.

TABLE 1
REVENUE OF ENVIRONMENTAL TAXES AND FEES IN FINLAND 1993–2000 (FIM MILLION)
(STATISTICS FINLAND 1996 & 2001)

	1993	1996	1998	2000
Energy taxes, of which	8 404	12 714	15 306	15 435
Carbon dioxide component	1 005	1 375		
Energy component	–	890		
Basic tax	7 399	10 449		
Electricity tax	656	–	–	–
Motor vehicle tax	1 609	3 611	5 259	6 295
Vehicle licence tax ('sticker tax')	–	1 110	1 198	1 306
Vehicle fuel tax ('diesel tax')	885	929	1 042	1 074
Oil waste tax	21	20	20	20
Charter flight tax	111	–	–	–
Oil pollution control fee	34	29	33	32
Waste tax	–	41	182	198
Disposable drinks packaging tax	16	52	60	73
Soft drink surtax	19	9	9	7
Fertiliser tax	516	–	–	–
Pesticide fee	6	6	10	10
Water protection tax	2	3	3	3
Total	12 279	18 524	23 122	24 453

Measured in terms of the amount of environmental taxes levied relative to GDP, Finland ranks well above the OECD average. In 1999 these taxes and fees equalled 3.4 per cent of GDP [*Statistics Finland, 2001*].

In Finland, all taxes and fees that have an environmental impact are regarded as 'environmental taxes', though not all of these are itemised in the state budget. Many of these taxes and fees were imposed for reasons other than environmental protection. Environmental effects are most marked on the surtaxes levied on alcoholic beverages and soft drinks, the environmental energy surtaxes, the waste-oil disposal fee, the oil pollution control fee and the waste tax.

Tradable permits have not been used in Finland. In EU politics, Finland has been quite sceptical towards the EU-wide emissions trading scheme for greenhouse gases. The Finnish industry has been especially very critical, and the government has until now mainly followed the views of industrial groups.

Secondly, voluntary environmental agreements (VA) have been brought into use, but they have not become very popular. In Finland, the application of VAs has been slow in comparison to other small European neo-corporatist countries such as Denmark and the Netherlands. Because the traditional regulation has followed the consensual policy style (negotiated rule-making) with quite good environmental results, there has not been an acute need for voluntary approaches. VAs between public authorities and industry have been carried out in relation to four different policy objectives: the reduction of the use of CFCs (1987–88), the reduction of packaging wastes (1995), the promotion of energy conservation (the first round in 1992 and the second round in 1997) and the remediation of contaminated soil (SOILI agreement in 1996) [*Sairinen and Teittinen, 1999*]. Recently, plans have been made to use the voluntary approach in environmental permit legislation. In addition, the private landowners (in practice the forest owners) have been able to strike a kind of voluntary agreement with environmental administrators concerning the conservation of valuable habitats on their own land.

Thirdly, the industrial sector has moved increasingly towards voluntary environmental management systems such as EMAS and ISO. Companies have joined the global ISO 14001 environmental system since 1995 and the EMAS since 1996. To date, ISO has awarded nearly 530 environmental certificates to Finnish companies and EMAS has awarded 35. In Finland EMAS companies can receive discounts on permit processing costs if their permit processing is faster than normal.

Fourthly, eco-labelling has become an integral part of Finnish environmental policy during the 1990s. Originally, the ideas for product labelling in Finland were based on experiences in the Federal Republic of Germany. Their 'Blue Angel' label was a well-known example. The most important eco-labels in Finland are the Nordic eco-label, EU eco-label, Luomu for organic food products, Norppa for eco-energy and eco-certification for forest products.

Fifthly, this author would also include environmental impact assessment systems (EIA) to the list of NEPIs because they are 'new' to Finland. The EU adopted EIA in 1985 and Strategic Environmental Assessment in 2001. In Finland, the process of drafting the EIA-law gave rise to many conflicts. After 1994, EIA practices in Finland very successfully introduced a comprehensive assessment procedure that also includes social impact assessment, strategic impact assessment and wider participatory practices.

Finnish Environmental Policy

The national policy structures and in some amount also policy contents have clearly influenced the usage of different policy instruments in Finland. The traditional policy structures have developed in order to use mainly command-and-control regulation towards increasing pollution and nature conservation needs. In practice, the Finnish consensual policy style has in some policy fields (mainly pollution policies) meant the development of negotiated rule-making.

Policy Structures

Since the beginning of the 1970s, the development of environmental legislation in Finland has occurred along the same general lines as in the other Nordic countries, although some national characteristics remain. In the background, the growing welfare state, modern environmental movement and emerging international environmental concern provided ideological and political possibilities for public intervention. The time-period 1970–86 has been described as a 'period of environmental institutionalisation' in Finnish environmental policy [*Sairinen, 2000*].

The period describes the era of establishing the modern environmental policy, its basic administrative institutions and legislation. The founding of separate and broad-based environmental ministry in 1983 (the Ministry of the Environment, ME) and new environmental legislation received lots of political resistance, but in the long run the establishment of modern environmental institutions was inevitable. Its agenda included pollution policies, land-use planning, nature conservation and housing. This signified a significant centralisation of environmental decision-making. After the founding of the ME, the environmental policy system was developed at the regional and municipal levels. Compared with international developments, the independent environmental administration was developed relatively late in Finland.

The dominant instrument of governance during this period was legal regulation [*ME, 1988*]. New purification technologies were developed and applied. While end-of-pipe technology was the dominant policy strategy, a more preventive policy strategy was being applied in the area of pollution policies. Private companies made significant environmental improvements as they redesigned their industrial processes.

Strong sectoral interests and political disagreements led to the sectoralisation of the environmental legislation and permit systems. Thus, Finnish environmental legislation has been composed of a number of individual acts that refer to only one specific sector of environmental protection. This development led to a variation in the aims, remedies, supervisory systems, penal provisions and permission procedures set out in the individual acts [*ME, 1988*].

During the first decades of its existence, legal regulation was a highly appreciated mode of governing within the ME [*ME, 1988*]. Thus, it seems that the tradition of administrative legalism has also characterised the young environmental administration. New ideas on environmental policy integration and instruments had to wait for the introduction of the international debate on sustainable development in the late 1980s.

EU membership has had a big influence on the Finnish environmental policy structures. First, Finland has tried to anticipate forthcoming EU regulations. Secondly, legislation in particular has been extensively developed by reforming the Forest Act (1996), the Nature Conservation Act (1996) and the Extractable Land Resource Act (1997). A new Environmental Protection Act (1999) revised the entire environmental permit system to correspond to the IPPC directive of the EU. It created an integrated system for the prevention of pollution, which now includes earlier separate water legislation. Special emphasis is on applying the principle of best available technology (BAT), risk management and the efficiency of energy use. In addition to new legislation, new policy tools have been brought into use because of the pressures and examples from the EU's side [*Sairinen, 2000*] (see below).

Advancing regulatory reform has always some effects on national policy structures. In Finland, it has clearly distributed environmental governing power to other ministries than the ME. For example, the formal preparatory mandate of environmental taxation belongs to the Ministry of Finance and the voluntary agreements can be developed under several ministries. Thus the regulatory reform seems to have a tendency to decentralise the environmental policy system.

Policy Style

The Finnish environmental policy style during the period of 'institutionalisation' – and also after that – can be described as two-dimensional: the conflicting (adversarial) nature conservation and consensual pollution policies [*Sairinen, 2000*]. It can be said that the adaptation of new policy instruments has mainly followed the adversarial style. Only the voluntary agreements have been developed on a more on consensual basis.

On the other hand, the official policy targets have frequently emphasised Finland's proactive role in European environmental policy, but in political practice the reactive role has been most common. Finland's environmental policy style in the EU (after 1995) has been called pragmatic realism [*Lindholm, 2002*]. A reactive attitude has been decisive also in the adoption of new policy instruments. It can be said that Finland has been proactive only in the case of energy and carbon taxation. In the following the Finnish environmental policy styles are analysed in more depth.

In spite of long-standing traditions, it has always been difficult to promote the integration of nature conservation interests in other policy sectors such as forestry, agriculture and land use planning in Finland. The cultural importance of landownership and the strong role of the rural political parties and interest groups has given rise to much conflict over nature-conservation issues at the national policy level. Nearly all the various conservation programmes have a history of conflict. In these policy fields, the policy actors have been divided into sharply confronting policy networks.

On the other hand, Finnish pollution policies – especially air and water pollution policies – have been based on the 'consensual policy style' between different actors ranging from the industry to environmental organisations. In these policy fields, the public governing mode has been based on legal state regulation, but in the manner of negotiative problem-solving. At first, the content of emission control activities and regulations were negotiated between different actors, and consequently the government or permit authorities made their decision on the basis of those regulations. This policy style has also been called 'negotiated rule-making' in contrast to 'command-and-control regulation'. The use of structural changes favourable to emission reduction and by fitting pollution control investments to the timetables of major process retrofits constituted an effort to avoid additional costs.

National 'neo-corporatism' in the context of the Nordic welfare states is an obvious example of the development of the consensual style. The formation of the policy style can also be attributed to the national economic-political structures. The production structure based on forest and steel industry has been largely nature-consuming, energy-intensive and polluting. Environmental protection policies and the nationally important export industries have traditionally represented very contradictory interests. Thus, the environmental administration has had difficulty in keeping a strong hand in regulating these activities. On the macro-political level, ensuring the price competitiveness of the forest and other export industries has been the fundamental doctrine, which has prevailed over other policy interests. In environmental administration, the most efficient perspectives to environmental governing have required negotiative capacities and a consensual mentality.

The environmental consequences of Finland's consensual policy style have been quite good in the areas of both air and water pollution [*Sairinen, 2000*]. It can be argued that this success within the regulatory system to some extent prevented the more active development of new instruments. The consensual policy style has provided possibilities for informal actor relations inside the regulatory system, to the extent that industry has not been very interested in the voluntary approaches.

Similarly, the environmental administration was at first so satisfied with the systems of legal regulation that the concepts of EIA and environmental taxation had to wait some time (during the late 1980s) before they were more readily accepted. Thus, it can be argued that the administrative-legalistic style has in some cases delayed the use of new policy instruments. This notion has links to the more general features of Finnish administrative culture. In Finland, the dignified traditions of civil servants have included attending to administration 'according to infallible principles of law'

[*Stenvall, 1998*]. This 'rule of law' ideology has influenced the forms of public governing in Finland for a long time.

Many influential officials in the ME have been committed to the legalistic culture, and initially showed no interest in developing new measures. The new instruments all differ markedly from the classic model of regulation. It has been claimed that in this kind of regulatory reform, the government refrains from using any instruments of formal power, that is, from enacting legal norms. Instead, the authorities enter into questionable negotiations with the polluters or trust the steering power of market prices. The Finnish environmental administrators were not familiar with these types of new governing mentalities.

The Content of Policy

During the initial phases, the key sectors of Finnish environmental protection concerned water protection and issues of forestry. Water and forest resources were of special interest in Finland because their utilisation has played such an important role in the development of the national economy. Hence it follows that water and forestry administrations enjoyed a central position and a strong organisation in national politics. This also influenced the development of environmental institutions and governing. For example, the integration of water and environmental legislation has been a very difficult task.

But during the 1990s, the change in the content (or quality) of environmental problems has influenced widely the choice of policy tools. As the significance of point pollution sources has diminished, diffuse pollution (traffic, agriculture) has become more important and at the same time the need for using the new policy instruments has increased.

The process of Europeanisation has meant deep changes in the Finnish environmental policy content. The traditional national standards, important policy questions and the level of general environmental policy have maintained their position, but at the same time the basic systems and practices have been efficiently adjusted to the EU ones. Several EU directives have had considerable positive impact on Finnish environmental legislation. Many directives have forced Finland to adopt stricter rules addressing such issues as urban waste water, nitrates and habitats than had previously been in place.

Clearly the most problematic area for Finland has been that of nature conservation. Generally speaking, Finland has kept to its traditional policy instruments in nature conservation. This includes sectoral and centralised planning and strict protection of nature areas. EU nature directives such as the Bird and Habitats Directives and the Natura 2000 programme, turned out to be stricter than had been anticipated among different stakeholders.

The first Natura proposal attracted more than 14,000 complaints and increased the already-existing criticism among the rural population against EU directives and the bureaucracy of the Union. The EU's nature protection regulations have caused remarkably longer planning and legal processes in many big infrastructure projects than the domestic ones used to be. There are new obligations for impact assessment and the exceptions are more difficult to obtain. This has meant a real strengthening of the arguments about the role of nature protection in Finnish politics. At the same time, some new governing patterns have emerged. In the Natura process, new ideas of biodiversity policy, such as a flexible system of protection, have been brought into use. There exist now nature areas which are simultaneously under protection and in active economic use. But it has taken several years for stakeholders to trust in this new logic.

Why Are NEPIs Being Adopted?

The change in the choice of policy instruments is a world-wide trend, but the reform has been especially dramatic inside the EU. In addition, behind the regulatory reform of environmental policy there can be seen at least two larger societal trends: deregulation and ecological modernisation [*Mol et al., 2000; Liefferink and Mol, 1998*]. In its different modes, the ecological modernisation theory has stressed the increasing importance of economic and market dynamics in ecological reform and the role of innovators, entrepreneurs and other economic agents as social carriers of ecological restructuring, in addition to state agencies and new social movements.

In Finland, the regulatory reform has been advanced by very pragmatic policies without clear reference to general environmental policy strategies, such as sustainable development or ecological modernisation. Policy reforms are more the result of pragmatic needs, domestic conditions, pressures from the EU and a desire to experiment, and less the result of some grand, widely accepted strategy. Of course, the general strategic debate on new governance modes has influenced also the Finnish environmental politics. Thus, the ideological policy climate has been positive for new instruments at least from the mid-1990s.

The situational political trends and economic conditions have also influenced the development of NEPIs. For example, in the early 1990s, environmental taxes were a popular trend in Finnish politics and at the same time the state was facing serious fiscal difficulty in the middle of an economic crisis. Thus, the NEPIs became an attractive source of new revenue.

The role of EU law and policy has been very important when introducing the NEPIs in Finland. For example, in the cases of EIA-law and voluntary agreements, anticipation of the EU membership has remarkably advanced the reforms. In the case of carbon tax, the EU policy is vulnerable to criticism because of its inconsistencies. It seems that the EU's legal environment has complicated rather than facilitated the implementation of national carbon taxes, although the EU has favoured these new tools in its general progammes.

In Finland, as in other Scandinavian countries, the need for reducing income taxes has paved the way for the introduction of energy and carbon taxes on a wider scale than would have been the case otherwise. In this sense, it can be argued that fiscal considerations have created opportunities for NEPIs. But we can also ask, how far is it rational to connect the state of the environment to the legitimacy crisis of income taxation? What happens if there are no further political needs for revenue-recycling, but there are clear needs for improvement in the state of the environment? It seems that in Finland, the political willingness for further increases in energy taxation has diminished remarkably after the better economic situation since 1997. In addition, it is still unclear how the possible development of emission trading is influencing willingness for developing carbon and energy taxes.

The regulatory reform has not been an easy policy process in Finland. The policy formulation of the EIA law, carbon taxation and forest certification systems have been heavily disputed, and the voluntary agreements have not become general. Only the development of eco-labels and environmental management systems have represented quite consensual policy processes. The carbon taxation and the EIA law were disputed inside the government and also between the different ministries.

It is important to notice that every policy instrument has its own supporters and opponents. The role of the Ministry of the Environment in promoting regulatory reform has varied depending on the policy instrument in question. It seems that the ME (or part of it) was initially skeptical or critical towards the new instrument in question, but has gradually adopted a more supportive attitude. In the field of voluntary agreements, the sceptical attitude continued over a longer period. In the beginning, both the legalistic attitude and the lack of new competence made it difficult for environmental authorities to support new policy tools. It is evident that regulatory reform calls for new kinds of expert systems and knowledge base among the administrators. The initial professional structure of the employees of the ME was based on the need for developing natural scientific knowledge of environmental problems and on the use of regulatory policy instruments. Thus, during the regulatory reform the ME has needed to recruit new professions such as planners, economists and sociologists.

The Finnish environmental groups have always supported the development of strong legal regulation. During the 1970s and 1980s, the environmentalists often criticised the consensual policy style for the possibility of regulatory capture. On the other hand, the main environmental associations were satisfied with the opportunity of participating in the various committees. When regulatory reform began to gain momentum, the main environmental groups remained cautious. Environmental taxation is one new policy instrument that they have been supporting from the beginning. Environmentalists also supported the EIA and eco-labelling. But, they have been critical towards VAs, because of the closed policy processes, the opportunity for regulatory capture and the weak results.

During the 1970s, Finnish industry criticised the broadening of environmental legislation and proposed more flexible systems of environmental permits. During the 1980s, the polluters became used to the new environmental obligations and negotiative routines (see above). When the debate on the need for regulatory reform began, Finnish industry showed little interest. Industry criticised both the EIA systems and environmental taxation. The voluntary agreements and ecolabels have been most suitable new instruments for the Finnish industry. At the same time, however, industry has argued that the negotiated rule-making style has been very successful and pleasant for them. On some occasions, they have also stated that free-riding has been less of a problem in the existing regulatory system than it is under more voluntary schemes.

The landowners and agricultural interest groups have traditionally been very active opponents of increased environmental governing. In any case, the new instruments have not involved these actors as much. With regard to the EIA, the agricultural policy networks took a very critical stand, although its direct effects on these policy areas were minor. Organic farming and its labelling systems were at first criticised. But nowadays, public attitudes have changed.

NEPIs in Finland

In the following, four cases of Finnish NEPIs are described and analysed: carbon tax, voluntary agreements, eco-labels and EIA. The cases illustrate the national policy features and the benefits of NEPIs.

Market-Based Instruments

The Finnish environmental taxation has been most actively implemented in air pollution policy. The biggest part of the revenues comes from energy taxes. The total revenue of energy taxation was FIM 8.4 billion in 1993, 12.7 billion in 1996 and 15.4 billion in 2000 [*Statistics Finland, 1996, 2001*]. The first economic instruments against air pollution were adopted in the late 1980s, when the price of catalytic converters was subsidised by the reduction of taxation on cars. After that Finland was the first country in the world to introduce the carbon tax in 1990. Afterwards, the structure of the carbon tax has changed several times and has been the target of major political debates during the 1990s. The revenue from carbon tax was FIM 1 billion in 1993 and 1.4 billion in 1996. After 1996 the carbon tax component has been much lower, because the energy tax model was changed towards normal consumption tax.

Efforts to increase the availability of lead-free gasoline is an example of the combined use of legal and economic instruments as well as voluntary measures. The production and import of leaded gasoline, with an octane number lower than 92, was prohibited by the government in 1989. This product was consequently substituted by lead-free fuel at almost all the 2,000 filling stations in the country. At the same time, the use of lead-free gasoline was generally encouraged through tax reductions. Today, almost all gasoline sold in Finland is lead-free.

In the following, the main features (three phases) of Finnish carbon tax policy are analysed more closely. During the first phase (1989–90), the carbon tax was brought onto the political agenda [*Sairinen, 2000; Bragge, 1997*]. During the second phase (1991–94), the carbon tax was raised in 1993 and in 1994 it was restructured. The 75/25 tax model was established: 75 per cent of the tax was based on the carbon content and 25 per cent on the energy content of the primary energy source. An important reason for introducing an energy tax component into the tax system was to take into account the externalities involved in nuclear power. The problem of a pure carbon tax is that it confers a fiscal advantage on nuclear power production. This structural change, which was later considered very advanced by the environmentalists, took place after relatively short political combat and successful broad-based committee work.

During the third phase (1994–96), the structure of the energy taxation was altered by decreasing the role of carbon taxes [*ME, 1994*]. A definite turn took place in 1994, when many important policy actors such as the Ministry of Trade and Industry and the Ministry of Finance, lost faith in the EU's ability to adopt a carbon-energy tax. Thus they did not trust any more to the quick development of the EU-based carbon tax system. Simultaneously, the EU Commission started to criticise the Finnish system: it claimed that the Finnish tax imposed on imported electricity was against trade agreements. In practice, this claim meant that the whole energy tax system would have to be reformed. Mainly because of the insistence of the Green Party inside the government, the reform of the energy and carbon tax was made in such a manner that parts of the carbon tax were preserved and the total level of taxes was increased remarkably. The increase was partly compensated through income tax relief. As a political solution, the result was the first sleight of hand towards *ecological tax reform*. But at the same time, the non-environmental nature of the lower carbon tax rate is evident. The changes made to the system can be seen as an indication that decision-makers pay more attention to the needs of large power producers' interests than those of environmental protection.

In the case of carbon taxation, the ME was at first a significant policy actor and mediator. The adoption of shared-responsibility and consensual-problem-solving styles, where all the stakeholders participated in the policy process, moved the preparations forward. When criticism towards increasing energy taxes was growing, the ME lost its role. As a result of several factors, a policy model evolved where the responsibility for the preparation of energy taxes was centralised to the MF backed by the MTI. More than once, the ME unsuccessfully tried to be admitted to the administrative working groups.

The environmental authorities have emphasised the need for environmentally-oriented taxation, in which tax proceeds are of secondary importance, whereas tax and energy authorities have stressed the fiscally-oriented approach and the international competitiveness of the Finnish companies. In the latter, the environmental impacts are relegated to side-effects. It has even been claimed that if environmental taxes are introduced without considering their implications for the overall balance of the fiscal system, they are likely to run into administrative and political opposition [*Määttä, 1997: 191*].

The environmental benefits of carbon taxation have not been examined in depth in Finland. In the public debate, it has been taken for granted that these taxes are beneficial for the targets of national climate policy. However, the industry has been sceptical of its effectiveness at producing concrete results. A Government working group on environmental taxation recently assessed the effects of environmental taxes [*Talousneuvosto, 2000*]. The results showed that the energy and carbon taxes have reduced carbon emissions by over 7per cent (57 million tonnes) during 1990–98. In electricity and heat production, the reduction was mainly the result of replacing coal and oil with natural gas and wood. Although the price flexibility of the energy demands of the industry was assessed as small, the reduction of energy demand has been remarkable, because the tax on fossil fuels has risen seven-to eleven-fold. Although these results include some uncertainties, overall, they show that carbon taxation has had clear environmental benefits in Finland.

Voluntary Agreements

In Finland, voluntary environmental agreements are quite a new and poorly developed instrument. They have not been part of mainstream Finnish environmental policy-making. The use of VAs has mainly been based on *ad hoc* practices and on individual cases rather than on planned strategic decisions made at ministerial or governmental level [*Sairinen, 2000; Sairinen and Teittinen, 1999*]. The key initiators have been certain industrial branches and individual administrators.

In total, 18 voluntary agreements have been concluded in Finland. Nearly all of them (14) were first negotiated at branch level between the ME or the MTI on the public side, and between branch associations on the private side. The aim of these negotiations was to integrate the individual enterprises into the process at a very early stage.

Most of the agreements are not legally binding. All the agreements where the ME is a signatory (CFC, SOILI, packaging) were initiated by the companies rather than by environmental authorities. The energy conservation agreement is an exception, because the VAs have achieved a significant role in the national energy conservation programmes and the responsible official has been the Ministry of Trade and Industry (MTI). Attitudes towards voluntary approaches have been clearly more positive in the MTI than in the ME. Underlying these differences is the fact that the MTI also has had a more positive attitude than the environmental authorities toward deregulation.

Finnish environmental administrators have not actively promoted the use of VAs. Problems of the agreements mentioned in the strategy plan 'Environmental Programme 2005', prepared by the Ministry for internal use in 1995, include weaknesses as regards supervision, sanctions and openness. According to the Ministry, agreements can be used mainly to support other forms of control:

> An agreement concluded by branch associations does not judicially bind companies belonging to an association. For agreements to be binding, they should be concluded with individual industrial plants and this would be complicated because of the great number of companies ... From the point of view of citizens obtaining information, the fact that the preparation of agreements is generally not public is problematic. After all, the agreement process cannot compensate control based on legislation and administrative measures. The extensive use of the agreement process seems to require a binding and general set of rules which would encourage companies to join the agreement and ensure that companies outside the agreement or companies which do not comply with the agreement do not obtain competitive advantage over companies that comply with the agreement. The distribution of information and the adequate opportunities for all instances to participate are matters which should be well defined in legislation [*YM, 1995: 121–2*].

This statement reflects the strong need for legal restraint. This legalistic tradition emphasised the controlling role of the state and the use of judicial administrative means of control as primary instruments of public power. Because the number of agreements within the environmental administration has been very small, none of the sets of rules or instructions for the use of agreements that were mentioned in the statement has been developed.

The process of preparing VAs have been very consensual. There have been no serious disagreements about the targets and contents of the agreements during preparation. In each case, the voluntary approach was a new governing task both for the public authorities and for the private sector. Thus, the authorities merely seemed to be putting the matter to the test; it seems that in this new situation they were more interested in establishing a consensus than in engaging in real negotiations.

The newness of this particular tool and the administration's weakness as a negotiator can be seen in the vagueness of the agreed targets, the strong role of the industry in preparing the agreement, the defects of the monitoring systems, and in the confusion over the role of third parties, among other things. In this situation, there is a definite risk that the administration alone is unable to control the use of the agreements and the goals of the policy sufficiently. In research, such a phenomenon is called regulatory capture [*Leveque, 1996d*]. This attitude was especially noticeable in the case of the packaging and energy conservation agreements, where industry had a good bargaining position which it used to influence the contents of the agreements.

At the political level, the environmental movement and the Green Party have both been suspicious of voluntary agreements. No opportunities for their adoption were created during the 1990s because environmental organisations strongly criticised the Minister representing the Greens for the packaging agreement. Thus the reasons for suspicious attitudes towards voluntary approaches can be found both in the administrative culture and in everyday politics.

Internationally, the VAs have been criticised for their disregard of certain basic democratic requirements, including parliamentary scrutiny and the rights of environmental or other interest groups to participate in the policy formulation process [*Liefferink and Enevoldsen, 1997*]. In Finland, the policy processes concerning voluntary agreements have been quite closed and they have focused mainly on the negotiations between the contracting parties. There is almost no public debate on VAs, and the general public has almost no knowledge of their existence, with the exception of the case of the packaging agreement, where the working groups established by the Ministry included members from non-contracting parties. There have been disagreements with other policy actors in two cases.

The Finnish VAs have been such short-lived and incremental ad hoc practices that it is often quite difficult to assess the environmental policy results quantitatively. It is also difficult to distinguish the results of different policy instruments used simultaneously. While quantitative analysis is difficult, the results and effectiveness of the agreements can be assessed in qualitative terms.

The first round in 1992 of the energy conservation agreements was poorly organised and the results were merely modest. The second round of these agreements started in the autumn of 1997. The main positive results from the first two years have been that many industrial companies and municipalities have joined the framework agreements, and energy conservation has come to be recognised as an important issue by the public.

Both the packaging and CFC agreements were in force only for a very short period of time. In both cases, the results are difficult to distinguish from the results of the administrative regulations which displaced the agreement. On the other hand, in these cases the agreements can be seen as a first stage towards stricter and more general legislation. The packaging agreement can also be seen as a basis for the present recycling and reuse system.

Eco-labels

The *Nordic eco-label* with its white swan logo is the most well-known eco-label in Finland. The label was founded in 1989 by the Nordic Council of Ministers. By the year 2001, the Nordic eco-label had awarded about 200 licences. In Finland, the *EU eco-label* has not yet become as popular as the Nordic eco-label. The *Luomu* label is the official label for organic food products certified by the public Finnish inspection authority. The labelled product conforms to the regulations of the European Union concerning organic food production. The Plant Production Inspection Centre grants the right to use the label. Currently, organic food production in Finland makes up approximately six per cent of all land under cultivation [*Finfood, 2002*].

'*Norppa recommends eco-energy*' – eco-labelled electricity markets were opened in September 1998. An eco-energy label means that the supplier can provide energy and services satisfying the Finnish Association for Nature Conservation's (FANC) recommendations. The basis for this kind of eco-label was founded through the new Electricity Market Act. This Act provided companies and private consumers with the opportunity to freely purchase their electricity from the power company of their choice. This means that everyone can decide what kind of energy they want to pay for. Energy utilities marketing eco-energy are expected to invest in the future in further renewable energy production plants, product development, and the raising of the level of such energy in their own production profile. An exception is that of new hydropower construction, which is not supported by the Nordic nature conservation NGOs. In respect of hydropower, investments are required to be targeted at waterway restoration work.

Eco-labelling for forest products is of considerable interest for the future of sustainable forest management, not just in Finland or in Europe but worldwide. The development of forest-certification in Finland has been full of disagreements. The environmentalists and forest companies have developed their own alternative certificates.

Other Instruments: Environmental Impact Assessment

In Finland, the process of drafting the EIA law gave rise to many conflicts. Inspired by the international debate, the need to include EIA into Finnish environmental systems was first studied by a working group as early as in 1981, but the active phase was not entered into until the early 1990s [*ME, 1992*]. The political and economic integration of the country into the EU launched the preparation of the EIA law in Finland and finally forced its introduction. Without pressure from the EIA Directive and the Commission, enacting the EIA law might have taken even longer. At the same time, connections established with international – especially North American – research in this field revealed the content of EIA and the shortcomings of the Finnish environmental permit system [*Leskinen and Turtiainen, 1987; Sairinen, 1991*].

During the entire policy process, the preparations of the EIA law were strictly in the hands of the ME. Other Ministries first participated in the work of the working group, and then negotiated with the ME regarding the disputed issues. The whole case was based on an adversarial policy style. There were two main policy alternatives presented. The main causes of dispute were the scope of application, the need for an assessment schedule, the need and content of hearing and notifying procedures, the obligation to work out alternative project plans, the content requirements of the environmental reports as well as the role of the liaison authority. During the long drawn-out disputes, the Ministry of Agriculture and Forestry prepared its own 'lighter' draft law as an alternative to the ME's proposal. Finally, the model of the ME was accepted by the government, and soon after also by Parliament in May 1994 [*Sairinen, 2000*].

The main issues in the final disputes involved fundamental differences of opinion on questions concerning the definition of democracy and the environmental and social preconditions of technological development. The importance of the democracy argument can be illustrated by the fact that the media treated the EIA reform primarily as an issue of participatory democracy, and the environmental dimension was given only secondary importance [*Puustinen, 1996*].

As a societal phenomenon, the adoption of the EIA system entails the institutionalisation of comprehensive environmental analysis as an integral part of the normal planning and decision-making procedures. In Finland, the EIA law has been very successful in attaining this aim by introducing a comprehensive assessment procedure that also includes future needs regarding social impact assessment, strategic impact assessment and wide participatory practices. This type of reform in environmental governance implies the normalisation and intensification of public and expert discourse on environmental impacts. Thus, it is no wonder that the Finnish environmental administration deemed the EIA law to be the most important environmental law of the 1990s. On the other hand, the EIA law has also had a profound impact on the content of local democracy and the role of citizen organisations in planning procedures.

Conclusion

Instrument reform has not been easy to achieve in Finland. The policy formulation of the EIA law, carbon taxation and forest certification systems have been heavily disputed, and the voluntary agreements have not become general. The carbon tax case indicates that the relationship between the different ministries seems to be vulnerable to conflict, because of their very different mentalities in environmental governing. All in all, the NEPIs in Finland have been used and developed not because of common strategy, but because of the desire to experiment (voluntary agreements), situational power relations (carbon taxation) or international pressures (EIA law). Of course, the EU membership, deregulation trend and new administrative cultures have produced general pressures to advance the regulatory reform.

In Finland, the NEPIs have usually served a so-called 'support function', which means that they have been used in order to support traditional instruments. For example, in climate policy the VAs and taxation are used together with standard setting and regulation. In some cases, VAs provide a 'bridging function' that is, a precursor to legislation or until the need for another form of environmental control (its content, form and continuity) and the content and conditions of the industrial sector's own environmental activities, have been settled.

Whether the new policy instruments in Finland are really new or just a refinement of what was going on before depends on the perspective of the assessor. Industry and also some environmental authorities have argued that we have already done the same thing before but in another way (such as environmental assessments before the EIA Act or negotiated rule-making before VAs). On the other hand, eco-taxes and environmental management systems have provided totally new governing dynamics. Overall, it is clear that when looking back to the early 1990s, the picture of Finnish environmental governing system has diversified and become more complex with several policy actors.

The process of regulatory reform also changes power/knowledge relations. It engenders a need for a fundamental change in the professional structures of environmental administration and other expert systems. For example, natural-scientific and judicial expertise is shifting towards multi-disciplinary understanding, where economics, planning professions and social sciences are also important for the governing practices.

On the other hand, the NEPIs have the effect of distributing influence and power from the state institutions to other policy actors such as private companies and consumers. As policy measures, they emphasise the ideas of shared responsibility, participation of stakeholders, subsidiarity and the market mechanism. This feature is a real challenge to the traditional policy structures because they have emphasised quite centralised modes of action.

The role of the Ministry of the Environment in promoting the regulatory reform has varied depending on the policy instrument in question. It seems that in the first phase, the ME (or part of it) has been sceptical or critical towards the new instrument in question. But gradually it has adopted a more supportive attitude. On the other hand, the NEPIs have clearly distributed the environmental governing power to other ministries. For example, the formal preparatory mandate of environmental taxation belongs to the MF and the voluntary agreements can be made under different ministries.

The Finnish environmental groups have always supported the development of strong legal regulation. When regulatory reform began to gain momentum, the main environmental associations were very cautious. Eco-taxes, EIA and ecolabels are new policy instruments that environmentalists have been supporting from the beginning. On the other side, the industry, agriculture and landowners have supported the voluntary approaches, but criticised eco-taxes and EIA.

Regulatory reform in Finland has clearly been restricted by national policy styles. Consequently, it has been quite difficult to alter the balance of the traditional regulatory system. The good environmental results of the consensual policy style have to some extent prevented the more active development of NEPIs. The consensual policy style has provided possibilities for informal actor relations inside the regulatory system to the extent that industry has not always been very interested in the voluntary approaches. Similarly, the administrative legalism has in some cases delayed the use of NEPIs.

The environmental administration and other policy actors have gained extensive experiences through the NEPIs. It can be argued that these experiences have normalised the regulatory reform. While some of the new policy instruments have become routine elements of the environmental governing system, others, such as the voluntary agreements, are still in the phase of experimental development. Simultaneously, knowledge about the new instruments has grown among different stakeholders. It can also be argued that the successful development of the NEPIs requires new epistemic communities with international foundations. This means that the expertise needed for developing new policy instruments nationally has to based on international expert networks. In the Finnish case, EU membership has clearly activated this kind of networking. But, as the general attitude towards reform becomes increasingly positive, it is also obvious that disputes will continue: the new policy instruments have very different kinds of features and images, which means that they have to be considered on an individual basis.

Given the traditional features of Finnish environmental policy, it can be expected that the use of NEPIs will grow in the future, but the policy process continues to be quite cautious towards new innovation. In this process, the effect of EU environmental policy is significant. As a pro-integration member country, Finland is willing to develop commonly accepted lines of governance. NEPIs will probably be developed in the form of taxes, eco-labels, certificates, environmental management systems and new planning patterns. In the field of nature protection, the voluntary and more flexible approaches are being brought into use. The state has no additional budget money for buying large nature areas for conservation. For example, there is a commonly accepted need to protect the biodiversity in the forests of southern Finland in particular, but the traditional way of governing is far too expensive.

REFERENCES

Bragge, Johanna (1997), *Premediation Analysis of the Energy Taxation Dispute in Finland*, Helsinki: Helsinki School of Economics and Business Administration, Acta A-130.
Finfood (2002), http://www.finfood.fi/finfood/luomu.nsf/pages/index_e.htm.
Kooiman, Jan (eds.) (1993), *Modern Governance: New Government–Society Interactions*, London: Sage.
Leskinen, Antti and Turtiainen, Markku (1987), 'Ympäristövaikutusten arviointiprosessi ympäristöpolitiikan välineenä', *Yhteiskuntasuunnittelu*, Vol.25, No.1, pp.3-6.
Leveque, Francois (1996a), 'Introduction', in Leveque (ed.) [*1996: 1–8*].
Leveque, Francois (1996b), 'The European Fabric of Environmental Regulations', in Leveque (ed.) [*1996: 9–30*].
Leveque, Francois (1996c), 'The Regulatory Game', in Leveque (ed.) [*1996: 31–52*].
Leveque, Francois (1996d), 'Conclusions', in F.Leveque (ed.) [*1996: 201–8*].
Leveque, Francois (ed.) (1996), *Environmental Policy in Europe*, Cheltenham: Edward Elgar.
Liefferink, Duncan and Enevoldsen, Martin (1997), *Joint Environmental Policy-making: The Emergence of New Interactive Approaches in Environmental Policy and Its Implications for Democracy*, paper for the 25th ECPR Joint Sessions of Workshops, Bern, 27 Feb.– 4 March 1997.

Liefferink, Duncan and Mol, Arthur (1998), 'Voluntary Agreements as a Form of Deregulation: The Dutch Experience', in U.Collier (ed.), *Deregulation in the European Union: Environmental Perspectives*, London: Routledge, pp.181–97.

Lindholm, Arto (2002), *Finland in EU Environmental Policy*, Helsinki: Edita/ The Ministry of the Environment.

ME (=Ministry of the Environment) (1988), *Environmental Protection in Finland: National Report 1987*, Series A 67/1988, Helsinki: Valtion Painatuskeskus.

ME (=Ministry of the Environment) (1992), *Environmental Impact Assessment; Report of the EIA '92 Working Group*, Helsinki.

ME (=Ministry of the Environment) (1994), *Interim Report of the Environmental Economics Committee: Environment Related Energy Taxation*, Working Group report 1994:4, Helsinki: Painatuskeskus Oy.

ME (=Ministry of the Environment) (1997), *Environmental Policies in Finland: Background Papers for the OECD Environmental Performance Review of Finland 1997*, Helsinki: The Finnish Environment 150, Edita.

Mol, A.P.J., Lauber, V. and J.D. Liefferink (eds.) (2000), *The Voluntary Approach to Environmental Policy: Joint Environmental Policy-Making in Europe*, Oxford: Oxford University Press.

Määttä, Kalle (1997), *Environmental taxes. From an Economic Idea to a Legal Institution*, Helsinki: Kauppakaari Oy, Finnish Lawyers' Publishing.

OECD (1997), *Finland. Environmental Performance Reviews*, Paris: OECD.

Puustinen, Sari (1996), *Toinen ympäristöjulkisuus: YVA-lakikeskustelu sanomalehdistössä*, Helsinki: Pro-gradu-thesis, Helsingin yliopisto, Viestinnän laitos.

Sairinen, Rauno (1991), *Ympäristövaikutusten arviointimenetelmät energia-alan suunnittelussa*, Espoo: Yhdyskuntasuunnittelun täydennyskoulutuskeskus, Julkaisuja B:64, Teknillinen korkeakoulu.

Sairinen, Rauno and Outi Teittinen, (1999), 'Voluntary Agreements as an Environmental Policy Instrument in Finland', *European Environment*, Vol.9, No.2, pp.67–74.

Sairinen, Rauno (2000), *Regulatory Reform of the Finnish Environmental Policy*, Espoo: Yhdyskuntasuunnittelun tutkimus- ja koulutuskeskus, Sarja A 27, TKK, 284 pp.

Sairinen, Rauno (2002), 'Environmental Governmentality as a Basis for Regulatory Reform: the Adaptation of New Policy Instruments in Finland', in A. Mol and F. Buttel (eds.), *The Environmental State under Pressure*, Oxford: JAI (an imprint of Elsevier Science), pp.85–104.

Statistics Finland (1996), *Finland's Natural Resources and the Environment 1996*, Helsinki: Ministry of the Environment, Environment 1996, 10C.

Statistics Finland (2001), *Finland's Natural Resources and the Environment 2001*, Helsinki: Ministry of the Environment, Environment and Natural Resources 2001: 3C.

Stenvall, Jari (1998), 'Professiot, asiantuntemus ja hallinnollinen ylivalta', in J. Mykkänen and I. Koskinen (ed.), *Asiantuntemuksen politiikka*, Helsinki: Helsinki University Press, pp.65–83.

Talousneuvosto (2000), *Ympäristö- ja energiaverotuksen käyttö Suomessa*, Helsinki: Työryhmäraportti, Valtioneuvoston kanslian julkaisuja 3/2000.

YM (=Ympäristöministeriö) [The Ministry of the Environment] (1995), *Ympäristöohjelma 2005*, Helsinki.

The Politics of Bounded Innovation: 'New' Environmental Policy Instruments in France

JOSEPH SZARKA

Introduction

French policy-making is characterised by a 'dual policy style' [*Hayward, 1982: 112*], which in the environmental domain involves a statist, top-down mode of policy formulation, conducted with 'heroic' flourishes by political entrepreneurs, allied to a pragmatic, bottom-up mode of implementation, based on 'humdrum' compromises with polluters. But the predilection for interventionist environmental policy-making has been moderated by meso-corporatist consensus, involving the ring-fencing of a policy domain, the emergence of organised private interests, and the establishment of public institutions exercising oversight.

In practice, this 'dual policy style' has translated into a multiplication of institutions and a fragmentation of responsibilities between, notably, the Environment Ministry, the water boards and the *Agence de l'environnement et de la maîtrise de l'énergie* (ADEME). This configuration has allowed the targets of environmental policy, particularly economic actors, multiple points of access to policy-makers and opportunities to influence policy development and implementation. This policy paradigm was supported from the 1960s by a comprehensive set of instruments, including not only regulation, but also hypothecated charges and voluntary agreements.

Given these early experiments, France was a pioneer in the use of 'new' policy instruments, though their usage proved unambitious in the 1970s and 1980s. However, better understanding of environmental pressures, the repercussions of international negotiations, the impact of the neo-liberal policy paradigm, as well as domestic political and institutional factors, led to a second phase of experimentation in the 1990s with eco-taxation and voluntary agreements. Under the Jospin coalition government (1997–2002), political ecologists – notably Environment Minister Voynet – spearheaded ambitious reforms which sought to renegotiate the meso-corporatist bargain and reconfigure environmental institutions. Eco-taxation, in particular, aimed to modify behaviour by firmer application of the 'polluter pays' and prevention principles, whilst generating revenue to implement the controversial project of the 35-hour week. However, the reforms were largely thwarted by the opposition of economic actors and the electoral defeat of the left in 2002.

Despite auspicious beginnings, usage of 'new' instruments has been limited compared to other OECD countries, with no radical break with past practice. On the one hand, familiar 'new' instruments (charges, contractual agreements) have been contained within long-standing policy paradigms, causing a dilution of their impact. On the other, unfamiliar instruments (such as emissions trading) have not been implemented at all.

Adjusted priorities with respect to the instrumentalisation of policy preferences have been the product of learning processes linked to greater political will and growth in institutional capacity. Consequently, explanations for the take-up of 'new' instruments will be contextualised within particular phases of policy development. The next section traces 'traditional' features of French environmental policy as regards policy styles, institutional structures and policy content. It develops the notion of 'dual policy style', explores the interplay between appearances of unilateral state intervention and the reality of bilateral meso-corporatist deals, and points up the distinctive way in which hypothecated charges have underpinned that bargain. The third section asks why 'new' environmental policy instruments (NEPIs) are being used, and discusses the impact of international and domestic factors on French policy reforms. The fourth section looks at NEPIs *per se*: it identifies the ways in which eco-taxation, voluntary approaches and eco-labels have been implemented over several decades, sets out the rationales associated with particular phases of usage, as well as assessing recent outcomes. The final section concludes that the impact of NEPIs has been limited in France, and discusses the reasons why long-standing policy paradigms have persisted.

French Environmental Policy

Policy Style

The characterisation of policy styles in France is problematic because of a disjunction between a stereotyped image and reality. France is often considered to have a 'strong' central state, capable of imposing its policy preferences in all areas of the polity. This reputation arises, *inter alia*, from economic and industrial policies frequently marked by interventionism and dirigism. However, it is worth probing the received idea of the 'strong' French state as a hyperactive and imposing policy actor.

Hayward [*1982: 112*] emphasised the existence of a 'dual policy style' in France, understood as 'the distinction between heroic and humdrum decision-making'. 'Heroic' decision-making involved 'a capacity for policy initiative, a potential for far-sighted planning and a propensity to impose its will' [*Hayward, 1982: 116*]. In French, the state's capacity for autonomous action is termed *volontarisme,* and in industrial policy this translated into *colbertisme,* namely state-sponsored entrepreneurship. Examples include the creation of the nuclear electricity generating sector, high speed trains (the 'TGV'), and aeronautics (Concorde, Airbus). Yet in many domains - such as health and education – the reality of the policy process tended to be 'humdrum', being merely dressed-up in 'heroic' language. The gap between entrepreneurial political rhetoric and mundane policy incrementalism points up the *trompe-l'oeil* character of much French policy making. This disjunction is particularly marked with regard to the environment, and explains why the literature assessing environmental policy styles has sometimes over-simplified the French case.

Promotion of the view of France as having an 'authoritative' policy style can be traced in various early strands of the environmental policy literature. Trilling [*1981: 74*] pointed to the importance of the 'active, *dirigiste* state' while the Economist Intelligence Unit report [*1990: 25*] characterised the French approach as administrative, imbued with scientific and technocratic confidence, and marked by centralism. More recently, this 'top-down' interpretation has been contested. Larrue and Chabason [*1998: 74*] affirmed that 'the main characteristic of the implementation of French environmental policy is that it is based on consensus rather than on imposition of constraints'. The existence of rival claims suggests a contradiction, but here too appearances prove deceptive. Arguably, the problem is an artefact arising from a conceptualisation predicated on supposedly exclusive modes of policy-making, each occupying a discrete quadrant of a policy matrix. But the French 'dual policy style', by its nature, cannot fit into one quadrant.

More specifically, this duality results from the interaction between an 'authoritative' and unilateral tradition (expressed at the formulation stage of environmental policy) and a system of neo-corporatist consensus (operating mainly at the implementation stage).[1] The French state maintained the appearances of a top-down policy mode, whilst in reality negotiating content and compliance with policy targets. The consensus that emerges from the negotiation process is best understood as a bilateral, meso-corporatist deal between government officials and sectoral representatives (rather than unilateral imposition or a multilateral agreement including civil society participation). Environmental meso-corporatism – involving the ring-fencing of a policy domain, the emergence of organised private interests entrusted with its stewardship, and the establishment of public institutions exercising oversight – developed particularly in relation to nature protection and the hunt lobby, and to industrial pollution control.[2]

Space here does not allow for detailed theoretical exploration of the 'varieties of corporatism',[3] but a useful outline of *corporatisme à la française* was provided by Muller and Saez [*1985: 135–6*] who identified three key features: (a) the sectoral representation of social interests, monopolised by a single organisation; (b) a close relationship between a sectoral 'corporation' and a specialised segment of the administration; and (c) a tendency to exclude other social actors and arms of government.

For Muller [*1990*] agriculture constituted the archetype of 'sectoral corporatism' because an interest group – the FNSEA (the main French farmers' union) – staked ownership over a sector and for long enjoyed an exclusive relationship with the associated organ of state, the Agricultural Ministry. With regard to environmental policy, Brénac [*1988*] and Gerbaux [*1988*] were among the first to develop extended analyses. The crucial point is that in a context of 'French-style corporatism', the *targets* of environmental policy had considerable influence on its implementation.

The underlying reasons for seeking meso-corporatist consensus were twofold. First, in the fields of nature protection and industrial pollution control, policy has mostly been implemented on a basis of 'delegated self-enforcement' [*Cawson, 1986: 38*]. Policy delivery depended on state representatives engaging the co-operation of largely private actors. Second, French institutional capacity for environmental policy-making has evolved slowly, unevenly and idiosyncratically. While apparently imposing new behavioural norms in an 'authoritative' mode, politicians and civil servants in fact delegated implementation by developing organisational structures that acknowledged the role of sectoral interests, and gave the latter institutionalised opportunities for influence.

Policy Structures

The central actor has been the French environment ministry but, because it is only one player in a complex institutional configuration, we also consider the *Agences de l'eau* and the ADEME.

The Environment Ministry: From its establishment in 1971, the Environment Ministry was conceived in terms of fulfilling a 'mission', namely to convince other ministries of the seriousness of environmental issues and co-ordinate their efforts. It was so woefully short of influence and resources that Robert Poujade, the first French Environment Minister, ruefully dubbed his office as *le ministère de l'impossible* [*Poujade, 1975*]. In the late 1970s and early 1980s, its very survival was in doubt. Ministerial appointments were rarely political 'heavyweights' and generally short-lived. The French executive tended to downplay the environment, at best co-opting political ecologists into government, notably Brice Lalonde who was made Environment Minister in the Rocard government (1988-1991), and Dominique Voynet (latterly replaced by Yves Cochet) who took the same portfolio in the Jospin government (1997-2002). Because of its insecure position within the executive, the Environment Ministry could not live up to the stereotype of the 'strong state'. However, it maintained appearances by a flow of 'top-down' legislation and regulation. In its early years, this included the 1975 Waste Act, the 1976 Nature Conservation Act and the 1976 Licensed Sites Act.

Over time, internal reforms enabled it to play a greater role. To improve effectiveness, the structure of the Environment Ministry, the organisation of its field services and its relationships to environmental agencies have repeatedly been modified.[4] By the 1990s, three core directorates had demonstrated their longevity – the Directorate for Nature, the Directorate for the Prevention of Pollution and Risks, and the Directorate for Water. Field services and specialised institutions report to these directorates. From originally having no field services, the Environment Ministry now has two sets, so improving policy delivery.

In his 1990 'green plan', Environment Minister Lalonde made provision for the establishment in each of metropolitan France's 22 regions of a *Direction régionale de l'environnement* (DIREN), specialising in nature conservation, architecture and town planning, and exercising a coordinating role regarding water. The aim was to bring an environmental dimension to infrastructural and housing projects, as well as consolidate water and waste management. Also, a part of the field services of the Industry Ministry was hived off and placed under the co-jurisdiction of the Environment Ministry, being relabelled as the *Directions régionales de l'industrie, de la recherche et de l'environnement* (DRIRE).

The DRIRE have responsibility for the enforcement of regulations on industry and the inspection of licensed sites. This expansion in institutional capacity proved crucial in enforcing the widening raft of European legislation. However, the impact of the reform was limited by several factors. These field services were small, with no organisation at the departmental level, making their officers dependent on colleagues attached to other ministeries. Further, the division of labour between the DIREN and the DRIRE consecrated the dissection of the environment into 'natural' and 'industrial' segments. Yet a number of resource utilisation issues – such as water – cut across this divide and call for a transversal response. But not only is the Environment Ministry segmented in terms of internal structure, the establishment of specialised institutions adds a further layer of compartmentalisation.

The Agences de l'eau: The 1964 Water Act established the river basin as the central unit of decision making. France was divided into six basins, each having a consultative committee (*comité de bassin*) and an executive board (*agence de l'eau*). Seeking to promote an efficient and responsible system, in 1964 the French river basin authorities were among to first to use economic instruments by setting charges on water. The *comités de bassin* determined who paid charges and set their levels, with decisions implemented by the *Agences de l'eau*. The proceeds are considerable: some 11.3 billion francs in 1996. This compares with the budget of 1.7 billion francs of the Environment Ministry for the same year. Moreover, the *Agences* have enjoyed considerable autonomy, with sole responsibility for the collection and spending of their revenues. The latter arise from two sources: abstraction and consumption charges, and pollution charges.

In principle, users pay not for water itself, but for the services and 'externalities' associated with its use, namely abstraction, treatment, distribution, collection, and clean-up. From inception, charges were based on the principle of hypothecation. In other words, their proceeds are earmarked as subsidies and loans to private firms and local authorities for capital investment in water delivery or treatment facilities. The most original feature of this system is that the water boards have served as the vehicle for redistributive policy *within the sector*.

For industrial users, pollution charges are proportional to water intake which acts as a proxy for discharge levels. Because norms are calculated with reference to industrial sectors (not on the basis of operating conditions in individual firms), the relationship between emissions and charges is approximate, and this uniform setting of charges means they are comparable to a tax. As such their levy is contrary to the French constitution, which holds that taxation is the prerogative of assemblies elected by universal suffrage. Despite their unconstitutionality, water charges have been paid by consumers and industrial users for decades (but not by farmers). The meso-corporatist strategy of negotiated agreements between governments and industry sector representatives was applied specifically to ease recalcitrant economic interests into the new system of water charges [*Martin, 1988: 118*]. This was achieved by the so-called *juste retour* (fair return), meaning that industrialists recoup what they pay in: the ratio of their subsidies to charges has been 109 per cent [*CGP, 1997: 103*].

Nevertheless, the system's success in environmental management terms was pointed up by the study undertaken by Andersen [*1994: 210*], who stated 'on the basis of the Dutch and French experiences, we can conclude that even modest earmarked taxes are in practice significantly more effective than the conventional view would lead us to assume'. Despite their successes, the complex operations of the *Agences de l'eau* came under scrutiny in the late 1990s, to which we return later.

The ADEME: In principle, the ADEME (the Environment and Energy Efficiency Agency) is the active arm of the Environment Ministry. It is a decentralised institution, with a branch in each French region. Its main tasks are to conduct research, levy environmental charges on industry and use the proceeds to sponsor cleaner technology by granting subsidies and soft loans. Its activities include waste management and recycling, the prevention and clean-up of soil contamination, the reduction of air pollution and noise, the pursuit of energy efficiency and development of renewable energy sources. Water is not covered by the ADEME, nor does it enforce regulations by inspection (entrusted to the DRIRE). Hence it is not a cross-media 'Environmental Agency' on the British model.

The ADEME is an unusually composite organisation, being the result of a merger in 1990 between three previously separate agencies for waste, air quality and energy. The merger constituted one of the few structural changes in French environmental policy delivery in recent years. Because of its origins, the ADEME in the early 1990s was responsible jointly to the Environment Ministry, the Industry Ministry and the Research Ministry. Although this threefold *tutelle* (reporting relationship) appears cumbersome, Pissaloux [*1995: 258–9*] argued that the rival claims of the different ministries neutralised one another, increasing the autonomy of the agency from each. The new institution brought together five income streams deriving from charges on household waste, industrial waste, industrial air pollution, used lubricants and aircraft noise. In addition, it received funding from each of its three *ministères de tutelle*.

However, given the budgetary strictures of the early 1990s, public funding as a percentage of total receipts fell from 69 per cent to 39 per cent; but because of increased receipts from its environment charges, revenues increased from 920 million francs in 1992 to 1047 million francs in 1996.[5] Consequently, in financial terms the ADEME became a powerful institution, and one relatively unencumbered by central government in the deployment of its revenues. Indeed, its funding status threatened to make it a competitor of the perennially impoverished Environment Ministry.

However, the ADEME's discretion in spending – and the setting of priorities – was limited by its internal decision rules. Copying the model of the *Agences de l'eau*, revenues have been hypothecated in a highly compartmentalised manner. For example, landfill charges went only towards investments in waste facilities, atmospheric pollution charges went only to reducing air emissions, and so on. Whereas large subsidies were allocated within sector – up to 70 per cent of total costs in some cases [*London, 2001: 151–3*] – cross-subsidies were debarred. Such sub-sectoral closure is part of the logic of the meso-corporatist deal: it 'sugars the pill' of environmental regulation and taxation for industrialists. But this degree of earmarking produced a rigid system.

Michel Mousel [*1995: 67*], a former chief executive of the ADEME, defined this approach as 'the French-style "polluter pays principle" according to which the sum paid by the polluter is established by reference to clean-up costs'. However, accurate and fair calculation of remedial costs is always problematic. Moreover, a contribution to clean-up may *not* be dissuasive for the polluter, who merely 'pays to pollute'. Further, one revenue stream can run up a surplus even as another suffers a short-fall in relation to needs.[6] These inadequacies led to calls for reform, to be discussed below.

The Content of Policy

In the 1970s and 1980s, environmental policy makers faced with urgent problems tried to harness old policy modes for new ends. This involved a 'command and control' style of environmental policy in order to accord with the traditions of the *dirigiste* state and with the new requirements imposed by EU directives. The appearance of 'authoritative' policy formulation enabled the Environment Ministry to save face, but the reality of policy implementation was as permeated by a 'logic of negotiation' [*Jordan and Richardson, 1982: 80*] as it was across the Channel. Thus the 'dual policy style' needed support from a gamut of instruments which embraced regulations, charges and voluntary agreements.

The 1976 act on *installations classées* ('licensed sites') strengthened the regulatory framework in relation to industrial sites known to cause high levels of pollution or hazard. Environmental protection was made an explicit requirement. The Environment Ministry was confirmed as the regulatory authority, with powers of administrative sanction in the event of untoward incidents (temporary stoppage or even plant closure on the orders of the prefect) as well as prerogatives for prosecution under criminal law. However, the underlying but unspoken rationale of French environmental policy towards economic actors was to persuade rather than punish. Roundabout means were found to encourage co-operation and compliance. Private sector actors were brought 'on board' by representation in public institutions such as the '*comités de bassin*', and a 'softly softly' approach instigated for the financing of environmental investments.

Thus environmental charges have been used to complement and buttress the regulatory regime. These have never been set so high as to be markedly dissuasive in their effect. Hypothecation of receipts for environmental protection purposes has been preferred, since firms who receive subsidies, loans and research grants offer less resistance to taxation. Because charges serve as the instrument for redistributive policy within industrial sector, negotiation is part of the policy process and hostility is defused. Indeed, industrialists have seen some advantages. Although it has forced pollution abatement investments on French firms, the state's recycling of revenues within sector has evened out competitive pressures caused by increased environmental liabilities. The closed circle of exchange relationships and meso-corporatist deals reinforce private actors as arbiters of public policy, and the legitimacy of their political influence is tacitly acknowledged.

In summary, French environmental policy from the 1960s has used both state-centred, 'command-and-control' regulation and market-based charges. For this reason, Héritier, Knill and Mingers [*1996: 2*] noted that 'France ... has long disposed of a "requisite variety" of instruments'. At this level, France can claim a pioneering role. Yet the policy mix for long remained ad hoc and lopsided, with NEPIs being under-utilised. A phase of renewal occurred in the late 1990s, however, whose causes will next be considered.

Why Are NEPIs Being Adopted?

In the 1990s, a number of 'drivers' propelled environmental policy reform. Generic factors included increased pressures on the environment, new threats (particularly climate change), greater public concern and mobilisation, and increased political activism. Green parties enlarged their electorate, entered into government coalitions and sought to revitalise environmental policy. Improvements were called for in relation to existing 'command and control' regulations, which had been criticised for their limited effectiveness and unnecessary expense incurred by state regulators and policy targets alike. The environmental policy mix was in need of drastic renewal. In the context of a shift to neo-liberal government occurring across the industrialised world in the 1980s and 1990s, market-based approaches became the new and dominant policy paradigm.

In the environmental domain, the neo-liberal policy paradigm was propagated by three international institutions. First, the Organisation for Economic Cooperation and Development (OECD) became the leading authority on 'best practice' and the main actor for its international dissemination. OECD analyses have been underpinned by the assumption that high levels of environmental performance are complementary to economic efficiency – the so-called 'ecological modernisation' thesis. This approach inherently favours market-based measures. Second, the 1992 United Nations Conference on Environment and Development, held in Rio, pushed the theme of sustainable development to headline status. The Rio convention on climate change led to the 1997 Kyoto protocol and the 2001 Bonn agreement, which set regional targets for the containment of carbon emissions. Attainment of this objective necessitated the identification of new instruments, such as emissions trading. Third, the European Community's goals of economic and monetary integration, open markets and enhanced growth, together with its commitment to preserving and enhancing the environment had led to a re-evaluation of its corpus of environmental directives and a gradual shift towards market-based measures. In 1991, the European Commission pioneered a tax proposal on carbon emissions from energy sources as the main plank of its climate change policy. Although the proposal for a Europe-wide 'carbon tax' stalled, successive rounds of negotiation kept it visible for much of the 1990s,[7] and the debate acted as a catalyst for policy measures at the national level.

In the French case, these developments are best understood as a set of enabling conditions, rather than as a series of cause and effect mechanisms. On the one hand, this is because French negotiators rarely played a proactive role in international negotiations on carbon emissions, often being content with special pleading (based on France's extensive recourse to nuclear energy which emits little carbon). On the other hand, where environmental policy review has occurred, its immediate triggers are found within the national political context.

France's statist tradition still provides a means for the expression of political will, providing that (a) ambitious leaders emerge on the political scene, (b) feasible policy options are identified, and (c) that the context of action is broadly propitious. In 1997, a concatenation of circumstances fulfilled these conditions. Subsequent to President Chirac's decision to call early parliamentary elections, the left won a surprise victory which led to a five-year period in government. The coalition government, headed by Prime Minister Jospin, brought together five left-wing parties, including the *Verts* (the French 'Greens') as one of the junior partners. Whilst his policy content proved innovative, Jospin's policy style remained in the interventionist mould. Similarly, Dominique Voynet – the new Environment Minister and leader of the *Verts* – embarked on a 'heroic', top-down overhaul of environmental policy.

Following the general trend towards market measures, her major innovation was an eco-tax known as the TGAP (*taxe générale sur les activités polluantes* – the general tax on polluting activities). It was intended to reinforce the 'polluter pays' and prevention principles by increasing the level of charges. Moreover, it proposed to end strict hypothecation, and allow more flexible use of revenues. In brokering this reform, Voynet tried to ride on a wave of criticisms expressed in relation to hypothecated taxation in general, and to the operations of the ADEME and the *Agences de l'eau* in particular.

General criticisms of hypothecation included the danger that arrangements with recipients become too cosy (with subsidies leading to over-investment, and companies who deserve to go to the wall surviving), that earmarked taxes can outlive their original purpose and funding is diverted to low order projects, that they distort the 'polluter pays' principle and restrict the implementation of the prevention principle. In addition, they create wealthy institutions whose bureaucratic structures may waste funds, whilst the Finance Ministry lacks flexibility in allocating revenues on a rational basis.[8] Criticisms specific to the French context included: the unconstitutional levy of taxation, the opacity of operations of the ADEME and the *Agences de l'eau*, doubts about their effectiveness (with public concern over air pollution by transport and water pollution by nitrates), and spiralling costs and prices.

The TGAP proposals were brought before parliament in the 1999 Finance Bill. Drawing on OECD studies, an accompanying report set out the arguments in their favour, and underscored the need for a coherent environmental taxation strategy to replace the piecemeal approach then prevailing. For example, the Bricq report [*1998*] had drawn up an inventory of some 75 eco-taxes. The TGAP aimed to 'modernise, unify and simplify' [*François-Poncet and Oudin, 1998: 85*], the eco-taxation maze. Its most radical aspect was a proposed break with hypothecation. No more would revenues be recycled solely within sector. Arguments based on the 'double dividend' provided the justification for this break.

One of the tax's main architects, the *Vert* Alain Lipietz [*1998, 2001*] maintained that the environmental dividend was attained when polluters were dissuaded from polluting (rather than by a system which financed clean-up costs). His argument effectively attacked the 'French-style polluter pays principle' with its earmarking of charges and the meso-corporatist bargain which underpinned it. But in challenging the favourable treatment enjoyed by economic actors, the *Verts* courted their hostility.

Also, a socio-economic dividend was to be attained by *diverting* a proportion of environmental levies to subsidies for the '35-hour week'. Employers who made an early transition to a shorter working work benefited from a reduction in their social security payments. This maintained the principle of fiscal 'neutrality' (namely, no overall increase in taxes on firms). The '35-hour week' policy was aimed at reducing France's high level of unemployment, an aim fully supported by the *Verts* who wished to demonstrate political competence and garner electoral support in domains beyond the 'single issue' of the environment. Thus the economic and instrumental justifications put forward for the new environmental tax were subtended by the wider political agenda of the *Verts*. This cocktail of 'drivers' and ambitions proved controversial.

NEPIs in France

Market-Based Instruments

The 1999 Finance Bill set out three phases for the implementation of the TGAP. With phase one in 1999, the charges levied by the ADEME on industrial and household waste, used lubricants, air pollution, and noise at airports were rolled up into a single tax. Ending the compartmentalisation of receipts allowed greater flexibility in their usage. Their levels were to be set by the Finance Ministry and Parliament, resolving the anomaly of unconstitutional levies. Receipts were to be incorporated into the Treasury budget, with a proportion returned to the ADEME via the Environment Ministry. This reinstated the Environment Minister's control over the ADEME, reducing the autonomy of the latter. Although potentially a source of friction between the two institutions, subordination was accepted in a constructive spirit by the ADEME's chief executive, Pierre Radanne (a long-time associate and nominee of Environment Minister Voynet). Thus a fiscal reform included a measure of institutional reconfiguration.

Phase two targeted water, and was scheduled for implementation in 2000. Aiming to offer financial disincentives to water pollution, the TGAP's coverage extended to fertiliser and detergent manufacture, and to gravel extraction from rivers. Important as these measures were, the core proposal was to bring the charges levied by the *Agences de l'eau* within the remit of the TGAP, following the model set in phase one with the ADEME (ending of strict hypothecation and subordination to the Environment and Finance Ministries). As such it was a bold proposal, both because of the scale of receipts (over 11 billion francs in 1996, ten times the revenues of the ADEME) and because of the political influence of the *Agences*. Given the consequences for the operation and autonomy of the latter, the proposal represented a major institutional reconfiguration.

Voynet felt empowered to initiate this 'heroic' reform because of public resentment in the 1990s towards water price hikes, especially in areas where supplies were contaminated by nitrates. The very critical report of the Commissariat Général du Plan [*1997*] had pointed to dysfunctional aspects of the operation of the *Agences*. The latter implemented an opaque redistribution of the environmental burden, which the CGP [*1997: 97–119*] called the *principe pollueur-sociétaire* (polluter co-operative principle). This system had two main components.

The first was that revenues were recycled as subsidies to investment in water treatment facilities. Although these subsidies were purportedly allocated on a 'best case' basis, the CGP [*1997*] concluded that the *Agences* were not attaining water quality objectives at least cost. The second component was that the consumers subsidised other users, especially farmers. The latter pay few abstraction charges (although their water consumption is the highest of any user group), and no pollution charges. The explanation stems not from the position of the farming lobby on *comités de bassin* (where it is numerically weak), but from its 'special relationship' with the Agriculture Ministry.

In effect, France's most corporatist regime gives privileged treatment to farmers in relation to water. Consequently Martin [*1988: 117*] described the water boards as *mutuelles,* namely organisations based on a sharing of burdens, rather than on bearing individual responsibilities. Thus the application of the prevention principle was acknowledged as too weak to produce major reductions in emissions.[9] Phase two of the TGAP aimed to improve prevention through making charges more dissuasive and more equitable by abolishing exemptions and redressing the balance for consumers.

Proposals went before the *Conseil des ministres* in October 1999 for a new water law to update the statutes of 1964 and 1992. Parliament was to decide on levels of water charges, so ending the constitutional anomaly which had allowed the *comités de bassin* to determine them. Parliament would continue to approve five-year spending plans for the *Agences de l'eau.* The latter, like the ADEME, would henceforth receive only a proportion of water revenues back from central ministries. Farmers were to be brought into the 'polluter pays' scheme, and some of the more questionable aspects of subcontracting to private water companies were to be reviewed.

However, during 2001 all of these powerful actors lobbied to protect their interests. The *Agences* refused to go down the route taken by the ADEME, arguing that their effectiveness would be impaired. In a political context where devolution of decision-making and budgets is increasingly favoured, the *Agences* could marshal arguments against proposals that were clearly centralising. The major water companies (Vivendi Environnement, Ondeo and SAUR) held out for their traditional (and lucrative) subcontracting arrangements, whilst French farmers reverted to their familiar stance of 'can't pay, won't pay'. In consequence, the proposals were considerably scaled back and the new water bill, as debated in January 2002, concentrated on the more technical aspects of water delivery. In the face of stiff resistance, major reform of policy instruments and institutional structures in the water sector was abandoned.

A similar story unfolded in relation to phase three, which centred on the energy sector. To improve energy efficiency and contain emissions of greenhouse gases (GHG), the French government in 2000 drew up a National Plan to Combat Climate Change. With the aim of stabilising GHG emissions in 2010 at a level consistent with undertakings made at Kyoto, three categories of preventive measures were drawn up. The first category (in principle using emissions trading and voluntary agreements) was designed to avert the production of 7 million tonnes of CO_2 equivalent, the second was a 'carbon tax' saving 6.7 million tonnes and a third contained 'long-term measures' (energy savings and use of renewables) to cut 2.27 million tonnes from projected estimates.[10] For the second category of measures, the instrument proposed was the 'TGAP-Energie' (corresponding to phase three of the TGAP).

The 'TGAP-Energie' was an eco-tax on intermediate energy consumption, intended for implementation as of 1 January 2001. Companies using over 100 tonnes of oil per year (some 40,000 in all) were to pay 260 francs per tonne of emitted carbon equivalent, to raise a projected 3.8 billion francs in 2001. However, due to their exposure to international competition, the most energy intensive firms were to be exempted from the tax, provided that they attained emissions reduction targets set out in voluntary agreements made with the authorities (discussed below). Failure to honour those agreements would lead to taxation on excess emissions. Farmers and food producers would be exempt, as would primary energy producers and chemicals companies. But nuclear-sourced electricity would be taxed, since Environment Minister Voynet [2000] had made the argument that the overall aim was to maximise energy efficiency.

Once again, eco-tax reform encountered the resistance of interested parties. A case was brought before the *Conseil constitutionnel* who, on 31 December 2000, struck down the 'TGAP-Energie' as unconstitutional since it failed to respect the principle of equality in taxation. The court ruled that the tax in its proposed form discriminated among categories of energy consumers and led to the perverse outcome that lower levels of consumption would incur higher levels of tax. In addition, the inclusion within the tax regime of nuclear-sourced electricity was ruled incoherent, given the modest GHG emissions produced. This set-back, together with the opposition of Finance Minister Fabius (who was promoting a tax-cutting agenda ahead of the 2002 elections) led to the sidelining of 'phase three'.

With the electoral defeat of the left in 2002, the TGAP went into limbo. Seduced by the elegance of their own arguments, the *Verts* had failed to see that the cross-linking of two controversial policies – the TGAP and the '35-hour week'– was a recipe for stalemate. The diversion of environmental revenue streams to a direct subsidy for employment generation proved a political error. Not only did it replace one kind of earmarking with another, but whereas the former was based on a long-standing consensus, the latter aroused general resentment. In the water sector, partisans of the *Agences de l'eau* claimed that the reform would destabilise a successful institution, farmers could lament that their livelihood was threatened by new taxation, whilst environmental groups were alienated by the proposed dilution of 'green' investment. Further, the political mishandling of water charging 'skewed the pitch' for a carbon tax which, in any case, had design faults. The abandonment of the 'TGAP-Energie' left a hole at the heart of national climate change policy.[11] Yet though the TGAP displayed failings, major environmental challenges did require an ambitious response. Hence it would be unfair to lay the blame exclusively on the 'naiveté' of greens in power. Persistent opposition to environmental policy renewal was a major cause of the debacle.

That opposition also arose in relation to the reform of excise on fuels. The original rationale of the latter had nothing to do with environmental performance, being designed as an efficient instrument for revenue generation. However, 'tax and spend' Finance Ministers have in recent years tried to justify increases in excise as environmentally beneficial, for example with the UK 'fuel escalator'. A comparable situation arose in France, where the *taxe intérieure sur les produits pétroliers* (TIPP), an excise tax levied on oil derived fuels, raised 144 billion francs in 1995. Though now sometimes called an 'energy tax', the TIPP is clearly a revenue raising tax – the fourth largest in France after VAT, income tax and corporate tax – and its proceeds go to the general budget. Attempts have been made to improve its environmental credentials by redressing the differentials between excise on petrol and excise on diesel.

France has one of the highest rates of tax on unleaded fuel in Europe and is the only European country where diesel has been taxed less heavily than unleaded petrol. To redress the balance, Environment Minister Voynet argued for a phased increase of diesel excise by seven centimes per litre per year between 1999 and 2005. This measure was implemented in 1999 and 2000. But when the oil price hikes of late summer 2000 prompted major demonstrations by hauliers, not only was the escalator abandoned but hauliers were given a total tax rebate of 35 centimes per litre of diesel for 2000 and 25 centimes in 2001 (*Le Monde*, 8 Sept. 2000, p.9). Yves Cochet (a *Vert*), nominated as Environment Minister in July 2001, announced his intention to reinstate the escalator. However, the Jospin government's fall in May 2002 closed this chapter of environmental tax reform by French political ecologists.

In summary, although some incremental improvements were achieved, a coalition of economic actors had successfully defended their interpretation of the meso-corporatist bargain by undermining the renewal of eco-taxation, whilst the institutional reconfiguration brokered by the TGAP had barely taken shape.

Voluntary Agreements

Voluntary agreements (VAs) in French environmental policy-making have mostly been limited to agreements arising from bargaining between a public authority and industrialists. Two main phases can be identified: an initial phase from 1971 to the mid-1980s bearing on pollution control, and a recent phase in the 1990s related to GHG emissions.

In the 1970s and 1980s, the Environment Ministry negotiated agreements with industrial representatives aimed at improving environmental performance. These were known as *contrats de branche* ('sectoral contracts'). The justification for this meso-corporatist approach was to ensure policy effectiveness by tailoring measures to circumstances and responding to industrialists' concerns over costs. The intention was not to replace the regulatory framework (since it provided the last resort of sanctions) but to find mechanisms by which its norms could translate into practice more efficiently, without placing excessive burdens on industrialists at a time when their competitive position was threatened as markets opened in Europe and around the world. Further, in its early years the Environment Ministry could not engage in strong-arm tactics against powerful economic interests, but needed incremental means to develop its authority.

Lascoumes [*1991, 1993*] showed how the Directorate for the Prevention of Pollution undertook negotiations with industrialists on a sector-by-sector basis. In a first round (1972 to 1977), the paper pulp, sugar beet, starch-making, distillery and wood-working industries signed agreements to reduce emissions to air and water, and received subsidies for pollution abatement investment. The second round (1977-81) involved the plaster and cement industries, meat renderers, asbestos and aluminium manufacturers. The aim was to reduce toxic wastes, but subsidies were not granted. A third round ran between 1981 and 1985. Lascoumes [*1993*] noted that the outcomes of these contracts depended on the relative strength (or weakness) of regulators in relation to particular industrial sectors, with the Environment Ministry enjoying a favourable balance of power against the unpopular and fragmented asbestos industry, but being poorly placed to deal with giant steel companies in a period of economic retrenchment.

Although these *contrats de branche* improved the environmental performance of targeted firms, their wider implications aroused criticisms. From the late 1970s, the European Commission questioned the distribution of subsidies as leading to market distortions. Further, although some contracts became public, the process was characterised by opacity. Its neo-corporatist orientation was flagrant in that civil society representatives were totally excluded. Following complaints by environmental groups, in 1985 the *Conseil d'Etat* (France's highest administrative court) ruled that contracts with steel-makers were invalid because 'during their period of operation, the three agreements effectively prevented the administration from enforcing more stringent requirements on the firms in question ... The Minister had renounced the prerogatives conferred on him by law.' The adverse ruling identified a case of 'regulatory capture' and led to a revision of policy. It made Environment Ministry negotiators more circumspect with respect to contractualisation. VAs had to exceed the regulatory framework by a substantial margin, and a clear rationale was required to justify contractualisation as superior to other policy instruments.

In the 1990s, VAs experienced a limited revival in a new context. Subsequent to the 1997 Kyoto protocol, governments sought GHG reductions. Given the difficulties in demonstrating tight causal links between emissions and harmful consequences (where the latter are typically distant in time and place), voluntary commitments were preferred to regulations. An EEA survey reported by the OECD [*1999: 51*] identified a total of 312 VAs in the EU in 1997, with the Netherlands having 107, Germany 93 and France only eight.

More specifically, during 1996–97 agreements were signed in France with branch organisations for the steel, glass, cement and plaster industries, setting targets of reductions in GHG emissions of between 5 per cent and 10 per cent in relation to the 1990 baseline [*MATE, 1999*]. A separate agreement was concluded with Péchiney, the aluminium giant, to reduce GHG emissions by 19 per cent, while Trois Suisses (distribution sector) opted for a 25 per cent cut. The oil company Elf unilaterally promised to reduce emissions by 15 per cent (*Le Monde*, 23 Nov. 1997, p.1). Such major industrial consumers of energy as Ciments Français and Lafarge (cement), Rhodia (chemicals), Saint-Gobain (glass) and Usinor (steel) also made commitments to reduce GHG output. According to government estimates, the industrial sector as a whole is close to meeting its 2010 target with a reduction to 41.5 million tonnes of CO_2 equivalent, from a baseline of 43.1 million tonnes for 1990 [*MATE, 2000*]. In summary, although VAs may have unrealised potential, in France the small number of agreements means that their positive impact has so far been limited.

Eco-labels

The history of eco-labels in France has been marked by the good intentions of policy-makers and much indifference by industrialists. The main eco-labels in existence are the 'NF Environnement' and the EU Eco-label, both administered by the *Association Française de Normalisation*. These voluntary schemes are based on a rigorous, multi-criteria analysis of the product life cycle, going from 'the cradle to the grave'. They propound the same objectives, namely to promote goods having a low environmental impact (in comparison to similar products), and to increase consumer awareness leading to well-informed purchases. However, from the inception of the 'NF Environnement' scheme, the question of the real purpose of eco-labelling was raised, namely whether the scheme intended simply to alert consumers to environmental performance differentials among comparable products or, more ambitiously, to reorientate manufacturing systems in a more sustainable direction [*Ventère, 1995: 71*]. Practice has since shown that the simultaneous attainment of the two objectives is problematic.

The schemes both date from 1992 and have similarities which, according to Beslin [*1993: 102*], are explained by the fact that the French model influenced the European Commission. By 2001, the 'NF Environnement' label covered 13 categories of products, with approximately 250 products certificated [*MATE, 2001*]. The product categories constitute an eclectic mix, including paints and varnishes, vacuum cleaners, detergents, bin-liners, coffee filters and envelopes. The European Eco-label stems from EEC regulation 880/92 and by 2001 had 12 fully-functional categories, with more in the pipeline. However, the incentives to take up either scheme are limited, given that the competitive advantage conferred is uncertain. Many established brands falling within existing product categories have not been certificated. In any case, most consumer goods fall outside the current product categories. In brief, the range of products covered is small, the speed at which new categories are created is slow, and take-up by industrialists is low.

A number of other quality labels exist in France, particularly in relation to agricultural and food products. Established in 1935, the '*appelation d'origine contrôlée*' is familiar to wine and spirits drinkers, with the scheme being extended to diary products in the 1960s, and to all food products in the late 1990s. The '*label rouge*' was established in 1960 and covers most foodstuffs, offering a guarantee of quality and taste. Set up in 1980, the '*agriculture biologique*' label certifies that a food product has been organically produced. In addition, labels exist offering information about the recycling potential of the product, of which some are international (for example, for paper and plastic) and some national (for example, the Eco-Emballages logo, related to the French state-sponsored scheme for the recycling of packaging). Finally, there are various logos invented by private firms to enhance the green credentials of their own products. Whether these merit the term eco-label is open to question. In consequence, the paradoxical situation arises where there are almost as many labels as there are labelled products. This compromises the value of 'official' schemes in the eyes of both consumers and industrialists.

In brief, the main schemes have met neither of their main objectives to any marked degree: consumers are barely better informed (and sometimes simply confused), whilst industrialists benefit from too few incentives to redirect their manufacturing systems towards greater sustainability. A reform of eco-labelling which concentrates on just one or the other objective may be the way forward.

Conclusions

The case studies analysed above demonstrate that the uptake of NEPIs in France has been fairly extensive, but their impact has been limited. To date, NEPIs have mostly been implemented in the context of market-centred policy-making: hence the fate of the former is related to the role of the latter. In France, the ideological momentum driving the swing from state-centred policies to market-centred measures was weaker than in Britain or the USA. The transition in France from a dirigist to a market-led economy has been pragmatic rather than enthusiastic. Indeed, the neo-liberal policy paradigm has been treated with a mixture of caution and suspicion by both the left and part of the right. Where they arose, market-based environmental measures came from unexpected quarters, principally the eco-tax championed by the *Verts*, and cannot be described as 'pure' neo-liberalism.

The rationale for the 'TGAP' included a 'radical left' dimension which was critical of the environmental performance of major economic actors, which was suspicious of the advantages enjoyed by industrialists under the existing meso-corporatist bargain, and which pointed the finger at the excesses of intensive farming. However, the application of this political philosophy – known in France as *social-libéralisme* since it combined social justice issues with neo-liberal measures – provoked a mixture of incomprehension and hostility.

The main architect of reform, Environment Minister Voynet, remained a prisoner of France's 'dual policy style'. By this is understood a top-down mode of policy formulation, conducted with 'heroic' flourishes by political entrepreneurs, allied to a bottom-up mode of policy implementation, based on 'humdrum' compromises with policy targets. In line with the traditions of 'heroic' policy-making, the TGAP was statist in character since it aimed to re-centralise environmental charges under the aegis of France's most powerful institution, the Finance Ministry. Although the increase in charges was intended to augment the deterrent effect on polluters, the ending of strict hypothecation meant that revenue streams would no longer flow directly to the main environmental institutions. Instead, they would go to the Treasury, which would finance the activities of those institutions by direct grant, while diverting part of the proceeds.

This complex reform failed because it provoked several categories of resistance: (1) tax rises are always unpopular with firms (who are adept at marshalling economic arguments against them); (2) the break with earmarking of revenues for environmental investments within sector compromised the meso-corporatist bargain, alarming industrialists whilst alienating environmentalists; (3) the diversion of revenues to the '35-hour week' was inherently controversial and (4) institutional reconfiguration 'by the backdoor' (particularly the centralisation of control over the *Agences de l'eau*) was considered illegitimate. An apparently 'technical' reform opened out into a highly political agenda, but due to the marginalised position of political ecology in France, its architects lacked the resources to bring it to fruition.

Yet the ambitions that motivated these measures were broadly proportionate to heightened environmental challenges. Dominique Voynet's espousal of sustainable development and her championing of climate change policy put her in the 'heroic' mould of French politics. But such environmental policy measures as were implemented during the Jospin government turned out to be 'humdrum'. These include tax reforms of which the most far-reaching components – the extension of the TGAP and recalibration of the TIPP – stalled. They also include a small number of VAs which, whilst enjoying a measure of success, are also latter-day instances of the meso-corporatist 'consensus'. Further, the *trompe-l'oeil* nature of the French 'dual policy style' persists, and is enlivened by new twists and turns. The market-centred measures normally associated with 'triumphant neo-liberalism' have been formulated by a component of the radical left (the *Verts*), their implementation has been conducted with 'authoritative' panache, but economic actors resisted and outcomes were modest.

Whilst France has experimented with NEPIs for several decades, their use has been contained within the long-standing policy paradigm. But where a novel instrument does not fit that paradigm it has largely been ignored. Emissions trading – one of the few new ideas to emerge in recent years – has made no impact to date in France. There appear to be three main reasons for this. First, questions are raised over both the feasibility and the ethics of 'pollution swaps'. Second, policy-makers are chary over committing themselves to emissions trading because controversies persist over energy sourcing. France remains reliant on nuclear-sourced electricity (low in GHG emissions but problematic in terms of waste disposal and risk), but the advantages of diversification (including gas) are understood. However, rigid emissions ceilings and tradable quotas would introduce greater uncertainty over the scope for medium-term diversification of energy sourcing. Third, inertia is maintained by the 'wait and see' attitude of the French authorities. This is due to the protracted nature of post-Rio climate change negotiations, and the shortage of substantive content in the EU policy frame.[12] Thus France still waits for an EU-wide initiative. With no 'heroic' proposals forthcoming, the French 'dual policy style' reverts to the 'humdrum'.

In summary, the main findings of this analysis are that long-standing policy styles remain a determining factor in policy formulation and implementation, that new instruments are only as effective as pre-existing national political and institutional opportunity sets allow them to be, and that outcomes remain heavily 'path dependent'.

NOTES

1. In 'meso-corporatism', interests are aggregated in terms of sector (such as industrial branch), with interest group representatives and state officials engaging in bipartite discussions. See Cawson [*1986: 106–18*].
2. This analysis is developed more fully in Szarka [*2000*] and Szarka [*2002: 132–9, 146–65*].
3. Cf. Schmitter [*1970*] and Cawson [*1986: 68–83*].
4. For details, see Prieur [*1994*].
5. These data are from Pissaloux [*1995: 260*] and République française [*1997: 42*].
6. The Adnot [*2001*] parliamentary audit was critical of this aspect of the ADEME's operations.
7. For discussion, see Zito [*2000*].
8. For further discussion, see Anderson [*1994: 206–8*]
9. Meublat [*1998: 79*] noted that 'it is more profitable for the polluter to pay the charge – and continue to pollute'.
10. Sources for these data are: Gouvernement français [*2000: 111–13*], Gouvernement français [*2002: 70–71*].
11. The French government's 'National Sustainable Development Strategy', produced in March 2002 for the Johannesburg World Summit, merely reiterated previous climate change policy. It acknowledged the collapse of the 'TGAP-Energie' proposals, and awaited future decisions at the EU level regarding energy taxation and emissions trading; see Gouvernement français [*2002: 70*].
12. Although some progress was made by the Sixth European Action Programme for 2000–2010 and by the approval of a European Sustainable Development Strategy at the 2001 Gothenburg summit.

REFERENCES

Adnot, P. (2001), *ADEME: la grande illusion*, Paris: Imprimerie nationale, Les Rapports du Sénat No.236.

Andersen, M. S. (1994), *Governance by Green Taxes: Making Pollution Prevention Pay*, Manchester: Manchester University Press.

Beslin, P. (1993), 'La marque NF Environnement', in S. Vigneron and C. Burstein (eds.), *Ecoproduit: concepts et méthodologies*, Paris: Economica, pp. 95–102.

Brénac, E. (1988), 'Corporatismes et politique intersectorielle: la politique de l'environnement', in D. Colas (ed.), *L'Etat et les corporatismes*, Paris: PUF, pp. 127–46.

Bricq, N. (1998), *Pour un développement durable: une fiscalité au service de l'environnement*, Paris: Assemblée Nationale, Commission des Finances, rapport d'information no. 1000.

Cawson, A. (1986), *Corporatism and Political Theory*, Oxford: Basil Blackwell.

CGP (Commissariat général du plan) (1997), *Evaluation du dispositif des Agences de l'eau*, Paris: Documentation française.

Economist Intelligence Unit (1990), *French Policy on the Environment. Unsung Achievements, Emerging Anxieties and Possible New Directions*, London: Economist Intelligence Unit, EIU Special Report No.2063.

François-Poncet, J. and J. Oudin (eds.) (1998), *La Taxe générale sur les activités polluantes: une remise en cause radicale de la politique de l'eau?*, Paris: Imprimerie nationale, Les rapports du Sénat No.112.

Gerbaux, F. (1988) 'Les politiques publiques peuvent-elles se passer du corporatisme? L'exemple de la montagne', in D. Colas (ed.), *L'Etat et les Corporatismes*, Paris: PUF, pp.147–59.

Gouvernement français (2000), *Programme national de lutte contre le changement climatique*, Paris: République française.

Gouvernement français (2002) *Propositions pour une stratégie nationale de developpement durable*, Paris: République française.

Hayward, J. (1982), 'Mobilising Private Interests in the Service of Public Ambitions: the Salient Element in the Dual French Policy Style?' in Richardson [*1982: 111–40*].

Héritier, A., Knill, C. and S. Mingers (1996) *Ringing the Changes in Europe: Regulatory Competition and Redefinition of the State: Britain, France, Germany*, Berlin: Walter de Gruyter.

Jordan, G. and J. Richardson (1982), 'The British Policy Style or the Logic of Negotiation', in Richardson [*1982: 80–110*].

Larrue, C. and L. Chabason (1998), 'France: Fragmented Policy and Consensual Implementation', in K. Hanf, and A.-I. Jansen (eds.) *Governance and Environment in Western Europe*, Harlow: Longman, pp.60–81.

Lascoumes, P. (1991), 'Les contrats de branche et d'entreprise en matière de protection de l'environnement en France', in C.-A. Morand (ed.), *L'Etat propulsif*, Paris: Editions Publisud, pp.221–35.

Lascoumes, P. (1993), 'Négocier le droit, formes et conditions d'une activité gouvernementale conventionnelle', *Politiques et management public*, Vol.11, No.4, pp.48–83.

Lipietz, A. (1998), 'Economie politique des écotaxes', in D. Bureau *et al. La Fiscalité de l'environnement*, Paris: Documentation française, pp.9–39.

Lipietz, A. (2001), 'Le double dividende de la pollutaxe', *Sociétal*, Vol.31 (1er trimestre), pp.79–81.

London, C. (2001), *Environnement et instruments économiques et fiscaux*, Paris: LGDJ.

Martin, Y. (1988), 'Quelques réflexions sur l'évolution des agences de bassin', *Annales des mines*, Vol.7–8 (July–Aug.), pp.117–19.

MATE (Ministère de l'Aménagement du territoire et de l'environnement) (1999), 'Engagements volontaires de réduction des émissions de gaz à effet de serre dans l'industrie française', http://www.environnement.gouv.fr/actua/cominfos/dosdir/DIRPPR/reducgaz.htm.

MATE (2000), 'Livre blanc sur les modalites de l'extension de la TGAP sur les activités polluantes aux consommations intermédiaires d'énergie des entreprises', http://www.gouvernement.fr.actua/...DIRGAD/fiscalite/energitaxe-annexes.htm.

MATE (2001), 'Les éco-labels', http://www.environnement.gouv.fr/actua/cominfos/dosdir/DIRPPR/ecolabel.htm.

Meublat, G. (1998), 'La politique de lutte contre la pollution des eaux', in B. Barraqué and J. Theys (eds.), *Les Politiques d'environnement. Evaluation de la première génération: 1971–1995*, Paris: Editions Recherches, pp.67–90.

Mousel, M. (1995), 'L'administration de l'environnement: agences et services déconcentrés de l'Etat en France', in Institut international d'administration publique (eds.), *Dossiers et débats. Délocalisations administratives. Politiques européennes d'environnement*, Paris: Documentation française, pp.65–70.

Muller, P. (1990), 'Les politiques publiques entre secteurs et territoires', *Politiques et management public*, Vol.8, No.3 (Sept.), pp.19–33.

Muller, P. and G. Saez, (1985), 'Néo-corporatisme et crise de la représentation', in F. d'Arcy (ed.), *La Répresentation*, Paris: Economica, pp.121–40.

OECD (1999), *Voluntary Approaches for Environmental Policy*, Paris: OECD.

Pissaloux, J.-L. (1995), 'L'Agence de l'environnement et de la maîtrise de l'énergie: un établissement public de type nouveau', *La Revue du Trésor*, Vol.5 (may), pp.251–61.

Poujade, R. (1975), *Le Ministère de l'impossible*, Paris: Calmann-Lévy.

Prieur, M. (1994), 'Le laboratoire français du rattachement environnement-gouvernement', *Studi parlamentari e di politica constituzionale*, Vol.104 (2e trimestre), pp.55–92.

République française (1997), *Projet de loi de finances pour 1998 – Environnement. Etat récapitulatif de l'effort financier consenti en 1997 et prévu en 1998 au titre de l'environnement*, Paris: Imprimerie nationale.

Richardson, J. (ed.) (1982), *Policy Styles in Western Europe*, London: George Allen & Unwin.

Schmitter, P.C. (1970), 'Still the Century of Corporatism?' *Review of Politics*, Vol.36, pp. 85–131.

Szarka, J. (2000), 'Environmental Policy and Neo-Corporatism in France', *Environmental Politics*, Vol. 9, No.3, pp. 89–108.

Szarka, J. (2002), *The Shaping of Environmental Policy in France*, Oxford: Berghahn.

Trilling, J. (1981), 'French Environmental Politics', *International Journal of Urban and Regional Research*, Vol.5, pp.67–82.

Ventère, J.-F. (1995), *La Qualité écologique des produits. Des écobilans aux écolabels,* Paris: AFNOR / Sang de la terre.

Voynet, D. (2000), 'Fiscalité, accords volontaires, permis négociables: quels outils pour le développement durable', http://www.gouvernement.fr./actua/...000/octobre/06-discdv-devdur-outils.htm

Zito, A.R. (2000), *Creating Environmental Policy in the European Union*, Basingstoke: Macmillan.

From High Regulatory State to Social and Ecological Market Economy? 'New' Environmental Policy Instruments in Germany

RÜDIGER K.W. WURZEL, ANDREW JORDAN,
ANTHONY R. ZITO and LARS BRÜCKNER

Introduction

For much of the 1980s, Germany has been portrayed as an environmental leader state [*Andersen and Liefferink, 1997; Liefferink and Andersen, 1998; Weale, 1992a, 1992b; Wurzel, 2002*]. However, post-unification Germany[1] has lost some of its environmental zeal whilst also coming under pressure from the European Union (EU) to reform its environmental policy which has relied heavily on detailed 'command-and-control' regulations often derived from the best available technology (BAT) principle [*Héritier et al., 1996; Knill and Lenschow, 2000; Pehle, 1997, 1998; Wurzel, 2003a, 2003b*]. International actors such as the Organization for Economic Cooperation and Development (OECD) and the World Bank have acknowledged Germany's formidable pollution control record but have urged a higher uptake of market-based instruments (MBIs) for cost-efficiency reasons [*OECD, 1999; World Bank, 1995*]. Demands for wider use of 'new' environmental policy instruments (NEPIs), namely MBIs (such as eco-taxes and tradable permits), voluntary agreements (VAs) and informational devices (such as eco-labels and eco-audits) have also been mounted by domestic actors in Germany during recent years [e.g., *UBA, 1999a, 1999b*].

There has been a significant degree of NEPI innovation in Germany. However, over time periods certain types of NEPIs have been used more heavily than others while the overall uptake has remained uneven across different sectors. VAs have formed part of modern-day German

The research underpinning this study was undertaken for a project entitled 'Innovation in Environmental Governance: A Comparative Analysis of New Environmental Policy Instruments' which was generously funded by the Economic and Social Research Council's (ESRC) Future Governance Programme under grant number L216252013. For more details see: http://www.uea.ac.uk/env/cserge/research/fut_governance/Home.htm.

environmental policy since it began in the late 1960s, although they have become much more widespread since the 1990s. Within the EU, Germany and the Netherlands have adopted by far the highest number of VAs [interviews, 2001; *EEA, 1997; Öko-Institut, 1998*]. However, in contrast to the Netherlands where VAs gave way to more formalised and legally binding so-called covenants, German VAs have remained legally non-binding. Germany acted as a pioneer when it set up the world's first national eco-label scheme in 1978. The so-called Blue Angel influenced other eco-labels and remained the world's most widely used scheme (in terms of the number of labelled products and services) until it was overtaken by the Nordic Swan in the late 1990s [*Jordan et al., 2002; Kern et al., 2000*].

Eco-taxes have been used, albeit sparingly, since the 1970s [*Andersen, 1994; SRU, 1978; Wurzel, 2002, 2003a*]. In the late 1980s, there was growing cross-party political support for ecological tax reform [*Schröder, 1989; Töpfer, 1989; UBA, 1994*]. However, for competitive reasons the German government was hesitant to make wide use of eco-taxes unilaterally and instead lobbied hard for the adoption of an EU-wide carbon dioxide/energy tax [*Wurzel, 1996, 2002; Zito, 2000*]. Until the late 1990s, Germany's uptake of eco-taxes remained moderate in comparison to Denmark, Finland, the Netherlands and Sweden [*Andersen, 1994; Andersen and Sprenger, 2000; EEA, 2000; OECD, 1999*] but it has been catching up since it introduced an ecological tax reform in 1999.

The pros and cons of tradable permits have been debated by environmental economists in Germany since the 1970s [*Siebert, 1976; SRU, 1978*]. However, by 2002, Germany had still not experimented with tradable permits on the national level despite half-hearted attempts by the Environmental Ministry to introduce this type of NEPI into the national policy instrument repertoire during the 1990s (interview, BMU official, 2001). Tradable permits were pioneered in America which insisted – against initial resistance from the EU and Germany in particular – on this NEPI being listed in the 1997 Kyoto Climate Change Protocol as a possible means of complying with greenhouse gases reduction targets. Within the EU, Denmark, Britain, the Netherlands and Sweden have all experimented with tradable permits. The German government managed to set up a working group on tradable permits in 2000. However, it has failed to adopt a national tradable permit scheme because of strong disagreements between the various stakeholders. Some German states (*Länder*) have therefore set up regional pilot schemes in order to gain practical experience before the EU's tradable permits scheme comes into operation in 2005.

Overall, Germany has gained considerable experience in the use of NEPIs although traditional regulation has remained the most important policy instrument in domestic environmental policy [*Kloepfer, 1998;*

TABLE 1
POLICY INSTRUMENTS IN GERMANY

Type of policy instrument	Extent of usage
Eco-taxes	First used in mid-1970s. Moderate use until the introduction of the ecological tax reform in 1999
Tradable permits	Not (yet) used on the national level
Eco-labels	Very high but declining moderately: 3,500 – 4,000 in the late 1990s
Voluntary agreements	Very high. About 130 by 2001.
Traditional regulations	Very high. About 800 environmental laws, 2,800 ordinances and 4,700 technical instructions. The highest estimates state up to 35,000 technical instructions

OECD, 1999; SRU, 2002; Weale et al., 2000]. Table 1 provides an overview of the different types of 'new' and 'old' policy instruments used in Germany.

The remainder of this study assesses when and why Germany has innovated with NEPIs. Section II analyses Germany's environmental policy structures, style and content while paying particular attention to the role of policy instruments. Section III identifies the most important drivers for and obstacles to NEPI innovation in Germany. Sections IV and V assess the development of the different types of NEPIs and their relationship with traditional regulatory tools. The final part examines the overall pattern of NEPI use while assessing the relationship between 'new' and 'old' policy instruments.

German Environmental Policy

Structures

The core institutional structures of the German environmental policy system were set up in the early 1970s [*Hartkopf and Bohne, 1983; Jänicke and Weidner, 1997; Müller, 1986; Weale, 1992a; Weale et al., 2000*]. They have remained remarkably stable despite the fact that a separate Environmental Ministry (*Bundesministerium für Umwelt, Naturschutz und Reaktorsicherheit – BMU*) was founded in 1986 [*Pehle, 1998*]. The BMU took over the environmental competences from the Interior Ministry (*Bundesministerium des Innern – BMI*) which had been responsible for environmental policy since 1969. The BMI was dominated by legally trained officials who felt most comfortable with traditional regulatory tools [interview, BMU official, 2001; *Holzinger, 1987*]. Compared to the BMI, the BMU employs a higher number of scientists. However, the BMU's recruitment of lawyers, who dominate the civil service within the federal administration in Germany, has remained high while environmental economists are still a rare species despite the fact that, in 1987–94, the Ministry was headed by Professor Klaus Töpfer (CDU) who was a trained environmental economist. Töpfer pushed for the wider use of eco-taxes, which had briefly flourished already in the 1970s [*Hartkopf and Bohne, 1983: 194–205*], but was unable to persuade Chancellor Helmut Kohl (CDU) of the merits of this policy instrument.

The Federal Environmental Agency (*Umweltbundesamt – UBA*) was founded in 1974. It provides the government with scientific advice. Since the late 1990s, the UBA has been headed by Andreas Troge, who is a trained economist. In the 1990s, the UBA carried out a major internal reorganisation in order to tackle more successfully cross-sectoral issues. It resulted in the creation of units such as 'transport and environment', the setting up of a separate unit for environmental policy instruments and the planting of environmental economists into all major specialist units (interview, UBA official, 2001). So far the BMU has shied away from reforming its internal administrative structures along similar lines. It therefore remains largely geared towards a media-centred (that is air, water and soil) approach to pollution control [*Müller, 2002*]. However, the BMU's climate change division, which is one of the few truly cross-sectoral units, has gradually evolved into the Ministry's main administrative unit for the use of NEPIs.

The Environmental Expert Council (*Sachverständigenrat für Umweltfragen – SRU*) was set up by the government as an independent advisory body in 1972. It called for the wider use of MBIs (and eco-taxes in particular) as early as the 1970s [*SRU, 1974, 1978*]. In recent years, the SRU has repeated its plea for MBIs [*SRU, 1998, 2000*]. However, in 2002 it warned against the demonisation of traditional regulatory tools while stressing their continued importance [*SRU, 2002*].

Federal Structures

Germany is a federal state in which the *Länder* have successfully defended their competences for water management and nature protection by blocking constitutional amendments that would have granted the federal government powers similar to those it had acquired for air pollution, waste management and noise pollution control during the 1970s. The asymmetrical allocation of environmental competences between the federal government and the

Länder has complicated the adoption of cross-sectoral approaches to pollution control [*Wurzel, 2002, 2003a*]. Policy instruments (such as certain eco-taxes) which affect the revenue allocation between the federal government and the *Länder* can lead to protracted negotiations.

Germany's bicameral system is biased towards incremental policy (instrument) evolution as major policy reform requires majorities in both the national parliament *(Bundestag)* and the *Länder* chamber *(Bundesrat)* which are often dominated by different political parties.

On the other hand, the *Länder* can provide additional opportunity structures for newly emerging policy actors (such as environmental interest groups and Green parties) and innovative policy experiments which, if successful, can be transferred to the federal level.

Environmental Regulatory Style

When tackling public policy problems, German governments are said to prefer a moderately active stance which relies heavily on consensus and consultation [*Dyson, 1982, 1992; Weale, 1992b*]. The traditional German policy style featured corporatist elements because government consultation extending primarily to employers and unions [*Katzenstein, 1987*]. Herbert Kitschelt [*1986*] has claimed that the opportunity structures are closed for environmental groups in Germany. Because they are often excluded from close involvement during the policy formulation phase, they have to rely on the courts during the post-decisional phase in order to influence the policy outcome. This strategy was facilitated by the fact that German environmental policy is characterised by a high degree of juridification which is the result of a strong state of law *(Rechtsstaat)* tradition [*Weale et al., 2000; Wurzel, 2002*]. However, the government actively encouraged the setting up of environmental groups during the early 1970s [*Hartkopf and Bohne, 1983*] while involving them closely in the running of the eco-label scheme.

Policy styles are not immutable to change although they usually evolve only incrementally due to structural constraints (that is, institutional structures and constitutional requirements) as well as deeply embedded cultural norms about the role of state within a country. The doctrine of the social market economy *(soziale Marktwirtschaft)*, which allows the state to set the framework conditions *(Ordnungspolitik)* for market actors, became a widely accepted macro-political action guiding norm in Germany after the economic miracle of the 1950s [*Dyson, 1982, 1992*]. It tried to combine both ordo-liberal and state interventionist ideas [*Dyson and Goetz, 2003*]. This resulted in a managed capitalist system which has often been referred to as Rhineland capitalism [*Hodges and Woolcock, 1993*] or the German model *(Modell Deutschland)* [*Harding and Paterson, 2000*]. The social market economy doctrine is compatible with Germany's preference for traditional regulation (that is, state intervention) and VAs (that is, self-regulation) which, as will be explained below, are often adopted in the 'shadow of the law' as industry aims to pre-empt government regulation.

Proponents of ecological modernisation, who challenged the conventional neo-liberal paradigm (which propagates the existence of a trade-off between stringent environmental regulation and economic growth) by claiming that ambitious environmental policy measures can be beneficial for both the environment and the economy, gained considerable cross-party support in Germany during the late 1980s [*Jänicke, 1993; Töpfer, 1989; Schröder, 1989; Weale, 1992b; Wurzel, 2002*]. They were the main driving force behind attempts to develop further the social market economy into a 'social and ecological market economy' *(soziale und ökologische Marktwirtschaft)*. However, the economic cost of unification, the recession of the early 1990s and the *Standort Deutschland* debate (which is about Germany's future as a production and investment location within the global economy) put proponents of ecological modernisation on to the defensive [*Weale et al., 2000; Wurzel, 2000; 2002*].

Since the late 1990s, the concept of sustainable development, which puts equal weight on environmental, economic and social concerns, has belatedly gained influence in Germany [*SRU, 2002*]. Compared to the ecological modernisation doctrine, the concept of sustainable development, which was popularised by the 1985 Brundtland report [*World Commission, 1987*] and later taken up in the EU's Fifth Environmental Action Programme [*CEC, 1993*], is less geared towards state intervention and puts greater emphasis on shared responsibility between stakeholders. The concept of sustainable development is still viewed with considerable suspicion by many BMU officials who are concerned that it might be used by, for example the Economics Ministry, to roll back environmental legislation (interview, 2001).

Policy Content

Germany is widely seen as a 'high regulatory state' [*Hèritier et al., 1996*] which has adopted a dense body of environmental laws [Kloepfer, 1998]. Some estimates put the number of domestic environmental regulations as high as 35,000 [*Müller-Brandeck-Bocquet, 1996: 130*], although this includes *Länder* laws and minor technical amendments (interview, UBA official, 2001). Many German environmental laws stipulate (uniform) emission limits derived from the BAT principle which can be traced to nineteenth-century Prussian trade ordinances [*Wey, 1982; Weale, 1992b*]. The wide use of the BAT principle in modern day environmental legislation has been encouraged by the adoption of the precautionary principle

(*Vorsorgeprinzip*) in the 1970s. The precautionary principle legitimises government action even in the absence of scientific proof where there is thought to be a significant risk that (irreversible) environmental damage would otherwise occur. However, a balance has to be struck between the precautionary principle and the principles of proportionality and co-operation which were all already adopted in 1971 environmental programme [*Hartkopf and Bohne, 1983*].

Why Are NEPIs Being Adopted?

Demands for greater NEPI innovation have grown significantly in Germany. However, there are also considerable obstacles to the wider use of NEPIs.

Drivers

First, traditional regulation is reaching its limits (in terms of efficiency and effectiveness) while environmental policy matures. At some point, diminishing margins of return are reached whereby it becomes ever more expensive to reduce the remaining pollutants. In Germany, traditional regulation has significantly reduced classic mass pollutants (such as sulphur dioxide and nitrogen oxides) which are emitted from major point sources (such as power stations and cars) [*Jänicke and Weidner, 1997; OECD, 1993; Weale et al. 2000; Wurzel, 2002*]. However, it has been less effective for tackling diffuse sources (such as agriculture) and substances which are emitted from a wide range of sources (such as climate change gases). Moreover, it has long been known that traditional regulation often leads to a considerable implementation deficit [*Mayntz, 1980*].

Second, increased competition within the EU's internal market and emerging global markets has led to the *Standort Deutschland* debate [*BMWi, 1983*]. It was further fuelled by the revolutionary changes in the former Eastern block countries which brought about low wage market economies within close proximity. Economic recession in the early 1990s and the huge cost of German unification have intensified the search for the most cost-efficient policy tools in the environmental field as well as other policy sectors. Since the mid-1990s, German governments have therefore again become more concerned about the possible negative impact of (environmental) regulations on the domestic economy while supporters of the ecological modernisation doctrine have been pushed onto the defensive.

Third, international actors such as the OECD [*1993*] and World Bank [*1995*] have urged Germany to make wider use of MBIs. In the early 1990s, the OECD [*1993: 206*] praised the '[r]emarkable progress ... [which Germany had made] in dealing with a number of the pressing environmental problems'. However, it also warned that '[c]urrent approaches, primarily based on country-wide uniform regulations and technological progress, may have to be supplemented'[*OECD, 1993: 208–9*].

Fourth, environmental policy 'has probably become one of the most internationalised policy fields with a universal tool-kit' [*Andersen and Liefferink, 1997: 19*]. Policy transfer and lesson drawing has become an important source for NEPI innovation [*Jordan et al., 2001; Kern et al., 2000*]. The transfer of tradable permits from the Kyoto Protocol to the EU and its member states is a good example.

Fifth, there is growing recognition that the role of states and governments is changing [*Böhret and Wewer, 1993; Jänicke and Weidner, 1997; Marin and Mayntz, 1991*]. Top-down policy approaches (including traditional 'command-and-control' regulations) are giving way to less hierarchical governance structures which are characterised by mutual dependencies between public and private actors, networking and learning from best practices. Market-based instruments, self-regulation and 'joint environmental policy-making' [*Mol et al., 2000*] have therefore become important watchwords also for German policy-makers.

Barriers

However, there are also formidable barriers which have prevented the full scale substitution of 'old' policy tools with NEPIs in Germany. First, amongst many German environmental policy-makers, traditional regulation is still regarded as an effective policy tool for dealing with pressing environmental problems [interviews, BMU and UBA officials, 2001; *SRU, 2002*].

Second, legally trained officials are often unfamiliar with and wary about untested NEPIs such as tradable permits which they consider as complex and ill suited for the German environmental policy system. Moreover, in the past, tradable permits have been denounced as unethical 'rights to pollute' by environmental groups while eco-taxes are (like all taxes) unpopular with the general public.

Third, some environmental policy-makers are concerned that the recent hype about NEPIs could lead to 'instrument shopping' which allows powerful industrial actors to escape or at least considerably delay the adoption of stringent environmental policy measures by pleading for extensive testing periods of 'new' policy instruments in order to prove their alleged superiority compared to traditional tools (interviews, BMU and UBA officials, 2001).

Fourth, some industrial actors actually prefer traditional regulation because it is relatively simple to administer, guarantees a level playing field for competitors and minimises free-riding because monitoring is relatively easy.

Finally, the traditional German policy style, structures and content militate against a wholesale substitution of regulation with NEPIs. Germany is a highly industrialised country at the centre of Europe which suffers from a high degree of ecological vulnerability [*Wurzel, 2002*]. German governments are also under considerable pressure to be seen as acting decisively also because public environmental awareness has traditionally been very high in Germany. Traditional regulation is a more easily understood and publicly visible policy tool (even if it sometimes amounts to little more than symbolic politics) compared to some complex and nationally untested NEPIs such as tradable permit schemes.

NEPI Use in Germany

Germany has gained considerable experience with NEPI innovation. However, while some types of NEPIs have been used extensively, others have been shunned.

Market Based-Instruments

Eco-taxes and tradable permits are generally the most important MBIs.

Eco-taxes: One of the earliest national eco-taxes is the waste water levy which was adopted in 1976 but implemented only in 1981 due to constitutional conflicts between the federal government and the *Länder*.[2] The waste water levy was only moderately effective because it was watered down due to industry opposition [*Andersen, 1994, 127–8*]. Moreover, the introduction of the BAT principle in the water management law greatly diminished the steering effect of the levy. In the late 1980s, Baden-Würtemberg introduced a moderate water extraction charge (*Wasserpfennig*). Similar charges were adopted by the other *Länder* in the 1990s.

The range and number of eco-taxes was extended incrementally and without an overall strategy until the late 1990s. They were adopted largely on an *ad hoc* basis as a reaction to new pollution problems and/or to generate revenue [*Andersen and Sprenger, 2000; OECD, 1999; EEA, 2000; UBA, 1994*]. In the 1980s, acidification and dying forests (*Waldsterben*) became a major priority of German environmental policy [*Weale, 1992b; Wurzel, 2002*]. The German government subsequently pressed for stringent regulation while making extensive use of fiscal incentives in order to encourage the speedy uptake of unleaded petrol and catalytic converter equipped cars. However, the German (as well as the Danish, Dutch and Greek) fiscal incentives were criticised as subsidies for particular technologies by Britain, France and Italy. The EU Commission therefore prohibited the level of fiscal incentives from exceeding the extra cost of the new technology [*Holzinger, 1994; Wurzel, 2002*]. Fiscal incentives fail to internalise the external pollution cost although they have often been used in combination with tax rises (on, for example, leaded petrol and cars not equipped with catalytic converters). They have remained an important tool in the German policy instrument repertoire as can be seen from the lower tax imposed on low sulphur fuel.

In the 1990s, Germany adopted an environmental leader role on the climate change issue. For most of the 1990s, Germany was governed by a Centre–Right (CDU/CSU/FDP) coalition government which strongly supported the introduction of an EU-wide carbon dioxide/energy tax but refrained from adopting such a measure unilaterally on the domestic level for fear of creating a competitive disadvantage for German industry [*Wurzel, 1996; Zito, 2000*]. An ecological tax reform was favoured by Environmental Minister Klaus Töpfer (CDU) and other leading Christian Democrats. However, Chancellor Kohl (CDU) opposed its introduction on a unilateral basis for competitive reasons. Germany therefore fell behind the other European environmental leader states such as Denmark, Finland, the Netherlands and Sweden which all adopted energy and/or carbon dioxide taxes in the 1990s [*Andersen and Sprenger, 2000*].

In 1998, a Red–Green (SPD/Greens) coalition government was elected which introduced the first stage of an ecological tax reform (*ökologische Steuerreform*) in April 1999. The ecological tax reform constituted a genuine NEPI innovation as well as an attempt to catch up with the environmental leader states. It consisted of five steps of tax increases on mineral oil, gas and electricity in order to reduce non-wage labour costs (that is, social security and pension contributions). The first step increased taxes on mineral oil by Euro 0.031 per litre, on gas by Euro 1.636 per mega-watt hour (MWh) and on electricity by Euro 0.01 per kilo-watt hour (kWh). The remaining four annual increases raised only the taxes on fuels for transport (by Euro 0.031 per litre) and electricity (by Euro 0.003 per kWh). As will be explained below, a political dispute soon broke out about whether the ecological tax reform should be terminated at an earlier stage (for example, after step four) or continued beyond the fifth stage. Moreover, generous exemptions were granted for the manufacturing industry and companies whose energy tax burden exceeds by the factor of 1.2 the reduction in social security contributions. No additional taxes were levied on the use of coal despite the fact it has a high carbon content. It was opposed by the SPD out of fears that it might otherwise lose votes from its stronghold constituencies in the coal-rich Ruhr area. Cogeneration of electricity and heat at a high efficiency level, local public transport, rail transport and natural gas as motor fuel received preferential treatment. The

German government had to ask the EU Commission for permission to be able to adopt subsidies for renewable energy sources (such as wind and solar power).

The principal idea behind the ecological tax reform was to increase the cost of resource consumption while reducing (the relatively high non-wage) labour cost. The intention behind the phasing in of the ecological tax reform in different steps was to allow companies to adapt gradually without damaging their economic competitiveness while sending out clear long-term signals about price increases for the use of non-renewable energy sources.

However, the annual increases soon generated considerable political opposition. BMU and UBA officials pointed out the foreign examples (such as the British fuel escalator) to defend the national eco-tax reform when it came under fire on the domestic level (interviews, BMU and UBA officials, 2000). From the late 1980s up to the early 1990s, cross-party support for the unilateral introduction of an ecological tax reform was rising while industry opposition become more muted. However, by the time the ecological tax reform was finally adopted in 1999, it had again become a controversial political issue. The main opposition parties (CDU/CSU and FDP) demanded the scrapping of the ecological tax reform after protests against rising fuel prices in Germany in 2000. The Christian Democrats (CDU/CSU) tabled a parliamentary initiative for the withdrawal of the eco-tax (*Öko-Steuerrücknahmegesetz*) in 2000 (interview in 2001). It was rejected by the Red-Green government which, however, adopted measures to compensate socially disadvantaged and politically influential groups by, for example, increasing tax allowances for commuters.

The introduction of the ecological tax reform was preceded by three waves of debates about the pros and cons of eco-taxes [interviews in 2001; *Reiche and Krebs, 1999*]. The first major debate, which took place in the 1970s, was largely limited to academic circles [*Binswanger et al., 1979; Hansmeyer, 1976; Siebert, 1976; SRU, 1974*]. Environmental economists (such as Karl-Heinz Hansmeyer from the University of Cologne, who also acted as the SRU's chairperson in the 1970s) propounded the theoretical advantages of eco-taxes (such as efficiency gains) compared to traditional regulation in the scientific literature. However, the academic debate (including the endorsement of eco-taxes by the SRU [*1974, 1978*]), had little overall impact on the (SPD/FDP) government as can be seen from the fact that the waste water levy was the only major national eco-tax in the 1970s.

The second major debate took place in the late 1980s [interviews, 2001; *Reiche and Krebs, 1999; UBA 1994*]. It differed from the earlier debate in two important respects. First, it explicitly linked eco-taxes and job creation.

Second, partly because of this link, debate was no longer limited to academic circles. In addition to their beneficial effects on the environment, eco-taxes were now promoted also as a means for making the economy more competitive by using tax revenue imposed on resource consumption to reduce labour costs (for example, cuts in social insurance and pension contributions). In the 1970s, the Swiss economist Christoph Binswanger coined, and Ernst Ulrich von Weizsäcker popularised in the 1980s, the phrase that 'prices must tell the ecological truth' [interviews, 2001; *Binswanger et al., 1979; Reiche and Krebs, 1999; Weizsäcker and Jesinghaus, 1992*]. Eco-taxes became seen as an important policy tool for the ecological modernisation of Germany [*Weale et al., 2000*]. However, the proponents of ecological modernisation (and eco-taxes) were forced onto the defensive due to the *Standort Deutschland* debate, the economic recession in the early 1990s and the cost of German unification.

In the mid-1990s a third major debate took place which started with the publication of commissioned scientific studies on the economic impact of eco-taxes. In 1995, the left-leaning German Institute for Economic Research (DIW) published a widely cited study which had been commissioned by Greenpeace [*DIW, 1995*]. The Federal Association of German Industry (BDI) subsequently commissioned a counter study from the Finance Institute at the University of Cologne which, however, failed fully to reject any beneficial effects for the job market from ecological tax reform [*Reiche and Krebs, 1999*]. In the run-up to the 1998 elections, environmental groups staged a major public campaign in favour of an ecological tax reform which was fiercely opposed by industry. The general public also remained highly sceptical about the need for an ecological tax reform.

Demands by leading Green Party politicians during the 1998 election campaign to raise petrol prices to DM 5 within ten years aroused much public controversy [interviews, 2001; *Raschke, 2001: 217*]. The SPD's chancellor candidate, Gerhard Schröder, was keen to avoid adverse public opinion for his party. He set the upper limit for the increase of one litre petrol at six Pfennig [interview, Finance Ministry official, 2001; *Reiche and Krebs, 1999*]. The election of a Red–Green coalition government in 1998, which came as a surprise to many pollsters, suddenly created a policy window for the adoption of an ecological tax reform at a time when cross-party and public support had already been falling. Especially the Greens and the left wing within the SPD (led by its chairperson Oskar Lafontaine) were determined to adopt such a tax. However, the introduction of the first stage had to be postponed by several months after the EU Commission objected to a number of exemptions (mainly for high energy users) and fiscal incentives for renewable energy sources (interviews, 2001). The German government wanted to adopt a road toll for lorries which use the motorway as early as 1990. However, it was overruled by the European Court of Justice on the grounds that it effectively acted as a discriminatory measure against foreign lorries. In 2001, the government announced a new plan for a lorry road toll which was passed by the *Bundestag* and *Bundesrat* one year later.

A few eco-taxes have also been introduced by local authorities (for example, parking charges). However, in 1995, the Federal Administrative Court banned the city of Kassel from imposing a levy on disposable tableware and cutlery as used in fast food chains on the grounds that it was unconstitutional. Constitutional requirements also narrow down the government's leeway in making use of the hypothecation (that is, earmarking) of taxes including eco-taxes. Hypothecated (eco-) taxes have to benefit the targeted tax payers which explains the German government's preference for general eco-taxes (interview, Finance Ministry official, 2001).

Tradable permits: The start of the German academic debate about tradable permits can be traced to the 1970s [interviews, BMU and UBA officials, 2000 and 2001; *Sandhövel, 1994*]. Economists (such as Hans-Werner Hansmeyer [*1976*], Horst Siebert [*1976*] and Holger Bonus [*1975*]) had expounded the virtues of tradable permits (in terms of cost-efficiency) early on but generated little academic and no political support for this policy tool. Tradable permits arrived on the German government's political agenda only in the late 1990s and mainly as a response to the Commission's proposal for an EU-wide tradable permit scheme which in turn was a reaction to the Kyoto climate change protocol [*CEC, 2000, 2001*]. BMU and Economics Ministry officials used the threat of an imposed EU solution (the EU directive on tradable permits can be adopted by qualified majority) to set up a working group on tradable permits in late 2000.

Tradable permits still suffer from a lack of wide societal acceptance in Germany. For ethical reasons environmental NGOs for long rejected tradable permits which they perceived as a 'licence to profit from pollution' (interview, NGO representative, 1995). However, in recent years attitudes have begun to change within the German environmental movement. According to one BMU official (interview, 2001) 'there have been meetings [of the tradable permits working group] when environmentalists demanded the introduction of tradable permit schemes … [with] pretty much the same arguments that had been used by industry … in the 1990s'.

German industry is deeply split on the use of tradable permits which made the discussions within the working group arduous. Energy intensive industries and the chemical industry in particular are fiercely opposed to tradable permits while demanding the continued use of tried and tested VAs. However, other industries such as the banking sector, which would be involved in running tradable permit schemes, strongly support the adoption of tradable permits (interviews, 2001). The disagreement came to a head when the chemical industry walked out of the tradable permits working group in late 2001 (interviews, 2002). During the 2002 election campaign, Chancellor Schröder (SPD) also opposed tradable permit schemes while Environmental Minister Jürgen Trittin (Greens) clearly favoured their introduction. Frustrated by the slow progress on the national level, some of the *Länder* have started to set up their own tradable permit pilot schemes. It is unlikely that the German government would have edged (albeit slowly) towards the adoption of tradable permits without the EU Commission's proposal for an EU-wide scheme.

Even amongst proponents of tradable permits there is considerable disagreement as to the best design of national and EU-wide schemes (interviews in 2001 and 2002).The most important sticking points relate to the initial allocation (that is, should they be for free (so-called 'grandfathering') or allocated in an auction?), the imposition of target limits (that is, should so-called caps be imposed?) and whether participation should be voluntary or compulsory. Tradable permits represent a highly technical policy instrument which requires considerable expertise from stakeholders who want to influence the design of a particular scheme. The German experience shows that the setting up of tradable permit schemes is a resource intensive exercise which may be a long drawn out process in a country that favours a consensual policy style.

The BMU made three half-hearted attempts to set up tradable permits pilot schemes in the 1990s. However, these attempts 'were blocked by industry although it had demanded the use of market-based instruments for many years' (interviews, BMU and UBA officials, 2001). In the late 1980s, Germany gained limited experience with compensation schemes under the Technical Instructions Air. The compensation schemes allowed companies to exceed emission limits for existing plants if they were compensated for by over-achievements in new plants. However, the label 'market-based' was attached to compensation schemes mainly by government officials who were keen to be seen as having developed innovative policy tools at a time when market instruments had become fashionable [*Zittel, 1996: 198–9*].

Voluntary Agreements

Within the EU, Germany and the Netherlands have adopted by far the largest number of VAs [*CEC, 1996; Öko Institut, 1998*]. In the late 1990s, the EEA [*1997, 29*] put the total number of German VAs at 93 while an UBA-commissioned study listed 97 [*UBA, 1999a*]. More recent estimates put the number of VAs at around 130 (interview, UBA official, 2001). The first (health-related) VAs even pre-date modern day German environmental policy. In the early 1960s, the Association of German Automobile Industry (VDA) put forward VAs to reduce carbon monoxide emissions from cars [*Wurzel, 2002*].

The range of VAs 'concluded in Germany remains the broadest in any member state' [*EEA, 1997, 30*]. They cover issues such as the reduction of energy consumption, the phasing out of harmful substances and the early introduction of low sulphur fuels. In Germany, VAs have taken different forms ranging from *ad hoc* informal self-declaratory statements by industry to well publicised negotiated agreements between industry and the government. Even the terminology varies between *freiwillige Vereinbarungen* (voluntary agreements), *Absprachen* (agreements) and *Selbstverpflichtungen* (self-binding commitments) with the latter term being used most commonly.

German VAs are legally non-binding; most of them do not trigger sanctions if they are not complied with [*CEC, 1996; EEA, 1997; Öko-Institut, 1998; UBA, 1999a*]. Moreover, VAs tend to stipulate few monitoring requirements although there are important exceptions such as the climate change VAs that are monitored by an independent research institute which publishes an annual report [*BDI, 2000; Buttermann and Hillebrand, 2000*]. German VAs are often adopted 'in the shadow of the law' because industry wants to pre-empt government legislation by offering a VA instead. However, sometimes VAs are combined with traditional regulation (as has been the case with regard to the 'green dot' waste recycling scheme) and eco-taxes. VAs therefore fit the German tradition of 'regulated self-regulation' [*Paterson, 1989: 284*].

In 1994, the importance of VAs increased significantly when a Centre-Right (CDU/CSU/FDP) government adopted a coalition agreement which stated a general preference for VAs above traditional regulatory instruments [*UBA, 1999a: 30*]. The Red-Green coalition government which came to power in 1998 was initially highly sceptical about VAs. However, it soon accepted a relatively wide range of different VAs including the renewal and extension of the climate change VA in 2000 [interview, UBA official, 2001; *BDI, 2000*].

The non-binding character of VAs has been criticised by environmental NGOs which, however, have toned down their criticism in recent years [*Öko-Institut, 1998*]. Environmental NGOs demand greater transparency, better monitoring and sanctions in cases of non-compliance.

Critics of VAs have pointed out that they can lead to collusion between industry and government or regulatory capture. UBA officials (interviews, 2001) argued that 'a "negative" VA came into being between the oil industry and leading politicians from the SPD/FDP coalition government with regard to unleaded petrol. The oil industry committed itself voluntarily to reducing the lead content in petrol in exchange for a government promise not to adopt legislation for the introduction of unleaded petrol.' Unsurprisingly this 'negative' VA was never published (interviews, BMU and UBA officials, 1993 and 2001 respectively).

VAs have been most widely used for products. Industry often commits itself to the voluntary reduction and/or phasing out of certain substances in order to avoid government regulation. VAs can also be found in the energy and waste sectors. VAs in the transport sector relate mainly to the early compliance with EU standards for (unleaded and low sulphur) petrol and emission limits ahead of the stipulated deadline.

The *Länder* have also adopted a considerable number of VAs. The so-called environmental pact Bavaria *(Umweltpakt Bayern)* consists of several VAs which had been negotiated between regional industry umbrella organisations and the Bavarian *Land* government [*UBA, 1999*]. The Bavarian Prime Minister and chancellor candidate for the CDU/CSU, Edmund Stoiber (CSU), suggested during the 2002 national election campaign that the environmental pact Bavaria could act as a model for the federal level (*ENDS Daily*, 29 July 2002).

The German government has committed itself to relatively ambitious carbon dioxide emission reduction targets (25 per cent by 2005 compared to 1990) under the UN Kyoto Protocol. The BDI and several sector-wide industry umbrella groups adopted VAs to reduce carbon dioxide (and other greenhouse gas) emissions in 1995, 1996 and 2000. The 1995 climate change VA was widely criticised as unambitious and vague. It was supplemented by a more ambitious VA one year later and updated in 2000. The climate change VAs became a kind of show case for industry which wanted to prove that VAs can work even for highly complex policy problems which involve a large number of actors. Industry would therefore have suffered 'a considerable loss of credibility if it had withdrawn its VA after the Red–Green coalition government adopted an ecological tax reform within a few months of coming to power' (interview, industry representative, 2001). Industry perceives VAs as an alternative to regulation while most BMU and UBA officials view them mainly as a supplementary policy tool.

Eco-labels

The German eco-label scheme, which became known as Blue Angel, was set up in 1978. It quickly developed into a highly successful scheme and influenced similar national schemes which were adopted at a later stage [*Jordan et al., 2002; Kern et al., 2000*]. The Blue Angel is a voluntary third-party scheme which is organised under private law and licensed by the German Institute for Quality Assurance and Labelling (RAL). RAL is a self-financing agency which administers the scheme while charging evaluation and licence fees. The eco-label jury, which is made up of a wide range of stakeholders, decides which products and, more recently, services should be awarded the Blue Angel. The UBA merely comments on the applications. Anyone, including foreign companies, can put forward suggestions for new product and service groups.

Environmental groups have traditionally played an influential role within the eco-label jury. This has greatly contributed towards the public's trust in the Blue Angel which remained Europe's most widely used eco-label (in terms of the number of products and services labelled) until it was overtaken by the Nordic Swan in the late 1990s. At its peak in the mid-1990s, the Blue Angel could be found on more than 4,000 different products. However, by 2001 the number of labelled products and services had fallen to about 3,500. In 2002, the UBA and eco-label jury announced that it was time to give the Blue Angel scheme a face lift. It is not yet clear whether the recent downturn is merely a temporary blip which is broadly in line with earlier ups and downs (interview with UBA official in 2001).

Over time, the institutional structures and procedures of the Blue Angel scheme have remained remarkably stable although there has been an increase in the number of assessment criteria and a greater emphasis on life-cycle analysis. However, the Blue Angel has continued to aim for simplicity and transparency rather than a complex cradle-to-grave approach.

Energy-saving products (such as light bulbs) and products which avoid waste (such as recycled paper) have featured prominently within the Blue Angel scheme. There are market pressures which have led companies to apply for the Blue Angel out of fear that they might otherwise lose the market share to eco-labelled products from competitors. This explains the high number of eco-labelled paints in Germany. Some BMU and UBA officials consider the eco-label as a market instrument (interviews, 1992 and 2001). However, eco-label schemes constitute only soft policy instruments for two main reasons. First, participation in the scheme is voluntary. Second, market pressures exist only if consumers recognise the label *and* are prepared to base their purchasing decisions on the eco-label [*Jordan et al., 2002*]. Voluntary informational environmental policy tools can exert market pressures on producers only in markets with high environmental awareness.

The recent proliferation of multinational, supranational and especially company eco-label schemes has led to some confusion amongst consumers (interview, UBA official, 2001). However, the Blue Angel scheme still enjoys a high degree of recognition and legitimacy amongst the German public. The same cannot be said about the EU's eco-label scheme which was established in 1992. By 2002, only two German companies had applied for the EU eco-label which is barely known in Germany.

Other Policy Instruments

The German government was initially opposed to the adoption of the EU's environmental management and eco-audit system (EMAS) despite the fact that voluntary informational tools (such as the Blue Angel) had already been used in Germany. However, since EMAS has come into force, German companies have made up almost two-thirds of all EMAS applications.

Despite considerable NEPI innovation, Germany remains a 'high regulatory' state [*Héritier et al., 1996*] which has made heavy use of traditional environmental regulation [*Reiche and Krebs, 1999: 62; Kloepfer, 1998; Weale et al., 2000*]. The highest estimates amount to approximately 35,000 technical regulations [*Müller-Brandeck-Bocquet, 1996: 138*]. However, one UBA official (interview, 2001) dismissed this and similar estimates as 'futile number games [which] put forward grossly inflated figures by taking into account also the environmental laws of the *Länder* - and there are now 16! In essence we have [in Germany] about eight or nine major environmental laws which are specified further by technical instructions and detailed implementation laws'. According to BMU estimates there were approximately 800 environmental laws, 2,800 ordinances and 4,700 technical instructions in place in the mid-1990s [*Reiche and Krebs, 1999: 63; Andersen and Sprenger, 2000: 14*].

Environmental subsidies have also played an important role within the national environmental policy instrument repertoire. They can take the form of fiscal incentives for less polluting products, direct subsidies for companies or research funding. Recent examples include fiscal incentives for low-sulphur petrol, subsidies for renewable energy use and funding for research into fuel cells. However, EU membership has severely constrained the use of environmental subsidies in Germany.

Conclusion

The German environmental policy system exhibits a considerable degree of NEPI innovation. Some policy actors have pushed hard to achieve a transformation of Germany's 'high regulatory' state (which makes wide use of regulation and VAs) into a social and ecological market economy (which relies more heavily on MBIs). However, traditional regulatory instruments and VAs still play a dominant role.

Demands for wider use of MBIs have increased significantly since the 1990s. The *Standort Deutschland* debate, economic recession in the 1990s, the cost of unification and increased competition (from the EU's internal market, Eastern and Central Europe and the global marketplace) have acted as important drivers in the search for more cost-efficient policy tools and MBIs in particular. Moreover, leading politicians (such as Environmental Minister Töpfer) and bureaucrats have promoted the use of MBIs within the German government. The UBA's internal reoganisation in the 1990s has made the institution more open to the consideration of NEPIs. External actors such as the OECD and the World Bank have also urged Germany to use more MBIs.

However, the uptake of NEPIs within the domestic policy instrument repertoire has remained uneven. The use of VAs predates the beginnings of modern day German environmental policy although their use has increased significantly since the mid-1990s. Germany acted as a pioneer with regard to eco-labels when it adopted the world's first eco-label scheme in 1978. Germany's record on eco-taxes is more mixed. Eco-taxes were used only moderately (compared to other Northern European environmental leader states) until the first stage of the ecological tax reform was introduced in 1999. The ecological tax reform was very much the result of the surprise election of Germany's first Red–Green coalition government in 1998. The previous Centre–Right coalition government abstained from the unilateral adoption of an eco-tax reform and instead lobbied hard for the EU-wide adoption of a carbon dioxide/energy tax. Germany has not yet gained any experience with tradable permits on the national level. The Commission's proposal for an EU-wide tradable permit scheme (as one means of complying with the Kyoto protocol) led to the setting up of a working group on emission trading in late 2000. However, partly because the working group made little progress during the first year of its existence, the *Länder* started to set up pilot projects. Overall, NEPIs have been used mainly to supplement traditional regulatory instruments which still dominate German environmental policy.

NOTES

1. The term Germany refers to the Federal Republic of Germany both before and after unification which took place in 1990.
2. There are several earlier examples of taxes (such as road tax) on polluting activities. However, their primary aim was to generate revenue rather than to curb pollution.

REFERENCES

Andersen, M.S. (1994), *Governance by Green Taxes. Making Pollution Prevention Pay*, Manchester: Manchester University Press.
Andersen, M.S. and D. Liefferink (eds.) (1997), *European Environmental Policy. The Pioneers*,

Manchester: Manchester University Press.

Andersen, M.S. and R.-U. Sprenger (eds.) (2000), *Market-Based Instruments for Environmental Management*, Cheltenham: Edward Elgar.

BDI (2000), *Vereinbarung zwischen der Regierung der Bundesrepublik Deutschland und der deutschen Wirtschaft zur Klimavorsorge*, Berlin: Bundesverband der Deutschen Industrie.

Binswanger, H.C., Geussberger, W. and T. Ginsburg (1979), *Wege aus der Wohlstandsfalle. Der NAWU-Report. Strategien gegen Arbeitslosigkeit und Umweltzerstörung*, Frankfurt.

BMWi (1993), *Report by the Federal Government on Securing Germany's Economic Future*, Bonn: Federal Ministry of Economics.

Böhret, C. and G. Wewer (eds.) (1993), *Regieren im 21. Jahrhundert – zwischen Globalisierung und Regionalisierung*, Opladen: Leske & Budrich.

Bonus, H. (1975), 'Steuern als Instrument des Umweltschutzes', *Zeitschrift für die gesamte Staatswissenschaft*, No.131, p.540.

Buttermann, H.G. and B. Hillebrand (2000), *Klimaschutzerklärung der deutschen Industrie unter neuen Rahmenbedingungen. Monitoring-Bericht 1999*, Essen: Rheinisch-Westfälisches Institut für Wirtschaftsforschung.

CEC (1993), *Towards Sustainability. A European Community Programme of Policy and Action in Relation to the Environment and Sustainable Development, COM(94) 500*, Brussels: Commission of the European Communities.

CEC (1996), *Communication from the Commission on Environmental Agreements, COM (96) 561 final of 27 November*, Brussels: Commission of the European Communities.

CEC (2000), *Green Paper on Greenhouse Gas Emission Trading Within the European Union, COM(2000)87 final of 8 March*, Brussels: Commission of the European Communities.

CEC, (2001), *Proposal for a Directive of the European Parliament and of the Council Establishing a Scheme for Greenhouse Gas Emission Allowance Trading Within the Community and Amending Council Directive 96/61/EC, COM(2001)581 final, 23.10.2001*, Brussels: Commission of the European Communities.

DIW (1995), *Wirtschaftliche Auswirkungen einer ökologischen Steuerreform*, Berlin: Deutsches Institut für Wirtschaftsforschung.

DNR (2000), *German NGO comments concerning the EU Green Paper on Greenhouse Gas Emission Trading within the EU*, Bonn/Berlin: Deutscher Naturschutzring.

Dyson, K. (1982), 'West Germany: The Search for a Rationalist Consensus', in J. Richardson (ed.), *Policy Styles in Western Europe*, London: George Allen & Unwin, pp.17-46.

Dyson, K. (ed.) (1992), *The Politics of German Regulation*, Aldershot: Dartmouth.

Dyson, K. and K. Goetz (eds.) (2003), *Germany and Europe: A 'Europeanized' Germany?*, London: British Academy (in press).

EEA (1997) *Environmental Agreements*, Copenhagen: European Environment Agency.

EEA (2000), *Environmental Taxes: Recent Developments in Tools for Integration*, Copenhagen: European Environment Agency.

Ewringmann, D. and F. Schafhausen (1985), *Abgaben als ökonomischer Hebel in der Umweltpolitik*, Berlin: Umweltbundesamt.

Friedrich, A., Tappe, M. and R.K.W. Wurzel (2000), 'A New Approach to EU Environmental Policy-making? The Auto-Oil I Programme', *Journal of European Public Policy*, Vol.7, No.4, pp.593–612.

Hansmeyer, K.-H. (1976), 'Die Abwasserabgabe als Versuch einer Anwendung des Verursacherprinzipe', in O. Issing (ed.), *Ökonomische Probleme der Umweltschutzpolitik*, Berlin: Springer.

Harding, R. and W. E. Paterson (eds) (2000), *The Future of the German Economy. An End of the Miracle?*, Manchester: Manchester University Press.

Hartkopf, G. and E. Bohne (1983), *Umweltpolitik 1. Grundlagen, Analysen und Perspektiven*, Opladen: Westdeutscher Verlag.

Héritier, A., Knill, C. and S. Mingers (1996), *Ringing the Changes in Europe. Regulatory Competition and the Redefinition of the State. Britain, France and Germany*, Berlin: de Gruyter.

Hodges, M. and S. Woolcock (1993), 'Atlantic Capitalism versus Rhine Capitalism in the European Community', *West European Politics*, Vol.16, No.3, pp.329–44.

Holzinger, K. (1987), *Umweltpolitische Instrumente aus der Sicht der staatlichen Bürokratie*, Munich: Ifo-Insitut für Wirtschaftsforschung.
Holzinger, K. (1994), *Politik des kleinsten gemeinsamen Nenners? Umweltpolitische Entscheidungsprozesse in der EG am Beispiel der Einführung des Katalysators*, Berlin: Edition Sigma.
Jänicke, Martin (1993), 'Über ökologische und politische Modernisierungen', *Zeitschrift für Umweltpolitik und Umweltrecht*, Vol.16, pp.159–75.
Jänicke, M. and H. Weidner (1997), 'Germany', in M. Jänicke and H. Weidner (eds.), *National Environmental Policies: A Comparative Study of Capacity-Building*, Berlin: Springer, pp.133–56.
Jordan, A., Wurzel, R.K.W., Zito A.R. and L. Brückner (2001), 'The Innovation and Diffusion of "New" Environmental Policy Instruments (NEPIs) in the European Union and its Member States', Paper for the 'Human Dimensions of Global Environmental Change and the Nation State' conference organised by the Postdam Climate Change Institut in Berlin on 8–9 Dec. 2001.
Jordan, A., Wurzel, R.K.W., Zito, A.R. and L. Brückner (2002), 'Consumer Responsibility-taking and Eco-labelling Schemes in Europe', in M. Micheletti *et al.* (eds.), *The Politics Behind Products. Using the Market as a Site for Ethics and Action*, New Brunswick, NJ: Transaction Press (in press).
Katzenstein, P. (1987), *Policy and Politics in West Germany. The Growth of the Semisovereign State*, Philadelphia, PA: Temple University Press.
Kern, K., Jörgens, H. and M. Jänicke (2000), 'Die Diffusion umweltpolitischer Innovationen. Ein Beitrag zur Globalisierung von Umweltpolitik', *Zeitschrift für Umweltpolitik*, Vol.23, pp.507–46.
Kitschelt, H. (1986), 'Political Opportunity Structures and Political Protest: Anti-Nuclear Movements in Four Democracies', *Journal of Political Science*, Vol.16, pp.57–85.
Kloepfer, M.(1998), *Umweltrecht*, Munich: Beck.
Knill, C. and A. Lenschow (eds.) (2000), *Implementing EU Environmental Policy*, Manchester: Manchester University Press.
Liefferink, D. and M.S. Andersen (eds.) (1997), *The Innovation of EU Environmental Policy: The Pioneers*, Oslo: Scandinavian Press.
Liefferink, D. and M.S.Andersen (1998), 'Strategies of the "Green" Member States in EU Environmental Policy-Making', *Journal of European Public Policy*, Vol.5, No.2, pp.254–70.
Marin, B. and R. Mayntz (eds.) (1991), *Policy Networks. Empirical Evidence and Theoretical Considerations*, Frankfurt: Campus.
Mayntz, R. (ed.) (1980), *Implementation Politischer Programme*, Königstein: Athenäum.
Mol, A, V. Lauber and D. Liefferink (2000), *The Voluntary Approach to Environmental Policy*, Oxford: Oxford University Press.
Müller, Edda (1986), *Innenpolitik der Umweltpolitik. Sozial-liberale Umweltpolitik – (Ohn)Macht durch Organisation?* Opladen: Westdeutscher Verlag.
Müller, Edda (2002), 'Environmental Policy Integration as a Political Principle: The German Case and the Implications of European Policy', in A. Lenschow (ed.), *Environmental Policy Integration*, London: Earthscan, pp.57–77.
Müller-Brandeck-Bocquete, G. (1996), *Die institutionelle Dimension der Umweltpolitik*, Baden-Baden: Nomos.
OECD (1993), *OECD Environmental Performance Reviews. Germany*, Paris: Organisation for Economic Co-operation and Development.
OECD (1999), *Environmental Taxes and Green Tax Reform*, Paris: Organisation for Economic Co-operation and Development.
Öko-Institut (1998), *New Instruments for Sustainablility – The New Contribution of Voluntary Agreements to Environmental Policy*, Freiburg: Öko-Insitut.
Paterson, William (1989), 'Environmental Politics', in G. Smith *et al.* (eds.), *Developments in West German Politics*, London: Macmillan, pp.267–88.
Pehle, H. (1997), 'Germany: Domestic Obstacles to an International Forerunner', in Andersen and Liefferink [*1997: 161–210*].
Pehle, H. (1998), *Das Bundesministerium für Umwelt, Naturschutz und Reaktorsicherheit: Ausgegrenzt statt integriert?* Wiesbaden: Deutscher Universitätsverlag.

Raschke, J. (2001), *Die Zukunft der Grünen. So kann man nicht regieren*, Frankfurt: Campus Verlag.

Reiche, D. and C. Krebs (1999), *Der Einstieg in die ökologische Steuerreform*, Frankfurt: Peter Lang.

Sandhövel, Armin (1994), *Marktorientierte Instrumente der Umweltpolitik. Die Durchsetzbarkeit von Mengen- und Preislösungen am Beispiel der Abfallpolitik*, Opladen: Westdeutscher Verlag.

Schröder, G. (1989), 'Alternativen in der Umweltschutzpolitik', in H. Donner, G. Magoulas, J. Simon and R. Wolf (eds.), *Umweltschutz zwischen Staat und Markt*, Baden-Baden: Nomos Verlag, pp.43–58.

Siebert, H. (1976), *Analyse der Instrumente der Umweltpolitik*, Göttingen: Vandenhoeck & Ruprecht.

SRU (1974), *Die Abwasserabgabe – Wassergütewirtschaftliche und gesamtökologische Wirkungen. 2. Sondergutachten*, Wiesbaden: Rat von Sachverständigen für Umweltfragen.

SRU (1978), *Umweltgutachten 1978*, Bundestags-Drucksache 8/1938.

SRU (1998), *Umweltgutachten 1998. Umweltschutz: Erreichtes sichern – neue Wege gehen*, Wiesbaden: Der Rat von Sachverständigen für Umweltfragen.

SRU (2000), *Umweltgutachten 2000. Schritte ins nächste Jahrtausend*, Berlin: Der Rat von Sachverständigen für Umweltfragen.

SRU (2002), *Umweltgutachten 2002. Für eine neue Vorreiterrolle*, Berlin: Der Rat von Sachverständigen für Umweltfragen.

Töpfer, K. (1989), 'Ecological Modernisation of the Industrialised State: A Federal Perspective', in T. Ellwein *et al.* (eds.), *Yearbook on Government and Public Administration*, Baden-Baden: Nomos, pp.489–520.

UBA (1994), *Umweltabgaben in der Praxis*, Berlin: Umweltbundesamt.

UBA (1999a), *Selbstverpflichtungen und normersetzende Umweltverträge als Instrumente des Umweltschutzes*, Berlin: Umweltbundesamt.

UBA (1999b), *Anforderungen an und Anknüpfungspunkte für eine Reform des Steuersystems unter ökologischen Aspekten*, Berlin: Umweltbundesamt.

Weale, A. (1992a) *The New Politics of Pollution*, Manchester: Manchester University Press.

Weale, A. (1992b), 'Vorsprung durch Technik? The Politics of German Environmental Regulation', in Dyson (ed.) [*1992: 159–83*].

Weale, A., Pridham, G., Cini, M., Konstadadkopulos, D., Porter, M. and B. Flynn (2000), *Environmental Governance in Europe. An Even Closer Ecological Union?* Oxford: Oxford University Press.

Wey, K.-G. (1982), *Kurze Geschichte des Umweltschutzes in Deutschland seit 1900*, Opladen: Westdeutscher Verlag.

Weizsäcker, E.U. von and J. Jesinghaus (1992), *Ecological Tax Reform*, London: Zed Books.

World Bank (1995), *The German Water and Sewerage Sector*, Washington, DC: World Bank.

World Commission (1987), *Our Common Future*, Oxford: Oxford University Press.

Wurzel, R.K.W. (1996), 'The Role of the EU Presidency in the Environmental Field: Does It Make a Difference Which Member State Runs the Presidency?' *Journal of European Public Policy*, Vol.3, No.2, pp.272–91.

Wurzel, R.K.W. (2000), 'Flying into Unexpected Turbulence: The German EU Presidency in the Environmental Field', *German Politics*, Vol.9, No.3, pp.23–43.

Wurzel, R.K.W. (2002), *Environmental Policy-Making in Britain, Germany and the European Union*, Manchester: Manchester University Press.

Wurzel, R.K.W. (2003a), 'The Europeanization of Environmental Policy: An Environmental Leader State under Pressure?' in Dyson and Goetz [*2003*].

Wurzel, R.K.W. (2003b), 'The Europeanisation of German Environmental Policy: From Environmental Leadership to Partial Mismatch?' in A. Jordan and D. Liefferink (eds.), *The Europeanisation of National Environmental Policy* (forthcoming).

Zittel, T. (1996), *Marktwirtschaftliche Instrumente in der Umweltpolitik*, Opladen: Leske & Budrich.

Zito, A. (2000), *Creating Environmental Policy in the European Union*, London: Macmillan.

Much Talk But Little Action? 'New' Environmental Policy Instruments in Ireland

BRENDAN FLYNN

Introduction

While Ireland has, like other states, begun tentatively to explore the potential offered by new environmental policy instruments (NEPIs), the results to date have been unimpressive. It is true that some voluntary agreements emerged in the 1990s, principally in the waste sector, yet there are comparatively few market-based instruments. This may be changing, given there has been at least some expert debate on green taxes, and belated taxes on landfills and plastic bags had been agreed by mid 2002. Yet other than these small gains, one must stress the overall lack of innovation as regards NEPIs in Ireland. In a nutshell, there has been much talk, but little action. The 1990s, in particular, have been a decade of missed opportunities, coming at a time when the Irish economy has reached impressive rates of economic growth, allied with equally unimpressive environmental problems [*OECD, 2000a: 19;, Lehane, et al., 2002*].

The emergence of the large voluntary agreement on packaging waste (the REPAK scheme), and some smaller innovative voluntary approaches [*Flynn, 2002*], both suggest that voluntary instruments are perhaps the one NEPI that find wider political support in the Irish context. Some discussion is also offered here as regards Irish experiences with eco-labels and environmental management systems (EMS), but in both cases these reveal a relatively disappointing picture.

In summary, the Irish experience suggests that NEPIs do not appear to offer any 'short cut' to achieving a better style of policy for a state such as Ireland. Moreover, links between conventional policy instruments and NEPIs [*Golub, 1998: 22–3*], as well as the relationship between different NEPIs, both emerge as problematic themes in this Irish case. In particular, a weak implementation of conventional environmental regulation is undermining the REPAK voluntary agreement, while Irish industry lobbies appear to see voluntary agreements as an alternative rather than a complement to less popular market instruments.

Irish Environmental Policy

Policy Structures

Generally speaking, Irish governance can be characterised by its high degree of centralisation, especially as regards fiscal matters. Indeed the Irish Department of Finance exercises a powerful role as a 'first among equals' [*Fanning, 1978*]. The result of this is that important policy decisions with environmental consequences are mostly determined centrally at Cabinet or national Departmental level, including even the detailed implementation measures required for EU directives. Only a limited autonomous capacity is evident at the local government level.

Policy Style

Irish environmental regulation has unquestionably been one of the weaker, less developed EU policy regimes. A regulatory style that was conservative, minimalist, and heavily influenced by UK models has persisted well into the 1970s and 1980s [*Blackwell et al., 1983, Taylor and Horan, 2001: 371*]. While a modern environmentalist movement of sorts emerged in the late 1970s [*Tovey, 1993*], environmentalist groups remain small and politically marginal. These features, allied with some peculiarities of the Irish legal system, may account for an adversarial and litigious Irish environmental policy style at the implementation stage. This is a feature especially of the waste sector but also of land use, infrastructure and development planning policies, as well as the imposition of recovery charges for water, waste and road use. Conflict over these policy sectors has tended to place the central focus upon legislation and law as the predominant policy instruments.

The Content of Policy

Since Ireland's accession to the EEC (now the EU) in 1973, achieving compliance with EU environmental laws has become an increasingly strong driver of domestic policy change, although not the only one. For example, indigenous Irish efforts to encourage an Integrated Pollution Control (IPC) permitting system, matured during the 1990s well before the EU adopted a Directive on IPC. This was in part to facilitate the investment by large transnational firms, but also to address flaws that had emerged in permitting over the preceding decades [*Taylor and Horan, 2001*]. This IPC initiative has become the dominant environmental regulatory approach of the 1990s, and directly led to the establishment of the independent Irish Environmental Protection Agency (IEPA), to oversee this programme, although again not without some controversy [*Taylor, 2001, 1998*].

Note the policy paradigm here has been subtly transformed from one of traditional legalism towards a technical and industrial management model.

In this regard, much of the detail of policy implementation has taken on the character of IEPA firm-level inspections, reviews and a continually evolving practice of 'technical' negotiation of risk with potential industrial polluters.

It is important to point out here that the societal interest and sympathy for environmental policy in Ireland is significantly less than in other EU stats. Studies of Irish public opinion routinely continue to show that environmental protection is of lower concern for Irish voters [*DoELG, 2000c; Faughnan and McCabe, 1998*]. Moreover, this low-level of prioritisation is reflected in the fact that the environmental portfolio is bundled within a large Department of Environment and Local Government, which keeps only a small dedicated environmental policy bureau amidst its varied interests.

Summary

Irish environmental policy performance over the last three decades has been rather more reactive than proactive, even if the influence of the EU has meant that the content of policy has been modernised and now reflects a wider set of influences other than indigenous or British regulatory ideas. However, a serious deficit has also been revealed with regard to implementation of EU norms, and the regulatory enforcement capacity of the Irish state appears essentially weak [*CEC, 2000: 61, Grist, 1997, Galligan, 1996*]. Indeed Ireland, which accounts for just 1 per cent of the total EU population, appears to account for 10 per cent of the complaints submitted to the Commission for non-implementation of EU environmental directives [*Coffey, 2002*]. It is hard, therefore, not to get the impression of a 'thin' regulatory regime essentially overloaded and unable to focus on delivering key priorities in the environment sectors, never mind fostering NEPIs!

Why Are NEPIs Being Adopted?

Ireland's tentative engagement with NEPIs has been driven by a variety of factors most of which could be described as exogenous, although how domestic actors respond to such external policy signals is a vital determining factor of the overall mix of instruments.

First, there is the undoubted effect of the EU as a 'disseminator' of norms and policy ideas. For example the Packaging Waste Directive of 1994 was obviously instrumental in pushing the Irish towards exploring a German or Dutch style 'not-for-profit' commercial voluntary agreement to achieve packaging recycling targets. This EU role however is tellingly absent with regard to fiscal policy innovations (see below).

Second, another driver for policy innovation with regard to NEPIs has been 'policy transfer' from abroad, predictably from the UK, but also continental Europe, and intriguingly often involving non-governmental actors, such as environmental NGOs, industry and farming peak representative groups. For example, two small voluntary approaches, a farm plastics recycling scheme run by the Irish Farmers Association, and a bird conservation partnership project run by Birdwatch Ireland, both have drawn from UK connections [*Flynn, 2002*]. The recent decision to introduce a landfill tax, which has been used in the UK for several years, also illustrates this feature, as does the admission by REPAK that much future Irish recycling will have to take place in the UK, given that the capacity or economies of scale do not exist in Ireland [*O'Sullivan, IT, 2000a*].

A third driver for the introduction of NEPIs, in particular voluntary agreements, has been unease with the adversarial legalism of existing and conventional regulation, which heretofore has been based chiefly on conventional legal 'command and control' approaches. In particular, the Irish Business and Employers Confederation (IBEC), are keen to suggest that novel flexible policy instruments should be adopted to ensure a maximum of 'competitiveness' for firms without the bureaucracy inherent in legal approaches [*IBEC, 1997: 1.4*]. Interestingly however, IBEC are also hostile to green taxes for competitiveness reasons [*IBEC, 1997: 7.1–7.5, IBEC, 2001c*].

If these are the drivers that have sustained the introduction of NEPIs in Ireland, what are the factors that hold back further innovation? One can suggest that these are a disparate series of social and political features. Firstly, there is a low level of societal pressure for environmental regulation. One can also say there has been a dominant political consensus, nurtured within neo-corporatist institutional forums over the last decade under the discourse of 'social partnership', which continues to prioritise economic growth and 'competitiveness' concerns over ecological issues. Thus while ecological modernisation discourses have emerged, these tend to place rather more emphases on competitiveness considerations underlying environmental policies and rather less on a technical discourse of turning pollution into profits [*Taylor, 2001*].

One can say then that the Irish political/institutional structure itself has skewed the scope for innovation in particular ways. Because powerful industrial and agriculture lobbies, allied with a cautious civil administration, dominate such 'social partnership' relationships, and given that environmentalists are mostly weak within such structures, the level of interest in NEPIs remains patchy and uneven. Moreover, the small and marginalised environmentalist movement, precisely because it has these features, prefers then to continue to place faith in litigious and adversarial strategies at the implementation stage. Irish environmental policy style then retains its adversarial features, revealed in numerous policy controversies and (legal) conflicts over policy implementation, whilst at the same time the dominant actors attempt to forge a more technocratic consensus by which to manage ecological problems at the level of policy formulation and design.

NEPIs in Ireland

In this section, I consider Irish efforts with NEPIs under three headings: market instruments (including charges, taxes, and trading systems), voluntary instruments, eco-labels and eco-management systems.

Market-Based Instruments

Ireland's record during the 1990s as regards the introduction of green taxes and other types of environmentally friendly fiscal measures is marked by a small succession of essentially piecemeal efforts, of only limited effectiveness [*OECD, 2000a:110*]. While recent OCED figures suggest Ireland raises a respectable three per cent of GDP from green taxes, above the average of 2.7 per cent, in fact these figures include many taxes that are only indirectly 'green', and these data also reveal that the share of green taxes has actually declined between 1994 and 1998 [OECD Observer, 2001]. Moreover, it is revealing that Speck's evaluation of Irish eco-taxes could point to no dedicated Carbon, Sulphur, or specific pollutant focused taxes [*Speck, 2000*].

This is not to say that there has been no experimentation with green fiscal reforms. Indeed one of the puzzling things about the Irish case is that there has been quite a structured internal expert policy debate on green taxes. The Department of Finance has chaired since the late 1990s an internal Green Tax Group that in turn reports to an overall Tax Strategy Group [*DoELG, 2000a: 76*]. However, this has led to only small-scale policy change.

As regards charges for resource use, Ireland has stood out during the negotiations over the recent EU Framework Water Directive (2000/60/EC), in demanding a concession that domestic users of water would *not* be charged [*OECD, 2000a:110*]. In fairness, Irish administrators are quick to point out that this peculiarity is perhaps matched by other countries' willingness to grant exemptions from cost recovery, for example to agricultural users of water in some Mediterranean EU states. However, the real political cause for this Irish decision has more to do with political expediency.

Since the 1980s and 1990s, local Irish politics has been marked by almost continuous opposition to paying flat-rate water charges (in effect a regressive local services tax), which has led to complex centre-local governmental disputes and a low rate of cost recovery. For example only 75 per cent of water supply and 18 per cent of waste-water costs were recovered in 1994 [*OECD, 2000a: 110*]. In the last two years there have been attempts to push through a new generation of waste charges justified on the basis of the 'polluter pays principle', although again this has met with some determined local resistance. In other cases, a trend towards the privatisation of waste collection, foremost in rural areas, serves as a more direct means of ensuring cost recovery.

As of 2002, two major initiatives have been agreed which promise to alter this limited regime. The first is a landfill tax agreed in June 2002, and the second is a tax on plastic bags that came into effect in March 2002. The latter involves a 15 cent levy on plastic bags and provides funds for a dedicated and 'ear-marked' *Environment Fund* – the first use of such 'earmarking' by Irish authorities. This *Environment Fund* will be controlled by the Minister for Environment and Local Government, and will be chiefly used it appears to fund the building of new waste infrastructure, although spending on the improvement of regulatory enforcement capacity is also allowed. It is significant to point out here that the idea of a tax on plastic (shopping) bags in fact goes back to political commitments made by one of the leading political parties in the election of 1997, which is also an indication of how slow promises can take to turn into reality. Moreover, this proposal initially generated some resistance from the Irish plastics industry, who threatened legal action [*Timmins, IT, 1999*], although public reaction appears broadly positive.

Landfill still remains Ireland's preferred method for waste treatment, and successive governments have been keen to move away from this towards incineration/waste-to-energy and recycling, given that licensed landfill sites are estimated to reach capacity by 2007 [*Lehane et al., 2002: vii*]. The landfill tax that has emerged appears then to be a welcome development, with relatively limited exemptions, notably for those who operate an IPC licensed waste facility. Again its revenues will be paid into the *Environment Fund*. However, one may note that the initial rate of Euro 15 per tonne and the added stipulation that this may rise by no more than 5 Euro per tonne per annum, are both relatively conservative levels of taxation, given that consultants recommended an ultimate level of between Euro 30 to 50 euro per tonne. This implies that such a level cannot be reached until 2005, and perhaps much later given that it is at Ministerial discretion to increase the rate [*DoELG, 2002: pt.6*]. It is difficult to suggest how much income will be generated from these two new green taxes, with one study estimating that a landfill tax could yield circa 19–21 million Euro per annum [*Lawlor and Scott, 1997: 111*], although the eventual figure appears likely to be between 80 to 100 million Euro per annum.

One can suggest that the policy 'drivers' behind these innovations originate from a variety of sources: a need further to comply with EU norms; the failure of conventional regulation; and above all, the need to generate revenues for new waste infrastructure projects which will involve a shift away from landfill towards recycling and thermal treatment/energy recovery.

One other area where there has been at least some minimal innovation that is rhetorically justified on the grounds of ecological concern, has been with regard to the taxation of motor vehicles. Ireland operates a complex system of taxation on motor vehicles consisting of three elements: a once off charge called Vehicle Registration Tax which corresponds to pre single market excise duties; an annual Road Tax payable to local governments, and finally a sales tax (or VAT). In addition there are varying rates of excise duty permitted under common harmonised EU single market rules for various vehicle fuels [*TSG 2000/25, TSG 2000/49*].

Throughout the period 1997–2000, successive internal *ad hoc* Department of Finance led review groups, foremost the Green Tax Group, proposed modifications of these complex taxes on motoring. However, the only significant impact these groups appear to have won was in the Budget of December 1998, which introduced a VRT rate distinguishing between three categories of vehicle, in theory making higher powered and larger vehicles more expensive and smaller vehicles less so. There is some evidence that this has led to a slight increase in the sales of new 'small' cars [*TSG, 2000/25*]. However, because Irish vehicle numbers have dramatically increased, by as much as 60 per cent during 1990s [*Lehane et al., 2002: ix*], there is considerably more congestion. Regardless of size of car, emission and fuel efficiency performance tends to be abysmal in congested driving conditions, which must cancel out at least some of the gains from having a smaller and newer than average car fleet, with supposedly better emission control properties [*TSG, 1999/51: pt.29*].

Moreover, there are many measures which could be taken but which have not been adapted, such that one Tax Strategy Group working paper openly complained: 'it is necessary for this group to point out again that each year that a measure suggested is sidelined, the more pain that will arise after, as even more draconian measures are needed' [*TSG, 1999/51: pt.14*]. For example, successive tax strategy advice groups have pointed to the low level of VRT on commercial vehicles: only a flat charge is levied of circa 51 Euros. This is in effect a substantial subsidy to commercial vehicle fleets, which often use highly polluting diesel fuel. Yet even modest increases have been avoided, presumably to please this powerful constituency. Indeed, even where some increases have been offered in the Road Tax in Fiscal Year 2000, the specific increase of six per cent on commercial 'goods vehicles' was offset for many commercial vehicles by the abolition of the annual circa 32 Euro fee for Heavy Goods Vehicle (HGV) trailer registration. There can be little doubt that competitiveness concerns appears to govern the scope for reform in this sector [DoELG, 2000b]. In the same way, successive demands for the imposition of a tax on agricultural fertilisers has been rejected, with a derogation from the provisions of the EU sixth VAT Directive to ensure this position is maintained, due to the objections of the powerful Department of Agriculture and Irish farmers' lobbies [TSG, 2000/49: Pt.42, Collins, 1993].

While a few privately tolled bridges operate in the Republic of Ireland, no extensive system of road pricing has operated. This should change in the near future, as the current Irish National Development Plan (to 2006) envisages a major role for private capital, with investment recouped through regulated road tolls. However, a vigorous debate has emerged led by those opposed to conventional road pricing, who argue that a system of 'shadow tolls' would be fairer [McCall, 2001]. These would apparently involve motorists being given free access and only being 'shadow' metered, with the state exchequer paying the bill per trip to the private road financier. The theory behind this is to avoid a problem of diversions of car traffic towards non-tolled roads. However, this approach may be criticised as resulting in all taxpayers paying out of general revenues for the trips of individual motorists using expensive motorways. Moreover, because the latter do not have any incentive to alter their behaviour, the efficient use of the resource might be undermined, and congestion encouraged.

The major issue as regards energy tax throughout the 1990s has been whether any Irish government will extend sale tax (VAT) to all energy products at the Irish standard rate (21 per cent), and not at the current intermediate rate of 12.5 per cent. The thinking here is that a higher rate would promote more rational use, and greater energy conservation. However, VAT rates are a matter regulated by the EU as part of the single-market framework of rules, so the Irish do not have a completely free hand. In any event, domestic political sympathy for such a move is decidedly cool. Indeed, one Tax Strategy Group in a pre budget submission advocated precisely this, only to be roundly ignored [TSG, 2000/49: pts.15–16]. Moreover, the state electricity monopoly (ESB) has historically been forced under political direction to hold prices down for consumers [Sweeny, 1990: 115–40], which explains the political saliency of this issue.

This question of taxes upon energy more generally has finally been raised by the much belated National Strategy on Climate Change [DoELG, 2000a] which admitted that Ireland has some of the lowest prices for fuels and thus that scope for tax increases logically existed [DoELG, 2000a: 41]. This strategy clearly promises that green taxes and fiscal measures will have to be introduced, with tentative dates set for the years 2002 or 2003, but it is otherwise very short on details. Indeed, the case made for these is heavily hedged by a number of principles by which to govern any future green taxes regime [*DoELG, 2000a: 76*]. These principles will include, to name but a few: the maintenance of the stable economic environment and fiscal policies, allowing for advance notice, and providing policy certainty for industry and economic actors [*DoELG, 2000a: 27*]. It is revealing of the political sensitivity of this issue, that even before experiments have begun with green energy taxes, the official Irish position is to hedge and limit these by numerous qualifying principles.

More specifically, there are clear indications in this document that the final regime Ireland seeks to develop, will favour so-called 'downstream' taxation on energy products, upon energy consumers in effect, rather than on energy producers, suppliers and raw materials [*DoELG, 2000a: 29*]. International emissions trading, which heretofore Ireland has not experimented with, is promised to emerge to form a part of the Irish strategy on climate change, and since 1998 an Irish Emissions Trading Advisory Group has been established within the Irish Department of Environment and Local Government [*DoELG, 2000a: 26, 35*]. However, one can say this appears to be again a case of the Irish responding very much to EU leadership on this issue, following from various Commission proposals for an EU wide emissions trading regime by 2005 [*CEC, 2000a*]. Moreover, there have been no suggestions about the introduction of a tradable permits approach for other types of domestic pollution, which may be a reflection of the small scale of the Irish environmental policy regime, which has only a limited capacity to host and sustain a few policy initiatives and debates at any one time. The fact that the existing 'policy space' is already 'crowded' with the problems arising from the need to implement EU laws, the IPC approach, and some new voluntary agreements (see below), seems to limit the scope for policy innovation.

Voluntary Agreements

Ireland's experience with voluntary agreements can be characterised as still limited in number and of mixed success. Indeed, a recent study on the adoption of voluntary agreements across Europe, reveals that the REPAK agreement on packaging waste was the sole Irish example [*Börkey and Lévêque, 2000: 44*]. This has since been joined by a few other very small voluntary initiatives on bird protection and farms plastics mentioned before, and since 1999 an agreement by the Irish Detergents and Allied Products Association (IDAPA) has been in place, aiming to phase out phosphate based domestic laundry washing powders [*ENDS, 1999*]. As these appear to be working quite well, it is interesting to speculate perhaps that there may be some scope for an increase in the use of less ambitious small-scale voluntary agreements, given that influential industry voices, represented by IBEC, appear markedly to favour voluntary approaches over green taxes [*IBEC, 1997: 7.1–7.5; IBEC, 2001c*]. In contrast Irish environmentalists still often appear lukewarm about voluntary approaches, although there is at least the one example of a voluntary negotiated conservation project between Birdwatch Ireland and local farmers [*Flynn, 2002*].

However, unquestionably the most significant Irish voluntary initiative of recent years is the REPAK agreement, established in 1995 to meet the requirements of the EU Packaging Waste Directive, illustrating both how conventional law based regulation can encourage NEPIs, and the centrality of the EU role.

On first impressions, REPAK appears to have been a success, having attracted over 1,000 Irish firms [*O'Sullivan, IT, 2000a*]. It is of course possible for Irish firms to choose not to join REPAK and instead develop their own plan with local governments, although few have done this, meaning a significant subset of uncompliant firms probably exists. One source has suggested that as many as a quarter of potentially liable firms [*Shanahan, IT, 2001*] are 'free riding' and have not developed an adequate waste management plans with their respective local governments *in lieu* of REPAK membership [*O'Reilly, IT, 2001*].

This low level of compliance is revealed in the fact that by 2001, only *two* successful prosecutions had been achieved for breaches of the relevant legislation. It appears this low rate of enforcement may be due to legal problems inherent in the waste management regulations that underwrite the REPAK scheme, which were successfully legally challenged, a fact that aptly reinforces the earlier observation concerning the litigious nature of much of the Irish environmental policy style [*Shanahan, IT, 2001*].

What is striking here is that even a small weakness in the Irish enforcement of conventional waste laws, has reduced the viability and attractiveness of the REPAK voluntary agreement [*O'Brien, IT, 1999*]. In effect, REPAK is being held back by a rather old-fashioned failure of political willpower to enforce existing laws, wedded to a weak administrative institutional framework.

REPAK's woes also certainly relate to the structural weakness of Irish waste infrastructure, where almost 80 per cent goes to landfill, posing huge problems for any voluntary agreement. In contrast, within the more mature policy regimes such as in the Netherlands, the pre-existing base of infrastructure is already comparatively well developed. This serves to reinforce the claim made at the outset that NEPIs require careful co-ordination with the pre-existing regime of conventional environmental policy, including where appropriate a more realistic understanding of their limits.

While REPAK has managed to meet, and for several years actually exceed, the recycling target laid down for Ireland under the terms of the Packaging Waste Directive, this was never that demanding (25 per cent), as Ireland had negotiated a derogation. After 2001, the Packaging Waste Directive's normal targets became effective, requiring a recycling rate of 45–50 per cent by 2005. Volumes are estimated to rise from 200,000 tonnes to 450,000 tonnes of packaging waste. It is clear that Ireland does not now, or likely will have by 2005, adequate recycling capacity to deal with this. As a result waste will have to be exported, most likely to the UK [*Shanahan, IT, 2001; O'Sullivan, IT, 2000a*]. While this might reflect the small-scale of the Irish economy, and from an economic perspective may represent the most cost-effective solution, it is a serious indictment of the abilities of the Irish state and industry to meet their environmental responsibilities through voluntary instruments alone.

REPAK have also experienced difficulty with market conditions that have caused considerable uncertainty. For example, the market for recycled packaging waste has proven quite unpredictable, with many commodities barely profitable today that were two years ago. Timmins recounts how the rate of Irish glass recycling has actually dropped from a level of 47 per cent during the 1990s to circa 37 per cent in the 2000–2001 period because of a drop in the price of recycled glass [*Timmins, IT, 2000a*]. The result has been the need to pay subsidies to waste contractors to recycle such waste, as it has not proven profitable for them to do so under current market incentives.

Secondly, the booming Irish 'celtic tiger' economy of recent years has ensured an unexpected surge in waste packaging volumes, reflecting a 60 per cent increase in general waste volumes between 1995–2000 [*Lehane et al., 2002: vii–viii*], which means that the overall amount that REPAK must recycle has actually increased faster than initially projected. Thirdly, the collection of waste has proven problematic, and indeed REPAK appear to be now moving away from direct involvement in the collecting of packaging waste for recycling, preferring to leave this in the hands of independent waste contractors.

Another particularly worrying trend emerged when a Dublin based door-to-door recycling venture, *Kerbside Dublin,* which had operated for nine years and had reached some 90,000 homes, suffered a complete financial collapse in the spring of 2000 despite significant financial support from central and local government, as well as REPAK [*Timmins, IT, 2000b*]. As it was, this *Kerbside* initiative that was supposed to lead the drive to provide Dublin city with a sophisticated recycling collection and processing capacity, its failure must be seen as a serious setback.

Eco-labels

Ireland's track record with regards to Eco-labels and Environmental Management Systems (EMS) appears to be also mixed. Indeed prior to the arrival of the EU eco-label in 1992, Irish industry did not use any national eco-label system. It is perhaps a little strange that Ireland has not since developed any national eco-label, as both national and EU Eco-labels are allowed to co-exist. Indeed, both Spain and France have introduced national eco-labels since the adoption of the EU Eco-label regulation in 1992. Moreover, the new centre–right coalition government, which was formed after the general election in 1997, explicitly promised initiatives on eco-labels [*Muire Tynan, IT, 1997*] and it was recommended by an all-party Parliamentary Committee report on Sustainable Development [*JCSD, 1997: 95*], all to no avail.

Moreover, the EU Eco-label itself has proven a little disappointing, attracting complaints from some Irish industry representatives of excessive cost and complexity [*JCSD, 1997: 93*]. It is perhaps not surprising then that by 2001 only *two* Irish companies had achieved the EU recognised Eco-label, one of whose membership has since lapsed [*NSAI, 2001, NSAI interviewee*].

This somewhat disappointing picture as regards the specific EU Eco-label scheme should not be taken to mean that no other efforts at experimenting with eco-labelling as a general policy instrument have emerged in Ireland. In fact under the EU LIFE fund various Irish bodies, typically involving partnerships between state agencies, local governments, and local community groups, have since the mid-1990s experimented with local 'Beatha Environmental Quality Marks' which are *de facto* eco-labels for tourist districts.

However, one example where eco-labelling in Ireland has caused controversy relates to complaints by Irish environmentalists over the decision of the internationally recognised Forest Stewardship Council to award their eco-label to the Irish state forestry development company, Coillte [*O'Sullivan, IT, 2000c*]. The arguments of environmentalists in this case were that this state company pursued an unsustainable forestry policy.

As a result of this controversy, one cannot say that eco-labelling as an instrument has achieved complete acceptance. In fact it appears that where there is greater community, local and national input into the development of indigenous eco-labels, these may generate more interest and support.

Environmental Management and Audit Systems (EMAS)

As regards Environmental Management Systems (EMS), the Irish domestic regime was considerably complicated by the decision of the EU in 1993 to regulate this area with its own Environmental and Management Auditing Standards (EMAS) Regulation (No.1836/93). Prior to this, Ireland had developed its own indigenous EMS standard, IS310. Alternatively, some Irish firms used the British EMS Standard BS7750. The result has been some confusion between the plethora of standards. To implement the EMAS Directive, Ireland established a National Accreditation of Board (NAB) in 1997, which oversees the accreditation of all EMS. However, the actual evaluation work is carried out by either commercial UK auditors, or more often by a state-owned National Standards Authority of Ireland (NSAI). The NSAI is also the recognised Irish authority for firms to apply for the award of an eco-label as well.

Since 1996, the 'old' Irish environmental management standard IS310 and the British standards BS7750 have both been 'retired', and Irish firms can proceed for accreditation under the ISO14001 standard, which has been acknowledged by the European Commission and the European Standards Centre (CEN) as being equivalent to EMAS. However, this decision has not been uncontroversial with environmentalists, who point to the fact that ISO14001 does not require periodic publication of environmental performance, implying it is qualitatively inferior [*ENDS, 1996a*].

Interestingly, by way of contrast, the 'old' Irish standard IS310 can be considered quite good. Certainly it was more than adequate to meet the terms and conditions of the original EMAS Regulation of 1993, and some Irish sources involved in formal accreditation under ISO14001 now consider it to have been in many ways a superior norm, as it brought firms towards the point of publishing their results (NAB interviewee). Arguably, the decision by CEN, the Commission and the member states in 1996 to accept ISO14001 as a way of meeting the terms of the EMAS Regulation, has in effect involved a substantial deregulation of what was an adequate and evolving national EMS regime [*ENDS, 1996b*].

One distinctive Irish innovation as regards EMAS deserves mention here. This is the linking of the auditing process for Irish IPC licensing, introduced in 1993, with accreditation for EMAS/ISO14001 (NSAI interviewee). This is a considerable advantage to a firm for it reduces costs and lost labour by allowing Irish located firms to meet both of these regulatory standards at the same time if they so wish. However, the take-up of this distinctive innovation has been rather poor (NAB interviewee).

Why Has Ireland Been So Reluctant to Introduce MBIs?

What is arguably distinctive in this account of the Irish experience with NEPIs is the comparative absence of market instruments, whereas there are at least some positive developments with regard to voluntary agreements, eco-labels and EMAS. Green taxes and fiscal charges appear unquestionably much more politically controversial in Ireland, compared to other NEPIs. What can then account for the paucity of market instruments in Ireland?

First, one can point to the absence of a strong EU role in pushing market instruments. Second, the resistance of Irish business lobbies to market instruments has been critical, and made stronger within a neo-corporatist institutional framework that privileges consensual 'partnership' discourses in general. Within this institutional context approaches such as voluntary agreements are likely to be more appealing. Thirdly, one must note the traditional prudence of an Irish Treasury mindset, which has been reluctant to embark upon extensive exploration of green taxes, especially as the 1990s has already seen extensive reductions in income and capital taxes. Finally, one can say that the low base of public support for environmental measures allied with wider misgivings about taxation in general, has also held back the emergence of market instruments.

The Missing EU 'Push Factor'

Fiscal policy co-ordination remains a bone of contention between the recent centre-right Irish government (1997–2002) and the European Commission, especially as this relates to Ireland's low rate of corporation tax, perceived by some other states as unfair competition. Indeed, the Irish, along with other states, not only blocked further possible tax co-ordination measures at the Nice Treaty summit (2000), but also consistently opposed efforts at Green tax co-ordination (1996-97) and the Carbon Tax proposal of 1992 [*ENDS, 1996c*]. The result is that beyond the limits set down under harmonised VAT legislation, there is no EU regulatory 'push' factor comparable to the transposition and implementation of Directives, and this has meant a vital external 'driver' has been absent. This suggests the ability of the EU to encourage the uptake of fiscal instruments is fundamentally much more limited than for other types of NEPI. Moreover, because the broader question of EU wide fiscal policy has become so politicised and fraught [*Barry and Fitzgerald, 2001*], it is arguable that future Irish governments are ill-disposed towards a stronger EU role in this area *per se*.

Business Opposition

In considering why voluntary approaches are regarded as a more acceptable type of NEPI *in lieu* of market approaches, it is vital to reiterate that the highly competent and influential industry lobby group, IBEC, has repeatedly and strongly rejected green taxes and favours instead voluntary measures. Even Irish plastics industry representatives have sought to challenge the introduction of a tax on plastic bags both on the grounds that it could be in breach of EU laws [*Timmins, IT, 1999*], but also by making the point that they already pay fees to REPAK.

Recently, IBEC has grudgingly accepted the need for charges and borderline market approaches, but this is hedged with the usual competitiveness concerns. In contrast Irish environmentalists and environmental economists appear much less happy with voluntary initiatives and are instead interested in seeing green taxes emerge allied with tougher laws and enforcement [*Cunningham, 2001: 22*]. What is especially interesting here is that in the Irish setting voluntary approaches are seen by business, as an *alternative* to costly green taxes and market measures rather than being complementary. There is also perhaps a view that they provide a means of avoiding the adversarial risks of litigation. It would appear then that voluntary agreements have tended to displace the possible scope for market and eco-tax instruments in Ireland. The Irish case reminds us then that central to any understanding of the uptake of NEPIs and their success, must be an appreciation of a dynamic relationship between one NEPI and others, and between NEPIs and traditional regulatory approaches.

Another reason why such voluntary approaches find favour with IBEC and successive governments, is because they build quite naturally upon a wider pattern of neo-corporatist relations which Ireland has experimented with since the late 1980s, under the label, 'social partnership' [*Adshead and Quinn, 1998*]. For example, it is interesting to note that REPAK now openly talks about the need for 'partnership' between community groups, local governments, firms and national government, rather than stressing the supposed self-responsibility of industry alone.

The growing dominance, if not the debatable success of this 'social partnership' model [*Roche and Geary, 2000*], offers policy elites or 'insiders' the promise of moving away from the traditional adversarial policy style of Irish environmental regulation, and crucially has created a more favourable intellectual environment for concepts such as voluntary instruments to be accepted as new forms of 'partnership'. Note this does not mean environmentalists necessarily accept this, or that during policy implementation, legal conflicts will be avoided. Market instruments by way of contrast, because they tend to produce a more transparent distribution of policy 'winners and losers', with price tags attached, are less likely to be attractive in such an institutional setting. This is not to say that it is impossible to discuss green taxes within such frameworks, but it implies that such an approach will be qualified by competing concerns other than ecological protection [*DoELG, 2000a: 27*].

Treasury Opposition to Eco-Fiscal Innovation

Notwithstanding the evidence pointed to here of an internal debate within the Irish civil administration concerning green taxes and charges, a distinctive institutional culture remains in place that stresses caution towards innovation in fiscal policy [*Fanning, 1978*]. It is noteworthy that the actual fiscal policy innovations which Ireland has experimented with throughout the 1990s have taken a marked neo-liberal direction, in the form of significant reductions in capital and income taxes.

In theory, this might have provoked some interest in green taxes as a possible 'cash cow' to make up for lost revenues, but in practice the Department of Finance senior civil servants have probably exhausted their already low tolerance for fiscal innovation. One can say a default position of innate caution remains, based on the memories of dire public finances during the 1980s [*Geary, 1992*]. Moreover, note the rational motivation here would be to secure a predictable and continuous revenue stream from a stable tax base, whereas green taxes by definition may not provide this if target groups change polluting behaviour, reducing their liability, but also exchequer tax incomes. Indeed one Tax Strategy Group paper explicitly cautioned against this risk [*TSG, 2000/49: pt.12*].

Cultural Resistance to Tax Instruments

More widely still, it is perhaps not going too far to suggest that there is a widespread cultural antipathy towards taxation in Irish society, in part a legacy of the heavy burdens of the 1980s and perhaps the historic relative lack of wealth of Irish society compared to other EU states. This may also be a consequence of Ireland's semi-colonial historical development, whereby the role of the colonial state *qua* state, in having a legitimate claim upon private incomes was not fully respected. Of course, it is tempting to counter this with the observation that almost *all* taxpayers in *all* liberal democratic regimes display reluctance towards paying taxes, but this forgets variation in the deeply seated cultural views of the state and the 'public realm' across countries, or even within states. For example, it is perhaps not accidental that Nordic states have managed to experiment with green taxes quite quickly [*Vehmas, et al, 1999*], given that there is at least a wider cultural acceptance of high levels of taxation [*Kautto, 2001: 243*].

What evidence is there to support the claim that the Irish are instinctively wary of using taxation as a legitimate public policy instrument? Here recent Irish opinion and attitude survey research on environmental issues suggest only weak support for fiscal and market approaches. Indeed the number of persons willing to pay higher taxes to fund environmental protection may have actually dropped slightly from 24 per cent in 1993 to 20 per cent in 2000 [*DoELG, 2000c: 11–12*]. The Department of Environment and Local Government's own study of 2000 was forced to conclude that:

> there is a public and private morality when it comes to the environment, with people saying one thing and doing another ... When Irish people are asked for their reaction to possible Government policies and initiatives to protect the environment, the majority are in favour of spending public money on environmental campaigns ... When asked specifically, however, there is less individual willingness to make sacrifices, with less than one-fifth of people either willing to pay higher taxes, pay higher prices or makes cuts in their standard of living [*DoELG, 2000c: 6*].

However, this kind of research may be only suggestive, for on closer examination it actually implies that there is at least some scope for tax measures to be supported, but only as long as they result in no extra burdens on taxpayers – a so-called 'revenue neutral' constraint.

Conclusion

It must be said that even the limited set of NEPIs which Ireland has managed to sustain over the last few years, unquestionably represents a welcome departure from the traditional emphasis upon legal instruments of the preceding decades. Yet Ireland has now quickly reached a threshold where the success of one type of NEPI threatens to infringe upon the regulatory scope for others; voluntary instruments appear to have matured at the expense of market based approaches. Moreover, the relationship between conventional regulation and NEPIs remains poor in Ireland, and the scope for NEPIs to complement traditional legal approaches has not been satisfactorily explored. This can be seen in the weakness of enforcement of the packaging waste regulations of 1997 that underpin REPAK. Additionally, one can suggest that the IPC effort has for many firms and state regulatory authorities simply taken so much of their time and effort, that it means little energy has been left to explore NEPIs more substantively.

In conclusion, Ireland's experience with NEPIs is best characterised as a case of 'much talk, but little action', for while expert debate on green fiscal measure has emerged along with government commitment for action, in fact it is only recently that relatively small-scale green fiscal measures have been agreed. It is also particularly worrying that the leading example of a voluntary agreement, the REPAK scheme, now suffers major weaknesses in enforcement and implementation.

Intriguingly, Irish voluntary agreements appear to have been more effective when they have been less ambitious, smaller in scale and more focused. In the same way domestically developed small-scale eco-labels have proven reasonably effective instruments, although hardly decisive in addressing ecological problems. Finally, Irish domestic EMAS approaches were revealed to be proceeding adequately, but are now paradoxically made more complex and not necessarily better policy instruments due to EU involvement.

Beyond the institutional design of NEPIs, or the pro and cons of particular instruments, the Irish case suggests that much greater attention needs to be paid to the ideological, institutional and cultural factors which can impede policy innovation. While these involve a series of highly diffuse considerations, they do nonetheless place very real limitations upon the potential of NEPIs in Ireland. Above all, what appears to be most badly needed is a more balanced approach to integrating and adopting various types of NEPI, which can then be implemented on a realistic timescale so that they complement one another and fit in well with the existing framework of regulation.

It would appear that Ireland has a long way to go before her experience with NEPIs becomes well thought out, properly executed, and evolves to be a substantive engagement, rather than the patchy and mixed performance that is revealed to date.

REFERENCES

Adshead, M. and B. Quinn (1998), 'The Move from Government to Governance: Irish Development Policy's Paradigm Shift', *Policy and Politics*, Vol.26, No.2, pp.209–25
Blackwell, J. and F. Convery (eds.) (1983), *Promise and Performance: Irish Environmental Policies Analysed*, Resource and Environmental Policy Centre, University College Dublin: Dublin.
Barret, A., Lawlor, J. and S. Scott. (1997), *The Fiscal System and the Polluter Pays Principle: A Case Study of Ireland*, Aldershot: Ashgate
Barry, F. and J. Fitzgerald (2001), 'Irish Fiscal Policy in EMU and the Brussels–Dublin Controversy', in *Fiscal Policy in EMU: Report of the Swedish Committee on Stabilization Policy in EMU* Stockholm: Statens Offentliga Utredningar. Available at http://www.ucd.ie/~economic/staff/barry/papers/BFITZ.PDF.
Börkey P, and F. Lévêque (2000), 'Voluntary Approaches for Environmental Protection in the European Union – A Survey', *European Environment: The Journal of European Environmental Policy*, Vol.10, No.1, pp.35–54
Coffey, M. (2002), 'Ireland One of the Worst Polluters in Europe', *The Irish Times*, 23 Jan.
Collins, N. (1993), 'Still recognisably Pluralist? State-Farmer relations in Ireland', in R.J. Hill, and M. Marsh (eds.), *Modern Irish Democracy – Essays in honour of Basil Chubb*, Dublin: Irish Academic Press, pp.104–22.
Commission of the European Communities/CEC (2000), *Second Annual Survey on the Implementation and Enforcement of Community Environmental Law, January 1998 to December 1999*, Working Document of the Commission Services, Directorate-General for the Environment. Luxembourg: Office for Official Publications of the European Communities.
Commission of the European Communities/CEC (2000a), *Green Paper on Green House Gases Emission Trading within the European Union*, COM (2000) 87.
Cunningham, A.M. (2001), *Comparative Report featuring Three International Sustainable Waste Management Programmes, Including Feasibility in the Irish Situation*, Dublin:

Earthwatch/Friends of the Earth Ireland/VOICE – Voice of Irish Concern for the Environment.

Department of the Environment and Local Government   (1997a), *Sustainable Development: A strategy for Ireland*, DoELG: Dublin.

Department of the Environment and Local Government (DoELG) (1997b),'Waste Management (Farm Plastics)', *Environment Bulletin*, Issue 35, Aug., p.29.

Department of the Environment and Local Government (2000a), *National Climate Change Strategy – Ireland*, Dublin: DoELG.

Department of Environment and Local Government (2000b), '*Press Release – Dempsey Announces 'Greening of Motor Tax Rates'*, 6 Dec. Dublin: DoELG

Department of the Environment and Local Government (2000c), *Attitudes and Actions: A National Survey on the Environment*, DoELG: Dublin.

Department of the Environment and Local Government (DoELG) (2002), *Waste Management (Landfill Levy) Regulations 2002, Information Note and Guidance*, Dublin: DoELG.

ENDS/Environmental Data Services (1999), 'Phosphate Detergent Phase-Out in Ireland', *ENDS Report*, No.299, Dec.

ENDS/Environmental Data Services (1996a), 'ISO Under Fire over Environmental Standards', *ENDS Report*, No.260.

ENDS/Environmental Data Services (1996b), 'BS7750 Finally Recognised as Equivalent to EMAS', *ENDS Report*, No.253.

ENDS/Environmental Data Services (1996c), 'A New Momentum Towards Green Tax Reform', *ENDS Report*, No. 257.

Fanning, R. (1978), *The Irish Department of Finance, 1922–1958*, Dublin: Institute of Public Administration.

Faughnan P, and B. McCabe (1998), *Irish Citizens and the Environment: A Cross- National Study of Environmental Attitudes, Perceptions and Behaviours*, Dublin: EPA/Commission of the European Communities/ Social Science Research Centre, UCD.

Fenlon, R.M. (1983), 'The Water Pollution Control Act: An Evaluation', in J. Blackwell and F. Convery (eds.), *Promise and Performance: Irish Environmental Policies Analysed*, Resource and Environmental Policy Centre, University College Dublin: Dublin, pp.5–12.

Flynn, B. (2002), 'Voluntary Environmental Policy Instruments: Two Irish Success Stories', *European Environment: The Journal of European Environmental Policy*, Vol.12, No.1, pp.1–12.

Galligan, E. (1996), 'Case Notes', *Irish Planning and Environmental Law Journal*, Vol.3, No.4, pp.180–88.

Geary, P.T. (1992), 'Ireland's Economy in the 1980s – Stagnation and Recovery – a Preliminary review of the evidence', *Economic and Social Review*, Vol.23, No.3, pp.253–81.

Golub, J. (1998), 'New Instruments for Environmental Policy in the EU Introduction and Overview', in J. Golub (ed.), *New Instruments for Environmental Policy in the EU*, London: Routledge, pp.1–32.

Grist, B. (1997), 'Wildlife Legislation –The Rocky Road to Special Areas of Conservation Surveyed', *Irish Planning and Environmental Law Journal*, Vol.5, No.1, 87–95.

Irish Business and Employers Confederation/ IBEC (1997), *IBEC Environmental Policy*, Dublin: IBEC.

Irish Business and Employers Confederation/ IBEC (2001a), 'Waste Management Amendment Act 2001 is Enacted', *IBEC Press Release*, 24 March (http://www.ibec.ie/ibec/Press/Publicationsdoclib3.nsf).

Irish Business and Employers Confederation/ IBEC (2001b), 'Dempsey Proposes Levy on Land-Filled Waste', *IBEC Press Release,* 05 Nov. 2001 (http://www.ibec.ie/ibec/Press/Publicationsdoclib3.nsf).

Irish Business and Employers Confederation/ IBEC (2001c), 'Cool Heads Needed to Move Forward on Climate Change', *IBEC Press Release*, 11 April 2001 (http://www.ibec.ie/ibec/buspolicies/buspoliciesdoclib3.nsf/)

JCSD/Joint Committee on Sustainable Development – Irish Parliament/Tithe An Oireachtais (1997) *Report of the Joint Committee on Sustainable Development*, Stationary Office: Dublin.

Kautto, M. (2001), 'Moving Closer? Diversity and Convergence in Financing Welfare States', in Kautto *et al.* (eds.), *Nordic Welfare States in the European Context*, London: Routledge, pp.232–61

Lawlor, J. and S. Scott (1997), 'Environmental Services', in A. Barret *et al.* (eds.), *The Fiscal System and the Polluters Pays Principle: A Case Study of Ireland*, Aldershot: Ashgate, pp.85–124.

Lehane, M., Le Bolloch, O. and P. Crawley (2002) *Environment in Focus 2002: Key Environmental Indicators for Ireland*, Wexford: IEPA.

McCall, B. (2001),'For Whom the Road Tolls', in *Motoring 2002 – A Commercial Report – The Irish Times*, 27 Nov., p.12.

Muire Tynan, M. (1997), 'New Programme Addresses Seven Key concerns', *The Irish Times*, 20 June.

National Standards Authority of Ireland (NSAI) (2001), 'Eco-Label Awards Not To Be Sneezed at', *NSAI News-National Standards Authority of Ireland Newsletter*, No.3.

O'Brien, T. (1999), 'Big Firms that Fail to Recycle Face Prosecution', *The Irish Times*, 1 July.

O'Connell, S. (2001), 'Metropolitan Mayhem', in *Motoring 2002 – A Commercial Report – The Irish Times*, 27 Nov., p.11.

OECD (2000a), *Environmental Performance Reviews – Ireland*, Paris: OECD.

OECD (2000b), *Voluntary Approaches for Environmental Policy: An Assessment*, Paris: OECD.

OECD Observer (2001), 'Green Taxes' (available at http://www.oecdobserver.org/news/fullstory. php/aid/497/Green_taxes.html).

O'Reilly, A. (2001), 'Repak says Legal Loopholes Hindering Recycling', *The Irish Times*, 5 Oct.

O'Sullivan, K. (2000a), 'Repak in £300,000 Drive to Recycle Green Message', *The Irish Times*, 18 Feb.

O'Sullivan, K. (2000b), 'Campaign Planned to Reduce Landfill Dependence', *The Irish Times*, 18 Oct. 2002.

O'Sullivan, K. (2000c), 'Environment Groups Oppose "Green Label"', *The Irish Times*, 15 June 2002.

Roche, K. and J.F. Geary (2000), 'Collaborative Production' and the Irish Boom: Work Organisation, Partnership and Direct Involvement in Irish Workplaces', *Economic and Social Review*, Vol.31, No.1, pp.1–36.

Shanahan, E. (2001), 'Waste Disposal Law is ignored –Repak', *The Irish Times*, 6 Oct.

Speck, S. (2000), 'A Database of Environmental Taxes and Charges – Ireland', *The Eco-Tax Database of Forum for the Future* (London), available at: http://www.europa.eu.int/comm/ environment/enveco/env_database/ireland2000.htm

Sweeny, P. (1990), *The Politics of Public Enterprise and Privatisation*, Dublin: Tomar.

Taylor, G. and A. Horan (2001), 'From Cats, Dogs, Parks and Playgrounds to IPC Licensing Policy Learning and the Evolution of Environmental Policy in Ireland', *British Journal of Politics & International Relations*, Vol.3, No.3, pp.369–92.

Taylor, G. (2001), *Conserving the Emerald Tiger: The Politics of Environmental Regulation in Ireland*, Galway: Arlen Academic.

Taylor, G. (1998), 'Conserving the Emerald Tiger: The Politics of Environmental Regulation in Ireland', *Environmental Politics*, Vol.7, No.4, pp.55–74.

Timmins, E. (1999), 'Industry Says Bags Tax Would Breech EU law', *The Irish Times*, 21 Aug.

Timmins, E. (2000a), 'Recycling Revisited', *The Irish Times*, 7 May.

Timmins, E. (2000b), 'Kerbside by the Wayside', *The Irish Times*, 7 May.

Tovey, H. (1993),'Environmentalism in Ireland – Two Versions of Development and Modernity', *International Sociology*, Vol.8, No.4, pp.413–30.

TSG/Tax Strategy Group (1999), *Working Paper No.29, Environmental Tax Policy*, Interim Report by Chairman of Working Party (available at Department of Finance website: http://www.irlgov.ie/finance/Publications).

TSG/Tax Strategy Group (1999), *Working Paper No.36 on Vehicle Registration Tax* (available at Department of Finance website: http://www.irlgov.ie/finance/Publications).

TSG/Tax Strategy Group (1999), *Working Paper No.51 on Environmental Tax Policy* (available at Department of Finance website: http://www.irlgov.ie/finance/Publications).

TSG/ Tax Strategy Group (2000), *Working Paper No.25 on Vehicle Registration Tax* (available at Department of Finance website: http://www.irlgov.ie/finance/Publications).

TSG/Tax Strategy Group (2000), *Working Paper No.49 on Environmental Taxation* (available at Department of Finance website: http://www.irlgov.ie/finance/Publications).

Vehmas, J. *et al.* (1999), 'Environmental Taxes on Fuels and Electricity – Some Experiences from Nordic Countries', *Energy Policy*, Vol.27, No.6, pp.343–55.

Instrument Innovation in an Environmental Lead State: 'New' Environmental Policy Instruments in the Netherlands

ANTHONY R. ZITO, LARS BRÜCKNER,
ANDREW JORDAN and RÜDIGER K.W. WURZEL

Introduction

The Netherlands is usually regarded as an environmental 'leader' in the EU [*Liefferink, 1997; Andersen and Liefferink, 1997*]. This study confirms that the Netherlands generally has also led the transition towards the use of NEPIs. It examines the Dutch regulatory evolution and occasional innovation, from the 1970s until the present. Table 1 provides a snapshot of the NEPI usage within the Netherlands. It also offers an impressionistic assessment of its overall rank in the OECD context while specifically comparing its instrument usage to that of a comparative EU environmental pioneer, Germany.

There is some question as to what should constitute a dedicated, substantial environmental tax. If one excludes a number of tax amendments, the number may actually be smaller, more in line with the EEA [*2000*] document than the 25 listed in the CEC [*1999*] database. Interviews conducted in 2003 suggest that six is a closer number in terms of dedicated environmental taxes (that is, introduced not for funding public expenses but rather environmental objectives) in the Netherlands. Nevertheless, policy actors do view excise duties, for instance, on fuels and car ownership, as green taxes [*Heineken, 2002*]. Furthermore, the revenue gathered particularly from the Regulatory Energy Tax represents a significant percentage of the national budget.

The research underpinning this contribution was undertaken for a project entitled 'Innovation in Environmental Governance: A Comparative Analysis of New Environmental Policy Instruments' which was generously funded by the Economic and Social Research Council's (ESRC) Future Governance Programme under grant number L216252013. For more details see: http://www.uea. ac.uk/env/cserge/research/fut_governance/Home.htm.

The high number of covenants (Dutch officials are loathe to use the term 'voluntary agreements' as there is a clear legal obligation behind the agreements) in Table 1 reflects their widespread usage throughout the Dutch economic sector. Although only one dedicated environmental tradable permit scheme is going to come online in 2003 (a Nitrous Oxide trading regime), the Dutch have some previous experience with market permit schemes and are certainly well in advance of most OECD countries. Eco-labels are the main environmental instrument where the Netherlands fall behind the environmental leaders, particularly compared to the German Blue Angel and the Nordic Swan; the Dutch came comparatively late to this economic instrument. Finally, it is worth noting that the traditional command and control system remains in place across all the key policy themes that are the focus of the various Dutch National Environmental Policy Programmes.

The remainder of this paper provides an overview of the instruments. Section II details the traditional features of Dutch environmental policy. Section III explores the analytical reason for NEPI adoption. Section IV provides an overview of the NEPI usage while the final section examines and assesses the overall pattern.

TABLE 1
NEPIs IN THE NETHERLANDS

Type of Instrument	Number	Germany comparison	Overall Assessment of Number
Environmental taxes and charges of [*CEC, 1999; EEA, 2000*] significance	25	19	High, a clear leader particularly in terms budgetary
Tradable permits (Interviews, 2002)	One in environment (as of 2003); 4 in agricultural schemes	0	High, clear leader in this new area
Covenants/voluntary agreements [*interviews, 2002*]	100+	130	High, clear leader in this area
Eco-labels [*Stichting Milieukeur, 2002; Jordan et al., 2002*]	Product number: 90+	3,355	Low, compared to other key OECD labels

Netherlands Environmental Policy

Policy Structures

The Dutch have had a long-standing tradition of using decrees and licencing systems to deal with industrial hazards [*Bressers and Plettenburg, 1997: 113–14*]. In 1972, when the environment became a distinct policy agenda item, the Dutch government published a memorandum detailing the key environmental problems and a number of measures. The government followed this with a number of environmental laws, mainly organised in terms of sectors (for example, water) or particular problems (for example, noise pollution) throughout the 1970s. The acts normally took the form of a government decree issued under the aegis of the entire cabinet [*Liefferink, 1997: 219–20*]. The act provided framework legislation setting out general objectives, issues of responsibility and possible instruments [*Hanf and van de Gronden, 1998: 162–3*]. Actors seeking to conduct activities within the regulated area had to seek licences from the appropriate authorities. These licences were conditional on the actors taking certain measures to mitigate pollution.

Hanf and van de Gronden [*1998: 162–3*] note that this legal framework has evolved over time, with an increased focus on (1) integrating and harmonising the various regulations and license specification; (2) shifting the environmental strategy towards more preventative and sustainable solutions and (3) emphasising the need to handle problems in a cross-sectoral fashion. This process eventually produced the 1993 Environmental Management Act, which simplified the permit system to allow installations to confront the key environmental priorities in one licence [*Bressers and Plettenburg, 1997: 113–4*].

The Dutch system of planning is also important for understanding the framework in which instruments operate. By 1989, the Dutch environmental plans had evolved into large strategic documents involving all levels of government and target groups in society; these documents guide environmental policy, set broader objectives and long-term programme of action to achieve these objectives [*Hanf and van de Gronden 1998: 162–3*].

The Dutch political system traditionally has been geared to building political consensus among various societal groups [*Cohen, 2000*]. This pattern continues today with various groups being incorporated within advisory bodies [*Middendorp, 1991*]. The executive and the ministries are fairly segmented [*van Waarden, 1995: 341*]. The Dutch system has a proportional electoral system that enhances the role of smaller parties and the need to think in terms of inclusive coalitions. The system also spreads responsibilities and power across several layers of government: central, provincial and municipal [*Eberg, 1997*].

At the central level, van Tatenhove [*1993: 20–21, 33*] characterises Dutch environmental policy as reflecting a process of 'fragmented institutionalisation' where roles and powers are located in different organisations; five ministries are involved in the definition of environmental instruments. Given the Dutch tradition of independent ministries, this means that there must be a complex and sometimes costly effort to build consensus through an array of coordinating governmental networks and high level committees as well as struggles to gain influence [*van Tatenhove, 1993; van den Bos, 1991*]. Newly created in 1982, the Ministry for Housing, Physical Planning and the Environment (VROM) initially sought to have a substantial policy impact by promoting a strong regulatory approach [*Giswijt, 1987; van Tatenhove, 1993: 42–5*]. In the 1980s, however it increasingly sought to build a consensus approach with interest groups [*Liefferink, 1997: 223*].

Because of the shift towards using environmental taxes to generate national revenue, the Finance Ministry has a significant role in designing and operating key eco-taxes. Finally the Ministry for Economic Affairs, with its relationships to the business sector and its control of the energy and energy conservation portfolio, shares the responsibility with VROM for integrating environmental policy into economic activities [*Hanf and van de Gronden, 1998: 171*].

While the central government generally has the key role in defining standards and targets, establishing national legislation and regulations and instrument design, provincial and municipal authorities have considerable responsibility for implementing environmental policy [*Weale et al., 2000: 201; Bressers and Plettenburg, 1997: 117*]. The 12 provinces are responsible for implementing national legislation in their territories, for developing environmental policy and water management plans for their territory, for granting licences under the national Environmental Management Act and for helping manage water quality in provincial waters [*Hanf and van de Gronden, 1998: 172*]. The provincial role varies in terms of its scope, depending on the province and the policy sector.

Policy Style

The Dutch history of religious cleavages and support for the interests of farmers and merchants has left its mark on the general political desire to build consensus politics [*van Waarden, 1995: 335–6; Middendorp, 1991*]. The general policy attitude emphasises building consensus with a variety of actors, through consultation and co-operation (which is often established on a formal basis). Particularly significant in environmental terms is the emphasis on planning and trying to encourage self-regulation on the part of private groups [*Weale, 1992: 137*].

At the same time, the government took a relatively interventionist stance towards the environment in the 1970s, but many scholars contend that the increasing orientation towards self-regulation since the 1980s was an important shift away from top-down thinking [*Bressers and Plettenburg, 1997: 116*]. This led to an emphasis on involving actors from the target groups defined by the agricultural, transport, energy and refinery sectors [*Weale et al., 2000: 174–5*].

In terms of the reactive/proactive dimension, Weale *et al.* [*2000*] argue that the Dutch policy style increasingly has become anticipatory as the emphasis on long-term environmental plans involving government and the target group have emerged and evolved in the 1980s and 1990s. This pre-eminence given to planning also suggests the important rationalist nature of the Dutch process.

The Content of Policy

Dutch environmental policy includes a number of guiding policy principles, but it is difficult to say that one is dominant overall. Weale *et al.* [*2000: 171–2*] argue that two key principles operated in traditional regulation: the more significant best practicable means (BPM) and best technical means (BTM). The Dutch policy actors tended not to define these principles in statutes but rather in guidance issues for the water sector [*Faure and Ruegg, 1994: 45*].

With the reforms of the 1993 Environmental Management Act, more prominence was given to another principle in use, the As Low as Reasonably Achievable (ALARA) principle. The Act defines the principle in these terms: 'as far as negative consequences for the environment cannot be prevented by subjecting licenses to conditions, licenses must be subject to conditions which offer the largest protection possible against these consequences unless the request would be unreasonable' [*Faure and Ruegg, 1994: 45–6*].

Another set of principles that have become increasingly important in the development of instruments are the principles of internalisation and target groups in previous sections. It is notable that internalisation requires co-ordination between the various national ministries which have different linkings to the different societal groupings [*van Tatenhove, 1993: 47*]. In the 1980s these concepts were part of an increasing attempt to create new relationships between the state and society, as well as economic actors in a way that fits the Dutch policy style.

As to the types of instruments used, the command and control toolbox of the 1970s, with its framework legislation and licensing, remains a key aspect of Dutch environmental policy. The critical 1989 National Environmental Plan still has the traditional, and more onerous, regulatory procedures at the centre of the document [*Liefferink, 1999: 264*]. Thus the Dutch policy instrument philosophy is a mix of instruments, rather than a complete change. Since the 1980s, other instruments have gained importance, but they have tended to supplement and extend the traditional instruments. Dutch policy actors have shifted away from more 'physical regulation' towards more financial and social regulation. Financial regulation includes subsidies, compensation, deposits, levies and taxes while social regulation refers more to the idea of self regulation, through information, education, environmental reporting and accounting and covenants [*van Tatenhove, 1993: 30–31*].

Why Are NEPIs Being Adopted?

The most important factors include: a philosophical shift concerning the role of the state and the nature of regulation, learning about instruments being used in the environment and other fields, and finally events and directions taken at the EU and the international level. These factors will often interact in any given policy context, but they are examined separately in this section. Of these explanations, the first and the second have been the most critical.

Policy Learning: Shifts in Regulatory Philosophy

The general philosophical approach behind Dutch environmental policy changed substantially in the 1980s although these changes were compatible with the basic characteristics of the Dutch political system (showing the importance of institutions). Several domestic factors external to the environmental policy-making process provided both the opportunity and the spark for change.

By the 1980s, Dutch politics, as in other Northern European countries, was raising basic questions about the government role, particularly in the area of welfare policy [*Lauber, 2000*]. A new government of Christian Democrats (CDA) and Liberals (VVD) came into power in 1982, reflecting these feelings [*Hanf, 1989: 194–6*]. The government platform included the aim of reducing the scope of government responsibility and regulation while increasing that for societal/economic actors.

Simplifying or reducing regulations in all areas would reduce the burden on the overloaded government and increase efficiency. The VVD, which strongly reflected this viewpoint, held the environment portfolio. Pieter Winsemius, became environment minister in 1982, was a high-ranking VVD leader as was his successor, E. Nijpels. They believed that environmental regulations of the time could be burdensome to industry, which also made this case. The government gave a working group of

VROM and Economic Affairs Ministry officials the task of developing concrete proposals for regulatory streamlining [*Hanf, 1989: 197–9*].

Under Winsemius' leadership, the environment ministry pushed the concept of 'internalisation' (those actors who create environmental degradation should be responsible for solving the problems, and their self-regulation would be more efficient than government regulation) [*Weale, 1992: 138–40; Hanf and van de Gronden, 1998: 166*]. The philosophy underpinning this change was more than just a negative focus on reducing governmental regulation; it was a positive attempt to create a more efficient and effective environmental policy by involving more closely the societal actors and their particular interests, including market philosophy [*Liefferink, 1998: 94*]. Some authors [e.g., *Liefferink, 1998: 101; Enevoldsen, 2000*] consider this as evidence of the influence of ecological modernisation, which emphasises the importance of using market dynamics while restructuring the state and the market to reflect ecological values, in the Dutch learning process. External affirmation and momentum for the new Dutch approach came with the Brundtland Report, which enshrined the sustainable development principle [*Liefferink, 1997: 227*]. This shift in thinking is particularly important in understanding the Dutch move towards covenants.

Policy Learning in the Environmental Sector

Another reason that NEPIs appeared was that policy-makers and analysts had learned from previous experience. A critical example was the discovery that taxes could deliver environmental benefits. The Dutch had considerable tax instrument experience, notably the levy contained in the 1969 Surface Water Pollution Act [*Andersen, 1994: 148–9*]. This levy, imposed on both households and industry, did not have an environmental aim. But several policy studies in the late 1970s discovered that the charge was substantially altering business behaviour, leading them to reduce pollution levels. In contrast, other studies in the 1970s suggested that the command and control system had considerable implementation difficulties [*Bressers, 1990; Liefferink, 1997; Andersen, 1994*]. Also significant was the uneven imposition of licences on businesses that made relatively minor contributions, compared to major polluters. A 1985 study found that many Dutch provinces differed widely in prioritising air pollution and lacked the knowledge to assess licence applications properly [*Bressers, 1990: 83*].

Even before the 1982 government coalition came into power, Dutch central government was responding to academic and public criticism about the problems involving the licensing procedures and poor co-ordination between authorities [*Hanf and van de Gronden, 1998: 163*]. However, under Winsemius' leadership, an even greater effort was made to develop a comprehensive approach, based on holistic planning and the defining of sector-transcending environmental issues [*Hanf and van de Gronden, 1998: 165*]. In the 1980s, the Dutch government issued Indicative Multi-Year Plans, with the idea of coordinating environmental regulation and licensing in a way that prevented policy solutions in one policy media from simply transferring the problem to a different media [*Weale, 1992; Liefferink, 1999*]. The policies focused on specific sources of pollution, the target groups (for example, consumers, industry, farmers, etc.), for which particular policy packages would be developed. In order to fulfil the internalisation principle, policy designers would consult with the target groups and involve them in the policy formulation [*van Vliet, 1994: 42*].

External Influences and Pressures

Dutch officials learned from the experiences and instruments being used in other countries, usually in Northern Europe. Cases of wholesale borrowing are rare although the current VROM officials' examination of the Swedish concept of Environmental Zones for Trucks and Bases to regulate air emissions seems to be one such example (Communication , VROM official, 24 April 2002). While the European Union is less likely to generate 'new' instruments for a 'leader state' like the Netherlands, it also can constrain Dutch developments as the EU seeks to maintain its other objectives of protecting the Common Market from perceived trade barriers. The Dutch commitments to EU goals may force the instrumentation issues; the prime example of this is the Kyoto Agreement, which forced a serious examination of tradable permit systems. At the same time, the inability of the EU to decide on common instruments may also affect Dutch policy-making.

NEPIs in the Netherlands

Market-Based Instruments

Eco-taxes and levies: As shown by the discussion of the surface water levy in the previous section on policy learning, economic instruments have provided a useful element in resource conservation and maintenance in the Netherlands since the 1970s. The levy was also vital in provoking instrument learning by the 1980s. However, in the 1970s, the Dutch government created a number of other charges to generate revenue for protection of environmental resources. It is difficult to tell how much these other charges were modelled on the surface water levy although it is arguable that the levy was a relatively straightforward tool that the ministries could develop without too much innovation and policy borrowing.

Any aspects of learning were restricted to the instrumental level, as policy-makers focused on improving the implementation of regulation. In the 1970s, all of the Dutch economic instruments tended to take the form of fixed charge levies to collect revenue to pay for public services. The Netherlands and France were the European countries that applied this instrument the most widely [*OECD, 1980: 62, 91*].

The preference of fiscal charges over other forms of environmental taxation continued to dominate the Dutch policy approach in the 1980s. In 1987, the government targeted the use of manure with the creation of the Manure Act. The Act presented a number of strict prescriptions but also imposed a levy in order to finance research and environmental adjustments in the individual farms [*Dietz and Termeer, 1991: 128–31*].

Despite the economic sector's preference for charges as taxation instruments, the government imposed an environmental tax on all fuels in 1988 [*VROM, 1992: 6–9*]. It basic goal was to replace the system of individual, programme-specific levies. By 1984 there were seven levies in force with the possibility of twice that number being created to raise revenue for the sector-specific acts.

Several administrative factors combined with the changes in the national philosophy to motivate this change [Interview with VROM officials, 1993; *VROM, 1992: 7–9; Vermeend and van de Vaarten, 1998: 17*]. First, the fuel tax fulfilled the goal of integrating the fragmented policy areas and creating an integrated system of financing. Second, there was the desire to build more transparency (for the sake of the taxpayers) and simplicity (increasing administrative efficiency) in the mechanism. The current system was seen as being too complicated; the last levy enacted, a charge on industrial noise, was so complicated that its operating costs for both the government and industry exceeded the revenue generated [*Vermeend and van de Vaarten, 1998: 17; Snel, 2000*]. Several Government Memoranda prior to 1988 suggested the need for a simpler system.

The government chose fuels because it wished to change polluter behaviour in key areas of air pollution and noise nuisance. Significantly, the fuel tax, administered by VROM, was set at a modest rate, with the revenue earmarked for financing certain environment-related government expenditures. Thus, the fund-raising objectives of the levy remained the instrument's basic focus. This suggests an instrumental learning within a stable policy outlook concerning the tax's goal; the changes in regulatory philosophy also provided an impetus and a rationale for this change. Nor were all individual charges abandoned as the aircraft noise pollution charge remains [*Commission of the EU, 2000a; OECD, 1993*]. At the same time, the Dutch have a system of excise taxes on fuel and taxes on automobiles that can serve environmental purposes although, in the case of the car tax, for example, its green objective has been fairly indirect and implicit [*Vermeend and van der Vaarten, 1998: 77*].

In the 1990s there was a surge in policy interest in environmental taxation, with the new 1989 coalition between the Christian Democrats and the Social Democrats. During this period there was also some concern, which was expressed in the National Environmental Plan, about the state of the environment and carbon dioxide emissions. One of the new coalition's new positions was to increase environment expenditure, which would be financed by environmentally linked charges and taxes. The question of how to pay for the environmental objectives of the 1989 NEPP had been a significant issue in the debate over the Plan. There was a substantial increase in interest in alternative environmental policy instruments in the OECD and other international organisations; of greater importance to the Netherlands was the increased interest shown by the European Commission post 1992. This did not affect the Dutch adoption of taxation instruments directly (interviews, VROM official, 1993; Ministry of Finance official, 2001), but arguably it created conditions that lubricated the national discussion. Interestingly, the new regulatory tax adopted the price level for oil found in the Commission proposal [*Heineken, 2002*].

A more direct influence was the Commission attempt to prevent Dutch from lowering the VAT rate on electricity produced from renewable energy sources [*The Green Tax Commission, 1998*]. Here the EU is a further institutional constraint on Dutch instrument selection. In a more indirect fashion, the inability of the EU to agree on an EU wide tax raises concerns about overburdening Dutch industry and reducing its competitiveness [*Snel, 2000*].

Turning from the influences towards what was accomplished, Vermeend and van der Vaart [*1998: 4–5*] suggest that the tax introduced in the 1988–98 period did not result from a 'planned, systematic green tax reform'. Rather different elements, based on different rationales, developed at different times to give an overall pattern of incremental, pragmatic change. The fact that other Scandinavian countries, particularly Denmark, were experimenting with (rather different) environmental taxes may have given some rhetorical momentum to domestic reforms. The Dutch government, concerned with the economic difficulties of the 1980s and early 1990s, had taken an interest in utilising the revenues collected from an energy tax to lower the tax on labour; the idea of boosting employment and environment was seen as 'the double-edged sword' or more notably the 'double dividend' [*Heineken, 2002*].

After significant discussion, the Dutch Parliament agreed to several modifications of the 1988 fuel charge/levy.

The elections of 1994 saw the exit of the CDA, and the entrance of the VVD, the Social Democrats and Democrats 66. A majority in the 'Purple

Coalition I' supported the idea of an energy tax if a European version was not forthcoming by 1996 [*Heineken, 2002*]. One plank of the coalition agreement was to introduce a regulatory energy tax on the small usage of gas and electricity [*Vermeend and van der Vaart, 1998: 23–7*]. The new tax, which entered into force in 1996, was aimed at reducing carbon dioxide emissions from small users while maintaining the competitive position of the large industrial users (whose environmental behaviour was altered by the fuel tax). In doing so, the small user tax enabled the regulatory system to modify the behaviour of actors that could not be reached through the voluntary agreements. It was also the first Dutch environmental tax to have its revenue hypothecated to reduce other taxes, such as income tax.

The second Purple Coalition, formed by the same parties after the 1998 election, incorporated the Commission recommendations in their new government agreement. In preparation for the 2002 election, this government instigated a Second Green Tax Commission. This Commission issued a report that recommended the broadening of the tradable permit schemes and some new types of taxes (interviews, VROM officials, 2002).

Tradable permits: The Netherlands has been a clear European front runner in the area of tradable permits. While the United States has played a considerable role in pioneering this instrument in the environment sector, the Dutch agricultural policy actors showed a strong willingness to experiment with these instruments in four sectors (interview, Floor Brouwer, 2002). The most notable were the milk and manure systems. In the manure case, the 1987 Manure Act established the idea of free production rights, which can be seen as a version of tradable permits, allowing each farm certain rights to produce more manure than the government standard.

International influences have also shaped Dutch policy learning. The Kyoto Agreement has raised the instrument on the international agenda in a way that no country can ignore; furthermore it has led the Dutch government to accept reduction targets that will be difficult to achieve with the current tools while also protecting the competitiveness of Dutch export industries (interview, VROM official, 2002).

Whatever the likelihood of transnational systems being imposed on the Netherlands, certainly the international discussion of climate change has raised the Dutch level of interest about its environmental applicability (interviews, VROM officials, 2000). Dutch and other commentators viewed the US experimentation as a success worth investigating [*Grubb with Vrolijk and Brack, 1999: 90*]. Dutch officials have also monitored developments in the UK and Germany (interviews, Ministry of Economic Affairs officials, 2000, 2002).

Nevertheless, the Netherlands has maintained a theoretical interest in the instrument for some time, even before Kyoto. Even if the Kyoto agreement had never happened, there is strong evidence that the Netherlands would have experimented with tradable permits. In 1983, the Dutch government and industry sent a delegation to the United States to examine instruments there; this delegation came back with the idea of creating 'plant bubbles' for sulphur dioxide and nitrous oxide emissions from combustion plants [*Dekkers, 1999: 109–10*].

In 1990, the national government, together with the provinces and municipalities, agreed a covenant with the Electricity Board. This covenant allowed existing plants to be covered in a cost optimisation scheme that resembles emissions trading. In 1995, VROM decided to re-examine the means for restricting nitrous oxide and sulphur dioxide emissions. Throughout the year, government representatives explored various possibilities with industry, including tradable permits. Indeed it was industry, particularly the chemical industry, that decided to push the idea of a nitrous oxide system. The industrial discussions generated a study, published in 1997, which came to the main conclusion that major savings in the nitrous oxide emissions were possible with a tradable permit scheme [*Dekkers, 1999: 112–19*]. VROM officials thought that the scheme was a good idea because it would enable the Dutch policy process to gain some experience of how to operate such a system for environment purposes as well as to achieve acidification objectives (interview, VROM official, 2002). Since then the policy actors have produced the basic design in 2000, VROM and the Economics ministries then worked in detail with industry, particularly led by the VNO-NCW. The system will go into effect in 2003.

The NOx system is not an isolated Dutch effort to explore tradable permit schemes. Concerns about global warming and the serious impact of Dutch CO_2 reduction commitments led the Economics and Environment Ministers in the Purple Coalition II to create a CO_2 Trading Commission to study the problem of CO_2 and devise options for tradable permits. This coalition, which published its findings in February 2002, was composed of various stakeholders including industry and NGO representatives to formulate proposals to control CO_2 emissions in a trading system. The VROM officials pushed the idea of a CO_2 system forward, meeting initial reluctance from the Economics and Finance Ministries (Interviews, VROM, Finance Ministry and Economics Ministry officials, 2002). The Economics Ministry has become more persuaded as to the economic benefits for industry if flexibility is used in targets for the vulnerable large industries. Although this Commission was quite successful in helping push forward Dutch national thinking about tradable permits, especially with respect to

CO_2 emissions, the EU process and the Commission thinking have overtaken their recommendations. The Dutch Commission recommendations differed substantially from the European Commission proposals (or at least the suggested implications of the European Commission wording) on a number of points, such as the use of caps (*ENDS Daily*, 'Dutch CO_2 Trading System Proposed', 5 Feb. 2002). Despite these differences, the Dutch Commission and ministries have decided that it would be far more advantageous for the Netherlands to conform to and participate in a Europe wide system than to create a system only applicable in the Netherlands (Interviews, Economics Ministry and VROM officials, 2002). Nevertheless, the Dutch actors are continuing to develop a Dutch version of this instrument, with the intention that it acts as an interim instrument in case the EU project is substantially delayed or even abandoned.

Voluntary Agreements

The term 'voluntary' is intentionally highlighted in quotation marks because it does not capture the binding nature of the Dutch instruments. The Dutch use the term 'covenants' to describe their environmental agreements and it takes a stronger meaning in the Dutch context. An environmental covenant occurs when at least two parties, which usually include a government agency and a representative of an industrial sector, reach an agreement on the realisation of environmental targets [*Glasbergen, 1998: 133*]. A critical factor in these agreements is the continued presence and influence of the more traditional command and control option; covenants remain linked to the licensing system [*Börkey and Lévêque, 1998: 13*].

The origin and rapid growth of environmental agreements, or covenants, comes in the 1980s as the CDA and VVD government and VROM (under Winsemius' leadership) pushed the idea of self-regulation and internalisation as being more efficient than the sole reliance on traditional instruments. The extensive use of covenants was one of the major Dutch policy instrument innovations of the late 1980s. Voluntary agreements dovetailed with the policy philosophy shift of the 1980s, and also fitted well with both characteristic Dutch interest group patterns (see above) and the relatively open, consensus-building style of policy-making.

The first extensive attempt at developing an agreement between the government and industry came in 1986; the overall environmental issue, viewed as a test case for covenants, was the attempt to reduce the emissions of volatile organic compounds by over 50 per cent [*van Vliet, 1993: 114–15*]. In the course of discussions undertaken between 1985 and 1988, a working group of central and local authority officials met with industry representatives.

In contrast to this agreement with its comparatively far-reaching sectoral scope, the government agreed a number of these covenants with a company or particular type of industry concerning a specific substance/product, for example, an agreement with soap manufacturers concerning detergent phosphates, aerosol manufacturers concerning CFCs in spray canisters and bottlers on cadmium use. In the area of packaging waste, the government agreed a 1985 covenant with industry to stimulate recycling and decrease drinks packaging; in 1987, a covenant was reached to boost recycling and develop a deposit-refund system for certain refillable bottles [*Lauber and Ingram, 2000: 129*]. In general, most actors perceived the 1980s agreements, which could really be seen as fairly *ad hoc* gentlemen's agreements, as having considerable scope for improvement, in terms of defining strategies and responsibilities [*Glasbergen, 1998: 134–6; ELNI, 1999*]. Glasbergen [*1998: 135–6*] suggests that much of this development was an *ad hoc* process, with a strong symbolic content, intended to get industry to make further voluntary efforts to reduce pollution.

The 1990s saw a tremendous growth in covenants. The mainly product-related agreements signed before 1990 remain as do covenants involving single issues and single actors, such as the agreement on sulphur dioxide and nitrous oxides with power companies and agreements with oil companies concerning soil sanitation at gas stations [*Glasbergen, 1998: 137*]. However, there has been a rise in the number of cross-sector agreements resembling the VOCs agreement of 1996. The national environmental plans, with their integrative focus and target group strategies, provided some impetus for covenants to become 'multiple-issue and composite-actor' [*Glasbergen, 1998: 146*]. This evolution suggests some learning has occurred on the part of government authorities as well as business, on an instrumental level. Increasingly the agreements are held to be binding, in that the parties that sign the agreement enter a contract under private law although the wording of the contract may vary widely [*Öko-Institut e.V., 1998: 36*].

One of the most noted forms of agreements was the Environment and Industry Target Group Policy, created by VROM to translate national objectives into specific emission reductions by various industrial sectors. So far these agreements have been reached with the graphics industry in 1990 and 1993, the wood conservation industry in 1992, the primary metals industry in 1992, the chemical industry in 1993, the printing industry in 1993, the diary industry in 1994, the metals and electronics industry in 1995, the oil and gas extraction industry in 1995, the textile and carpet industry in 1995 and the paper and cardboard industry in 1996 [*de Hoog, 1998; VNO-NCW, 1999: 16*].

Looking at the sectoral scope of covenants various sectors, there are agreements on waste management, water pollution, energy/climate, health protection, air pollution, soil pollution, ozone depletion, timber as well as the multi-issue agreements; the main economic sectors include agriculture, hunting and fisheries, food and drinks manufacturers, tobacco manufacturers, industries manufacturing rubber and plastic products, the chemical industry, transport, storage and communication [*ELNI, 1999; EEA, 1997*].

The energy sector is an important example. By 1989, the Ministry of Economic Affairs had pushed the idea of covenants in promoting energy efficiency; avoiding regulatory burdens on the energy industries was a clear priority [*Öko-Institut e.V., 1998: 35*]. The initial talks involved the chemical industry, and served as a model for future energy efficiency discussions [*Enevoldsen, 2000: 73*]. This has led to the creation of Long Term Agreements (LTAs) with nearly 30 different industrial branch organisations (including base metals, building materials, chemical, light industry, food and drinks sectors and other industries) representing major consumers of energy [*Ministry of Economic Affairs, 1999: 7*]. The LTAS are focused generally on inducing a broad movement towards particular target ranges, where each party signs a Declaration of Intent, which is not covered under civil law [*Rietbergen, Breukels and Blok, 1999*]. Once the parties sign, the Ministry of Economic Affairs and the energy supervisory body NOVEM draw up an agreement with industry to create a Long Term Agreement, which sets out targets for the sector and establishes a monitoring system [*VNO-NCW, 1999: 18*].

Eco-labels

It is striking that, while tax instruments as significant policy instruments appeared in the 1970s and covenants in the 1980s, the Dutch only set up a national eco-label scheme in 1992. The fact that the Dutch economy is both small and open to international forces may have given Dutch actors less incentive to create a scheme. The different outlooks of VVD leaders who were in charge of the VROM in the 1980s help to explain both the initial reluctance and the later change of thinking. In 1989 eco-labels presented the government with a chance to do something more in the way of green instruments than was already being done. Dutch environmental groups also pushed for the creation of the national label (interview, VROM official, 2001) The Parliament pushed for this move, pressing the idea of a scheme to be included in the 1989 NEPP.

The Dutch eco-labels scheme is voluntary and organised under private law. The key policy actors are VROM and the foundation created to operate the system, the Stichting Milieukeur. The various societal actors all have a place in the foundation's committee structure. Although the Dutch model was quite late, it did not seem to be modelled on any other national eco-label. Nevertheless the policy actors took into account the existing criteria found in the EU eco-label and national labels, such as the German Blue Angel, after the Dutch label had become operational (Interview, VROM official, 2001; Communication, Stichting Milieukeur official, 2002). The Dutch model emphasises Life Cycle analysis. The Dutch have made some innovative moves, such as developing in 1995 criteria for foodstuffs, which was found to have public interest in a survey, and also reflect the importance of Dutch food and flower exports [*Jordan et al, 2002;* Communication with Stichting Milieukeur official, 2002].

Compared to other national labels such as the Blue Angel, the Dutch scheme has not seen a large adoption rate. This reflects the lack of interest on both the producer side and the consumer side. Bigger companies, which play a significant role in the Dutch export-oriented economy, are not attracted to the idea of individual labels when they are trying to develop brand marketing (interview, VROM official, 2002). Only niche firms with less known brands see a significant incentive to participate. And so the market share is relatively small. This feeds into the lack of awareness among consumers, with surveys finding that only roughly 30 per cent of Dutch inhabitants know about the national label (Interview, VROM official, 2002). The lack of a critical mass of products creates a vicious circle: companies have less incentive as consumer show little interest and enthusiasm. VROM remains supportive of the label as being one of a mix of tools, however, believing that the criteria established in the individual product labels will have an impact on non-participating firms. Nevertheless, the Milieukeur lacks the strong pushers, beyond the Environment Ministry, to have a dramatic impact.

Other Instruments

The Dutch system contains a number of instruments not included in the categories listed above. These tools had a significant presence even in the 1970s. This reinforces the notion of a Dutch instrument mix and having more than one instrument for any given environmental problem. For instance, in the 1970s the Dutch government started to develop information about energy saving to send to the private sector. This effort is a communicative instrument, that is, a policy tool that shapes the target group's behaviour by providing particular information [*Bressers, 1991: 86*]. In the energy sector, the government also instituted an investment grant scheme. This scheme provided subsidies and a system of soft loans as an incentive for industry to make investments in various energy-saving processes [*Bressers, 1991: 89–90*].

Although environmental taxation has received the strongest interest from both environmental policy actors and academics, the Netherlands has expanded the use of other financial instruments over the last decades. These measures include the modifying an old instrument of reimbursing employees for public transportation costs, incentives for companies to provide bicycles for employees, a carpool bonus, reimbursing the costs of computers for employees working at home, the free depreciation of environmental investments and energy premiums for environment friendly household appliances [*Vermeend and van der Vaart, 1998: 48–60; Snel, 2000*].

One particularly notable financial instrument was the creation of the Green Fund System (GFS) in 1992 [*van Bellegem, 2000*]. This scheme was the outcome of discussions between the government and the financial sector. The government's ambition was to promote new economic activities that demand high capital investment, for example, renewable energy projects, and so on. The system is based on an incentive scheme incorporated into the income tax paid by individuals. The income generated by investing in the Green Fund System projects is not subject to income tax, and entrepreneurs realise a lower interest rate for their investment. The GFS system operates as a soft loan system for green projects, and involves various stakeholders [*van Bellegem, 2000; Vermeend and van der Vaart, 1998: 60–61*].

Conclusion

From 1970–2000, the overall pattern of Dutch instrument selection is one that has kept numerous elements while changing certain fundamental perspectives. If we try to isolate patterns of learning in the three decades, we find a number of incremental changes at the instrumental level and one major philosophical shift. In the 1970s we see the public authorities learning more about command and control legislation and its implementation problems. The solution of using charges to gather revenue for regulation was considered as a serious policy option. In this decade, learning occurred largely at the instrumental level.

The 1980s witness a dramatic change in policy philosophy on two key fronts: the idea of bringing the private sector into the regulatory process and the integration of pollution abatement across environmental sectors. Several external forces combined to trigger this change: the economic difficulties of the 1970s, public reaction and dissatisfaction about the role of government, the political response of deregulation, and the election of coalition partners intent on enhancing both the economy and the environment while shifting the responsibilities of the actors involved. The philosophical change that did occur in environmental strategy is clear, but did this occur as a result of a particular set of beliefs we can isolate? Certainly there are distinct visions of how the world works visible, especially the questioning of the role of the state in society and the relationship of ecology and the market. Does the policy change suggest the influence of ecological modernisation? Mol [*1996, 313–14*] notes three key attributes to this approach: modern science and technology as central to ecological reform, the importance of economic and market dynamics in ecological reform, and the desire to amend the role of the state in environmental reform.

Certainly all three values are very strongly represented in the thinking of Winsemius and other policy actors during this time although they are translated into the Dutch institutional model. But there seems to be a larger, looser frame shift that incorporates the tenets of ecological modernisation as well as other points left out, particularly the issue of a holistic, cross-sector approach. Jachtenfuchs [*1996*] suggests the idea of a sustainability 'frame' (a set of beliefs) towards the environment. This seems better to encompass the holistic principles of both integrating policy sectors and internalising environmental problems [*Lenschow and Zito, 1998*].

Would the learning about sustainability and internalisation have occurred without the major external changes? Most actors had noted the flaws in the environmental legislation by 1980, so arguably it would have occurred in a much more slow, shallow and disorganised fashion. Nevertheless, the Dutch subsystem actors were beginning to consider larger issues of planning and the need to incorporate society actors in a more effective manner.

In terms of changes to the policy instruments, the change of beliefs did make the selection of voluntary agreements a strong option. The instrument also fits well with the structure, style and content of traditional Dutch environmental policy-making system (with its fragmented responsibilities) and the strong organisation of employer associations. The changes in fiscal instruments suggest that the major philosophical shift did not lead to a surge of taxation instruments. Voluntary instruments seemed to fit better with the Dutch consensual model of policy-making that decision-makers were trying to enshrine in the 1980s. The changes that did occur in the taxation system tended to be instrumental: for example, the confusing levy system was simplified as a result of analysing the old systems. The philosophical shift of the 1980s added new instruments but it also kept older alternatives, even if their usage and role has changed.

In the 1990s, there seems to be a considerable policy learning at the instrumental level about environmental taxation (culminating in the 1996 small user tax) and covenants; these instruments are more complex and nuanced in how they motivate actors and in their target objectives. The shift from levies to environmental taxes was propelled by domestic learning about improving the efficacy of the instruments and by the political necessity of protecting tax revenue. In contrast, the broader principle of tradable permits seems to have been stimulated by discussions and actions outside the Netherlands. Nevertheless, the ideas and schemes that the Dutch have generated have mainly reflected Dutch thinking.

The overall policy picture that emerges is that the Dutch have always tended to experiment with different instruments in order to protect the environment, but the instruments included in this policy mix or toolbox have increased in number and diversity, as well as policy design sophistication sice the 1970s. Crucially, the command and control system of licensing has not disappeared in favour of NEPIs. Instead the way these regulations are designed and how they link to other instruments has changed. Regulation no longer dominates the Dutch policy design, but is quite often linked to the voluntary agreements (sometimes implicitly through government threats of regulation). Other instruments have become more pervasive and more important, particularly the various forms of negotiated and voluntary agreements. Dutch policy actors unanimously reject the idea of one instrument being better than the others; rather they prefer a mixture of instruments to be tailored to the particular context.

REFERENCES

Andersen, Mikael Skou (1994), *Governance by Green Taxes: Making Pollution Prevention Pay*, Manchester: Manchester University Press.
Andersen, Mikael Skou and Duncan Liefferink (1997), 'Introduction: the Impact of the Pioneers on EU Environmental Policy', in M.K. Andersen and D. Liefferink (eds.), *European Environmental Policy: the Pioneers*, Manchester: Manchester University Press, pp.1–39.
Anderson, M.K and D. Liefferink (eds.) (1997), *European Environmental Policy: The Pioneers*, Manchester: Manchester University Press.
Börkey, Peter and Lévêque Francois (1998), *Voluntary Approaches for Environmental Protection in the European Union*, Paris: OECD.
Bressers, Hans (1990), 'Environmental Policy Instruments in Dutch Practice,' in *European Parliament DG for Research, Economic and Fiscal Incentives as a Means of Achieving Environmental Policy Objectives*, No.16, Luxembourg: EP, pp.79–96.
Bressers, Hans (1993), 'A Comparison of the Effectiveness of Incentives and Directives: The Case of Dutch Water Quality Policy', paper presented at the Conference 'An International Comparison of Achievements in Environmental Protection,' Berlin, 8–10 Jan.
Bressers, Hans and Loret Plettenburg (1997), 'The Netherlands', in M. Jänicke and H. Weidner (eds.), *National Environmental Policies: A Comparative Study of Capacity-building*, Berlin: Springer, pp.109–31.
Cohen, Maurie (2000), 'Ecological Modernisation, Environmental Knowledge and National Character: A Preliminary Analysis of the Netherlands', *Environmental Politics*, Vol.9, No.1, pp.77–106.

CEC (Commission of the EC) (1999), *Databases on Environmental Taxes in the European Union Member States, plus Norway and Switzerland. Evaluation of Environmental Affects of Environmental Taxes*, Luxembourg: Office for Official Publications.

CEC (2000a), *Database on Environmental Taxes in the European Union Member States, plus Norway and Switzerland*, Luxembourg: Office for Official Publications.

CEC (2000b), *Green Paper on Greenhouse Gas Emissions Trading within the European Union*, COM(2000) 87 final, Brussels: CEC.

de Boo, A.J. (1991), 'Financing the Environment: The Netherlands', in DocTer, *European Environmental Yearbook*, London: International Institute for Environmental Studies, 240–41.

de Hoog, Maarten (1998), 'Environmental Agreements in the Netherlands: Sharing the Responsibility for Sustainable Industrial Development', *UNEP Industry and Environment*, Jan.–June, pp.27–30.

Dekkers, Chris (1999), 'Trading Emissions and Other Economic Instruments to Reduce NOx in the Netherlands', in S. Sorrell and S. Skea (eds.), *Pollution for Sale: Emissions Trading and Joint Implementation*, Cheltenham: Edward Elgar, pp.109–23.

Dietz, Frank and Katrien Termeer (1991), 'Dutch Manure Policy: The Lack of Economic Instruments', in D. Kraan and R. in' tVeld (eds.), *Environmental Protection: Public or Private Choice*, Dordrecht: Kluwer, pp.123–47.

The Green Tax Commission (1998), *A Summary of its Three Reports 1995–1997*, The Hague.

Eberg, Jan (1997), *Waste Policy and Learning*, Delft: Eburon.

EEA (European Environmental Agency) (1997), *Environmental Agreements, Environmental Effectiveness*, Copenhagen: EEA.

EEA (2000), *Environmental Taxes: Recent Developments in Tools for Integration*, Copenhagen: EEA.

ELNI (Environmental Law Network International) (1999), *Environmental Agreements: The Role and Effect of Environmental Agreements in Environmental Policies*, London: Cameron May.

Enevoldsen, Martin (2000), 'Industrial Energy Efficiency', in A. Mol, V. Lauber and D. Liefferink (eds.), *The Voluntary Approach to Environmental Policy*, Oxford: Oxford University Press, pp.62–103.

Faure, Michael and Marieke Ruegg (1994), 'Environmental Standard Setting through General Principles of Environmental Law', in M. Faure, J. Vervaele and A. Weale (eds.), *Environmental Standards in the European Union in an Interdisciplinary Framework*, Antwerp: Maklu, pp.39–60.

Giswijt, August (1987), 'The Kingdom of the Netherlands', in G. Enyedi, A. Gijswijt and B. Rhode (eds.), *Environmental Policies in East and West*, London: Taylor Graham, pp.267–89.

Glasbergen, Pieter (1998), 'Partnership as a Learning Process. Environmental Covenants in the Netherlands', in P. Glasbergen (ed.), *Co-operative Environmental Governance*, Dordrecht: Kluwer Academic, pp.133–56.

Grubb, Michael with Christiaan Vrolijk and Duncan Brack (1999), *The Kyoto Protocol: A Guide and Assessment*, London: Royal Institute of International Affairs.

Hanf, Kenneth (1989), 'Deregulation as Regulatory Reform: The Case of Environmental Policy in the Netherlands', *European Journal of Political Research*, Vol.17, pp.193–207.

Hanf, Kenneth and Egbert van de Gronden (1998), 'The Netherlands: Joint Regulation and Sustainable Development', in K. Hanf and A. Jansen (eds.), *Governance and Environment in Western Europe: Politics, Policy and Administration*, Harlow: Longman, pp.152–80.

Heineken, Kees (2002), 'The History of the Dutch Regulatory Energy Tax', paper presented at the Third Annual Global Conference on Environmental Taxation, Woodstock, VT, USA, April 12–13.

Jachtenfuchs, Markus (1996), *International Policy-Making as a Learning Process? The*

European Union and the Greenhouse Effect, Aldershot: Avebury.

Jordan, Andrew, Wurzel, Rüdiger, Zito, Anthony R. and Lars Brückner (2002 forthcoming), 'Consumer Responsibility-Taking and Eco-Labeling Schemes in Europe', in M. Micheletti, A. Føllesdal and D. Stolle (eds.), *The Politics Behind Products: Using the Market as a Site for Ethics and Action*, New Brunswick, NJ: Transaction Press.

Lauber, Volkmar (2000), 'The Political and Institutional Setting', in Mol, Lauber and Liefferink [*2000: 32–61*].

Lauber, Volkmar and Verina Ingram (2000), 'Packaging Waste', in Mol, Lauber and Liefferink [*2000: 104–55*].

Lenschow, Andrea and Anthony Zito (1998), 'Blurring or Shifting of Policy Frames? Institutionalization of the Economic-Environmental Policy Linkage in the European Community', *Governance*, Vol.11, No.4, pp. 415–41.

Liefferink, Duncan (1997), 'The Netherlands: A Net Exporter of Environmental Policy Concepts', in Andersen and Liefferink [*1997: 210–50*].

Liefferink, Duncan (1998), 'New Environmental Policy Instruments in the Netherlands', in J. Golub (ed.), *New Instruments for Environmental Policy in the EU*, London: Routledge, pp. 86–106.

Liefferink, Duncan (1999), 'The Dutch National Plan for Sustainable Society', in N. Vig and R. Axelrod (eds.), *The Global Environment: Institutions, Law, and Policy*, London: Earthscan, pp.256–78.

Middendorp, C. (1991), *Ideology in Dutch Politics: The Democratic System Reconsidered, 1970–1985*, Assen/Maastricht: Van Gorcum.

Ministry of Economic Affairs (1999), *Long Term Agreement on Energy-Efficiency. Progress in 1998*, The Hague: Ministry of Economic Affairs.

Mol, Arthur (1996), 'Ecological Modernisation and Institutional Reflexifity: Environmental Reform in the Late Modern Age', *Environmental Politics*, Vol.5, No.2, 302–23.

Mol, A., Lauber, V. and D. Liefferink (eds.) (2000), *The Voluntary Approach to Environmental Policy*, Oxford: Oxford University Press.

OECD (1980), *Pollution Charges in Practice*, Paris: OECD.

OECD (1993), *Taxation and the Environment: Complimentary Policies*, Paris: OECD.

Öko-Institut e.V. (1998), *New Instruments for Sustainability – The New Contribution of Voluntary Agreements to Environmental Policy. Final Report*, Frieburg: Öko-Institut e.V.

Rietbergen, Martijn, Breukels, Maaike and Kornelis Blok (1999), *Voluntary Agreements – Implementation and Efficiency. The Netherlands' Country Study – Case Studies in the Sectors of Paper and Glass Manufacturing*, Utrecht: University of Utrecht.

Snel, Menno (2000), 'Green Tax Reforms: The Dutch Experience', paper presented at the Symposium on 'Green Fiscal Reforms in Europe', Paris, 10–11 Oct.

Stichting Milieukeur (2002), 'Certification Outlines,' http://www.milieukeur.nl/english/certification.php,3 June.

van Bellegem, Theo (2000), 'Green Fund System in the Netherlands', preprint, The Hague.

van den Bos, Jan (1991), *Dutch EC Policy-Making: A Model Guided Approach to Coordination and Negotiation*, Amsterdam: Thesis Publishers.

Van Tatenhove, Jan (1993), *Beleidsvoeringsprocessen in het Nederlandse Milieubeleid in de Periode 1970–1990*, Wageningen: Agricultural University.

van Vliet, Martijn (1993), 'Environmental Regulation of Business: Options and Constraints for Communicative Governance', in J. Kooiman (ed.), *Modern Governance*, London: Sage, pp.105–18.

van Vliet, Martijn (1994), 'Controlling VOCs by Government- Industry Consensus', *Greener Management International*, Vol. 6, April, pp.41–8.

van Waarden, Frans (1995), 'Persistence of National Policy Styles: A Study of their Institutional Foundations', in B. Ungerer and F. van Waarden (eds.), *Convergence or Diversity? Internationalization and Economic Policy Response*, Aldershot: Avebury, pp. 333–72.

Vermeend, Willem and Jacob van der Vaart (1998), *Greening Taxes: the Dutch Model*, Deventer: Kluwer.

VNO-NCW (The Confederation of Netherlands Industry and Employers) (1999), *Environmental Agreements in the Netherlands*, The Hague: VNO-NCW.

VROM (1992), *The Netherlands's Environmental Tax on Fuels: Questions and Answers*, The Hague: VROM.

Weale, Albert (1992), *The New Politics of Pollution*, Manchester: Manchester University Press.

Weale, Albert, Pridham, Geoffrey, Cini, Michelle, Konstadakopulos, Dimitrios, Porter, Martin and Brendan Flynn (2000), *Environmental Governance in Europe: An Ever Closer Ecological Union?* Oxford: Oxford University Press.

Policy Innovation or 'Muddling Through'? 'New' Environmental Policy Instruments in the United Kingdom

ANDREW JORDAN, RÜDIGER K.W. WURZEL,
ANTHONY R. ZITO and LARS BRÜCKNER

Introduction

The United Kingdom (UK) began to experiment with voluntary agreements (VAs) and market-based instruments (MBIs) much later than the so-called 'leader' states of the EU such as The Netherlands and Denmark. It was even slower than 'high' regulatory states such as Germany and those with a comparable environmental record such as France. This is not to say that the UK has not contributed to the debate about their use. On the contrary, British environmental economists such as David Pearce have been at the very forefront of academic discussions. The UK has also played an important part in encouraging the OECD to take an active interest in their adoption and assessment.

This delayed uptake can be traced back to a number of institutional factors: the UK's comparatively long legacy of regulation, which dates back to the mid-nineteenth century; the background of most civil servants and other policy elites (generally scientists, lawyers and so on, rather than economists); and the strong belief in the ability of regulation, if properly fine tuned, to resolve most domestic environmental problems. Political interest in environmental issues more generally, which remained at a low level throughout much of the 1980s, was not strong enough to kick-start innovation, be it with regulation or any other environmental policy instrument.

The deployment of 'new' environmental policy instruments (NEPIs) grew significantly in the 1990s, to the extent that the UK is now a world

The research underpinning this contribution was undertaken for a project entitled 'Innovation in Environmental Governance: A Comparative Analysis of New Environmental Policy Instruments' which was generously funded by the Economic and Social Research Council's (ESRC) Future Governance Programme under grant number L216252013. For more details see: http://www.uea.ac.uk/env/cserge/research/fut_governance/Home.htm.

leader in designing emissions trading schemes and other complex instrument packages that fit together different types of NEPI. None the less, the UK still has comparatively fewer VAs agreements than the norm in the EU and is much less enthusiastic about eco-labels than countries such as Sweden and Germany. The aim of this contribution is to assess how far the NEPIs adopted in the UK are genuinely 'new' as compared with pre-existing institutional forms and policy instrument types. The findings suggest that the UK's institutional setting has restricted and strongly conditioned the development and functioning of VAs. Until relatively recently, the same could be said of MBIs, but the arrival of tradable permits, complex policy packages and various other eco-taxes is indicative of a pattern of genuine innovation, which departs significantly from past practices.

The second section briefly describes the pre-existing structures, style and content of UK environmental policy, paying particular attention to the role played by policy instruments. The third section discusses the most significant factors that are driving the uptake of NEPIs in the UK, as well the barriers that stood (or still stand) in their way. The fourth section describes the current distribution of VAs, MBIs and other NEPIs in the UK. The final section compares the *status quo* with the traditional pattern of instrument use in order to assess the extent to which NEPIs in the UK are genuinely 'new' or not.

UK Environmental Policy

Policy Structures

The prevailing *structures* of environmental policy reflect the style and the underlying philosophy of action. Therefore in the past, the responsibility for determining the precise setting of individual instruments (which in most cases were regulatory – see below) was normally devolved to front-line officials working in technical agencies. Decentralised implementation was consistent with the contextual philosophy or paradigm of UK policy (see below), which could not have been applied by bureaucrats working at desks in London, Cardiff or Edinburgh. In the 1990s, these local agencies were gradually brigaded into a national Environment Agency in order to deliver simpler and more cost-effective regulation. The Agency inherited a long legacy of regulatory control from its predecessors that dates back to the mid-nineteenth century. However, it is now beginning to explore the potential of NEPIs [*Pearce et al., 2000*].

Central government's role was restricted to setting the legislative or policy framework, leaving the detailed aspects of policy fine-tuning and implementation to local officials. As far as policy instruments were concerned, informal, 'gentleman's agreements' were usually preferred to regulation (see below), which only ever set a broad *framework* for extensive local interpretation by technical experts working in a culture of secrecy and trust.

Policy Style

Voluntarism, discretion and practicability are the words that were traditionally used to characterise British environmental policy throughout the 1970s and 1980s [*Weale, 1997*]. As new problems emerged and became important, new laws were enacted and new agencies put in place. As it was sold to foreigners by British politicians, "the British approach" [*Waldegrave, 1985*] was predominantly reactive rather than anticipatory, tactical rather than strategic, pragmatic rather than ambitious, and case-by-case rather than uniform (see also RCEP [*1984*]). For policy elites in the UK 'muddling through' problems was inherently better than strategic, long-term planning [*Ashby and Anderson, 1981*]. It fitted with the UK's legal system (which relies heavily on common law), its informal and constantly evolving constitution, and the widespread desire to optimise pollution rather than minimise waste emissions regardless of their environmental impacts (see below).

The traditional *style* of policy in the UK has tended to be informal, reactive, gradualist and accommodative. Great emphasis has always been placed on consultation and negotiation, rather than imposition and confrontation [*Weale et al. 2000: 180*]. In operational terms, regulation proceeded on the basis of courteous negotiation between polluters and regulators operating in exclusive policy communities of experts (what Weale *et al.* [*ibid.: 181*] term 'club government'). Regulators preferred not to set standards which could not be complied with (the philosophy of 'practicability'). Curiously, this style of working had many similarities with the way in which some negotiated agreements are negotiated today. Critics, however, claimed that they adopted all too easily the norms preferred by those that they were supposed to be regulating.

The Content of Policy

It is actually quite difficult to identify an overall philosophy or *paradigm* of UK policy other than that pollution should be *optimised* (by limiting its effects in the environment) rather than reduced at source [*Weale et al. 2000: 177; Jordan, 2002a*]. Traditionally, the underlying principle is that standards should be 'reasonably practicable' that is, tailored to reflect local conditions and circumstances, the economic costs of abatement and the current state of technical knowledge [*Jordan, 1998a: 180–81*]. This approach was assumed to be more effective and more economically efficient than forcing all polluters to attain the same (that is, harmonised) statutory standards. This mode of working was staunchly defended by the scientific and political establishment [*Jordan, 2002a*]. In terms of the *policy instruments* used, regulation was generally preferred to taxes, subsidies and the sort of sectoral covenants that started to appear in The Netherlands, France and Germany in the 1970s. Crucially, British regulatory instruments were somewhat different from those used in continental European states and the EU. Whereas as the latter preferred fixed legislative standards and deadlines to ensure comparability of effort and to simplify the process of monitoring and enforcement, Britain usually opted for unwritten agreements with polluters, general legal guidelines and standards, and flexible implementation systems, which could be tailored to suit political and financial exigencies.

Summary

Policy elites were immensely 'proud' of these arrangements [*Hajer, 1995*]. A guide to national policy produced by the Department of the Environment (DoE – between 1997 and 2001, the Department for the Environment, Transport and the Regions (DETR) and, after restructuring in 2001, the Department for Enironment, Food and Rural Affairs (DEFRA)) in the late 1970s concluded that the UK was already 'at an advanced stage in the development and adoption of environmental protection policies' [*DoE, 1978: 1*]. In reality, environmental imperatives were (and in large part still are) subservient to the (perceived) need to address the country's long-term economic and industrial decline as a world power. Thus, the UK has never been a particularly 'green' member state. More often than not, the UK has 'taken' policies shaped elsewhere in the EU, rather than 'shaped' EU environmental policy in its own image [*Jordan, 2003*].

   These inherited features should, at least in theory, have militated in favour of many VAs. Depending on how one defines a VA, the UK could even be said to have pioneered the use of voluntary approaches. Yet, British VAs have generally been relatively small in number, informal (that is, non-legal) in nature, secretively negotiated, local in their implementation and highly flexible in their execution. Eco-labels and other instruments of moral suasion generally go with the grain of British practice. However, MBIs (at least those set centrally and transparently by central government) are alien to the guiding precepts and organising structures of UK policy.

Why Are NEPIs Being Adopted?

General Drivers

Since the 1980s, British environmental policy has undergone a slow but profound change, which has gradually produced a much more

'Europeanised' system of control. In general nowadays there is a much greater willingness to innovate with environmental instruments, more openness and formality in management matters, and greater recourse to legal action by the courts. Source-based legal controls are more common; the locus of control has shifted from 'front line' regulators to officials at higher levels, who try to adopt a more integrated view of problems; regulation is much more open and independent; the style of policy is much more formal and 'arms length'.

The reasons for this shift are many and varied [*Jordan, 1998a, 2003*]. First, the Europeanisation of national environmental policy has forced the UK to adapt its approach to reflect continental axioms of control. The effect has been most direct in relation to regulation primarily because the EU is a regulatory state. So far, the EU has not been a strong force promoting VAs and MBIs. This is partly because the UK has succeeded in clinging to the national veto in the Environment Council governing all tax matters, and partly because the EU has adopted very few VAs of its own. However, by setting strict targets, EU regulations (for example, the packaging waste Directive) have indirectly encouraged UK industry to experiment with NEPIs (see below). It is a measure of how far the situation in the UK has evolved, that the EU is now regarded as a constraint upon the UK's ability to innovate in the area of climate change (see below).

Second, the steady politicisation of environmental issues has increased the political profile of environmental instruments and exerted pressure on the government to impose constraints on industry. The public profile of regulation is higher than it was and there are widespread demands for greater transparency. Consequently, in the 1990s similarities began to appear between the way that domestic regulations (such as Integrated Pollution Control) were adopted, and the negotiated agreements used on the continent [*Jordan, 1993*]. On the other hand, the increasingly powerful environmental pressure groups in the UK have tended to resist the adoption of MBIs on moral and philosophical grounds; some remain deeply suspicious of VAs with industry [*Green Alliance, 2001*]. Many would sympathise with the IPPR's argument that 'there is [still] a shortage of any instruments of environmental protection, fiscal or regulatory' in the UK [*Tindale and Holtham, 1996: 22*].

Finally, new ways of thinking have emerged and become important. There is a widespread acceptance that many local environmental pollution problems (which are mostly regulated) are well under control, and a realisation that even highly sophisticated regulations (such as Integrated Pollution Prevention and Control) will not deliver sustainable development. It implies that environmental protection must involve many stakeholders (shared responsibility). In fact, industry recognises the scope for assisting in the design of instruments to ensure that environmental protection measures generate economic benefits (that is, ecological modernisation).

Specific Drivers

The increasing popularity of particular NEPIs such as environmental taxes and VAs is the outcome of several more specific pressures. First, in the 1990s, politicians began to search for other means to intervene in the economy and society, pushed by parliamentary committees, environmental economists and some environmental pressure groups. This dovetailed with a growing trend towards a more 'hollowed out' state. NEPIs fitted the liberal, market-led beliefs of the governing Conservative party in the 1990s and 'new' Labour post-1997 'Third Way' philosophy of promoting work and reducing pollution. MBIs and VAs are very much the environmental manifestation of these shifts from government to governance in the UK.

Second, the economic recession of the early to mid 1990s encouraged policy makers to search for more flexible and cost-effective policy tools. It is often said that the British like continental European standards of welfare provision but American rates of taxation. At one stage in the late 1990s, environmental taxes were used as a relatively uncontentious source of new revenue with which to square this circle. There are now signs that these and other so-called 'stealth taxes' have lost their anonymity and are becoming steadily more problematic to implement (see below).

Third, there is a growing cultural receptivity to new ideas emanating from abroad and especially the EU. Political interest has began to grow in how economic instruments, such as VAs, are used in and by other countries (that is, policy transfer/learning). The OECD and the EEA actively disseminate good practice at the European level, but the UK has often been an exporter of ideas about MBIs through the work of David Pearce and Wilfred Beckerman. In the UK, NGOs such as the Green Alliance [*2001*] and the Institute of Public Policy Research (IPPR] [*Tindale, 1997*] have sought to improve the environmental effectiveness of national policy by advocating new tools, but Greenpeace and FoE have tended to be more circumspect.

Finally, the EU and the United Nations have not directly imposed new tools on the UK, but they have accelerated the adoption of ambitious commitments in areas such as climate change, packaging waste and acidification, which have then encouraged the domestic political system to investigate innovative modes of response. In other words, they have provided an external impetus to innovate without specifying the precise instruments to use. For instance, Labour's 1997 decision to adopt a more ambitious carbon dioxide reduction target than that required by the Kyoto protocol [*Jordan, 2002b*] has spurred the UK to innovate with particular MBIs such as emission trading (see below].

Obstacles to Change

Many of the obstacles to change are also alluded to above. First, the traditional structure, style and content of British policy militated strongly against innovation. Policy elites in the UK have traditionally viewed eco-taxes with a mixture of suspicion and hostility. Many had grown up with regulation and were well versed in the art of using it to 'muddle through' problems. In 1972, the Royal Commission on Environmental Pollution (RCEP] looked at how innovators such as the USA, France and The Netherlands were using MBIs, and concluded that:

> We are not convinced that a system of charges would be so effective as [legal] consents ... [which] if properly policed, would guarantee a level of [environmental] quality ... The administration of a system of charges would need an expertise ... which we do not believe exists at present ... [The] Government should forthwith examine the case for adopting [MBIs]; but we do not believe that the case ... is already so well established as to justify ... a switch from consents to [MBIs] as the main device for controlling pollution [*RCEP, 1972: 67–8*].

Second, industry has often opposed the imposition of *any* type of environmental instrument whether it be regulation or one of the NEPIs. A British environment minister once claimed that '[I]ndustry in Britain has always opposed the concept of a general charging system whereby charges are imposed'. He continued:the rationale behind [British] policy... is based on a three-part premise of practicability, confirmed expert advice and pragmatism. We must make absolutely certain that we do not compromise on these objectives *by favouring the next popular theory that comes along* [*HL Hansard, Vol. 444, 5th Series, 14-1-11-83, cols. 1110–1112*] (emphasis added). Consequently, Britain stood aloof while continental European countries and the US began experimenting with NEPIs in the 1970s.

NEPIs in the UK

Market-Based Instruments

The UK can claim to have adopted one of the very first environmental taxes in the world when, in 1909, Lloyd George introduced a tax on petrol [*Tindale and Holtham, 1996: 22*]. However, since then progress has been extremely fitful. The publication of the 'Pearce Report' (which was commissioned by the DoE), in 1989 secured huge media interest in environmental taxes [*Pearce, Barbier and Markandya, 1989*]. A whole annex of a government White Paper on the environment published the following year (1990) explored the potential for applying them in the UK.

In the foreword to an update published in 1992, the Conservative Minister went as far as to promise 'a new presumption in favour of economic instruments rather than regulation' [*H.M. Government., 1992*].

The report itself added that 'new regulations should be limited to cases where economic instruments ... are either not available or require regulatory underpinning' Shortly afterwards, the DoE published a major review of the main policy options [*DoE, 1993*]. Again, the foreword written by the then Minister made several bold promises, but the rest of the report was much more cautious. There, civil servants warned there was 'no widespread body of empirical evidence to demonstrate that [MBIs] ... save resources', implying that they will only be used part 'with existing [legal] control remaining in place as a safety net' [*DoE, 1993: 53, 23*]. The adoption of NEPIs at this time was done in a very *ad hoc* manner. For instance, the two MBIs adopted in 1993 (higher road fuel duties and the ill-fated tax on domestic fuel) (see below) were not even mentioned in the 1992 White Paper [*ENDS, 226: 11*].

Developments in the 1990s: The economics divisions in the DoE had in fact been actively exploring the scope for implementing MBIs to control water pollution, sulphur emissions, waste generation, CFC usage and tyre disposal throughout much of the 1980s. Consultants were even hired to examine best practices in other countries [*ENDS, 120: 4*], and Ministers paid visits to other countries to learn at first hand. Yet, today, MBIs are still conspicuous by their absence from most areas of British environmental policy. The most well known are outlined in Box 1. According to Helm [*1998: 11*], the vast majority are 'implicit' economic instruments that is, they are primarily designed to raise revenue rather than to protect the environment *per se*. It is striking how few have been set using the kind of formal externality assessment advocated by the DoE's best practice guide [*DoE, 1993; 26; Seccombe-Hett, 2000: 117*]. It is also obvious that the vast majority target industry rather than households (that is, consumers) [*Seccombe-Hett, 2000: 123*]. Those that have (for example, Value Added Tax (VAT) on domestic fuel) have proved to be controversial because of the distributional impact on poor consumers.

The inertial factors are relatively well known [*Hanley et al., 1990; Tindale and Hewitt, 2000; Pearce et al., 2000*]. In addition to well-known design problems (for example, measuring the total externality effect), there are the following. First, there has been c*oncerted opposition from business* [*Tindale and Hewitt, 2000: 11*]. It is significant that the philosophy of ecological modernisation is still weakly rooted in Britain. British firms have generally regarded any form of environmental protection (economic or regulatory) as an extraneous constraint to be resisted. It is possibly true that

BOX 1
MARKET BASED INSTRUMENTS IN THE UK

Unleaded petrol differential (1987–2001)
A tax differential introduced to encourage the use of unleaded petrol. Having mostly done its work, it will soon be removed and replaced with a statutory ban.

Fuel duty escalator (1993–)
This automatic annual increase in road fuel tax was introduced by the Conservatives to raise revenue. It was raised by subsequent Chancellors but adjusted in 2000 to pacify petrol tax protestors and encourage low sulphur diesel.

Vehicle excise taxes
Lower taxes for smaller vehicles and cleaner lorries were introduced by Labour in 1999. These were subsequently extended in 2000 to cover a larger number of less polluting small cars. Various tax concessions for company car owners were progressively removed during the 1990s. A fundamental review of company car taxation was launched in 2002–3.

VAT on domestic fuel (1993–)
Raised by the Conservatives from zero per cent to eight per cent but a further increase to the higher level of 17.5% was hastily abandoned in the teeth of widespread concerns about 'fuel poverty'. In 2000 Labour announced that VAT on energy saving devices (including solar technology) would be reduced to the EU minimum of five per cent

The Landfill Tax (1996–)
Announced and then implemented by the Conservatives, this was the most significant innovation thus far. It aims to push more material up the waste hierarchy i.e. to increase recycling and waste reduction. Strictly speaking, the revenues are not hypothecated. However, some of the revenue is used to finance environmental measures through an Environmental Body. Another quantum is used to offset the cost of labour through a 0.2 per cent reduction in the National Insurance (NI) contributions paid by all employers. It is still the only environmental tax in the UK to be based on an externality study.

Packing recycling notes (PRNs) (1998–)
Designed by Volpak in 1998 to demonstrate compliance with the EU Packaging Waste Directive. It qualifies as a tradable permit because the PRNs are traded between parties (that is, those who over-comply can sell permits to those that under-comply) [*Salmons, 2002*]. Interestingly, the scheme is one of the first in the EU covering the waste sector. The market is quite localised in the sense that it is overseen by the Environment Agency, not the environment ministry. It is intended to promote recycling, but its long-term success is still questionable.

industry warmed to NEPIs in the 1990s as the lesser of two evils. However, even today, the main employers' federation, the Confederation of British Industry (CBI) [*CBI, 2002*], remains strongly critical of the UK's approach to deploying environmental taxes. Second, many sectors are already heavily regulated (for example, water) and there is an obvious unwillingness among politicians and bureaucrats to tamper with it. There is also wider 'societal lock in' [*Jordan, 2002a*] because polluters also have an intimate knowledge of how regulation operates and fear the uncertainty that innovation would bring. EU regulatory requirements have on occasions (see above) reduced the scope for introducing NEPIs.

Third, the coalitions advocating MBIs have been politically weak. Even environmental groups have traditionally mistrusted MBIs because they do not morally stigmatise pollution as strongly as regulation. Pearce *et al.* [*2000: 34*] conjecture that although most UK environmental economists support the use of MBIs, there are no think tanks that consistently advocate them in policy circles.

Fourth, there has been strong opposition from *cognate government* departments. In the past the Treasury flatly opposed the principle of hypothecation and it also doubted whether the efficiency gains from MBIs were high enough to offset their administrative costs. The agriculture and trade departments have often flatly opposed the introduction of *any* new environmental control as matter of principle.

Finally, indirect (or 'stealth') taxes have become almost as electorally unpopular as direct taxes were in the 1980s. The distributional impacts of new taxes are now strongly in the public eye. In a word, MBIs no longer represent an 'easy' new revenue stream for the Treasury to exploit. This means that new MBIs will have to: (1) publicly penalise the producer of the economic 'bad' being targeted; and (2) ensure that the losers from such an action should be no worse off that they would otherwise have been. Designing instruments that satisfy both these requirements is extremely difficult.

New Labour, new instruments? The arrival of a new Labour government with (relatively) ambitious environmental policies has added fresh impetus to the domestic debate about MBIs. By the end of its first term in office (1997–2001) a number of innovative proposals for new MBIs were poised to be (or had been) introduced (see Box 2). In opposition, Labour shifted its policy to incorporate NEPIs such as MBIs. Left of centre think tanks such as the IPPR and (under the Directorship of the environmental economist Michael Jacobs) the Fabian Society, played a particularly influential role in re-modelling Labour's stance on NEPIs so it fitted with the principles of ecological modernisation. One IPPR fellow, Stephen Tindale, was the secretary to the Labour Party's Policy Commission on the Environment prior to Labour's election in 1997. He is said to have briefed Labour's Treasury team on the merits of eco-tax reform. When Labour entered power he was hired as a special adviser to the DoE. Within weeks of entering power he organised an IPPR seminar on NEPIs which involved several key Ministers.

These initiatives soon bore fruit when, a few months later, the *Treasury* (that is, not the DETR!) issued a strategic 'statement of intent' on environmental tax reform although this fell short of the comprehensive plan for adopting specific MBIs demanded by the IPPR a few years earlier.

BOX 2
NEW LABOUR, NEW INSTRUMENTS?

The Climate Change Levy (CCL) (2001–)
Announced in the 1999 budget and implemented in 2001. Following opposition from industry, the DETR announced an 80 per cent discount for companies in highly energy extensive sectors that sign up to a negotiated agreement – the climate change levy agreement (CCLA) (see below). The title CCL is somewhat of a misnomer as it is really directed at the downstream use of energy rather than reducing the carbon intensity of energy use *per se*. Like the landfill tax, some of the revenues will be offset against employers' NI contributions. The CCL is expected to raise £1billion p.a. Around £150m will be channelled into a fund to pay for energy efficiency measures. It seems unlikely that the tax as it is currently conceived will deliver the emission savings needed to fulfil the UK's climate targets, so industry is bracing itself for future hikes.

An Aggregates Tax (2002–)
First mooted in 1998 but only began to achieve political momentum in 1999. The Quarry Products Association attempted to resist it by proposing a VA but the DETR regarded this as insufficiently ambitious. Most of the receipts are recycled to reduce employers' NI contributions, but a portion is being diverted to a sustainability fund which works to remove the barriers to re-using aggregates.

The Emissions Trading Scheme (2002–)
The initiative first came from industry as it searched for alternatives to the government's plans for a carbon-energy tax. It was mooted by a 1998 government (Marshall) report on options for limiting the business use of energy. Industry associations took the government by surprise when they formed an emissions trading group (ETG) in 1999 to produce a blueprint for a fully functioning scheme, as their preferred alternative to the government's CCL. Crucially, several of the 100 or so members (for example, BP) already had their own 'in house' schemes; the powerful London money market was also keen to be involved as it has designs on becoming the international trading body under the Kyoto Protocol. The start of trading (2002) was delayed several times as the complex inter-relationships between the scheme, the CCL, the CCLAs and the EU's plans for trading were painstakingly ironed out (see below). The government also had to find £215m as a financial incentive for businesses (most of whom wanted to sell rather than buy emission credits) to join the scheme. In phase two, these 'direct participants' will be able to trade with companies that are party to CCLAs. The government claims that trading will deliver five per cent of the total UK greenhouse gas reductions required by the Kyoto Protocol, but critics maintain that much of this reduction is either not real or would have happened anyway [*ENDS, 326: 25–9*].

ENDS report [*ENDS, 290: 17*] described the 1999 budget as 'indisputably the greenest yet.' As well as strengthening a number of existing measures, it contained concrete plans for new taxes on pesticides and aggregates.

These initiatives are undoubtedly evidence of genuine innovation. Many more new MBIs are being actively explored including a tax on plastic shopping bags, a variable charging system for household waste (households currently pay a flat charge for all their local authority services) [*ENDS, 322: 17*], and even distance-based lorry road user charges to replace the vehicle excise duty and the hugely unpopular fuel escalator (see above).

In spite of growing enthusiasm in parts of Whitehall (for example, the Treasury and the industry ministry) that were previously opposed to MBIs, there is still a rich 'unpolitics' of instrument use. For example, well-developed plans to introduce charging schemes relating to water quality and water abstraction are in abeyance. Plans for sulphur trading were proposed and then dropped when they conflicted with regulatory requirements [*Sorrell, 1999*]. Tradable permits for waste have also been mooted by the DETR as a means to achieve targets set by the EU landfill targets but planning is proceeding extremely slowly. Finally, in the spring of 2000 Blair intervened to halt work on a pesticides tax that had been under way since 1998 in order to placate farming groups after the BSE crisis. The DEFRA is currently discussing the possibility of brokering a series of VAs with relevant industry associations.

Voluntary Agreements

Although British policy has always been relatively voluntaristic, the UK has always been suspicious of the more structured VAs used in The Netherlands and Germany. That highly influential critic of British environmental policy in Europe, the House of Lords Select Committee on the European Communities [*HOLSCEC, 1980*] said they 'deserve careful discussion as their legal basis is unclear'. It continued: 'although they cannot be expected to replace legislation entirely, [they] may ... prove useful supplements'. By the mid-1990s, the UK government's opposition had softened, though it remained decidedly unconvinced. In the 1994 sustainable development strategy, it opined that: '[s]ome other countries have pioneered this approach but before it could be adopted in the UK, further work would be needed on the scope of such agreements and how they could be negotiated, implemented and enforced.'

In principle, industry is also broadly committed to voluntary approaches. However, when it comes to discussing the detailed *content* of VAs, views diverge somewhat. Some economic sectors have warmly embraced them whereas others have flatly opposed them. As might be expected, there has been more enthusiasm for negotiated agreements when industry has faced the prospect of an alternative instrument such as a tax! The CBI is concerned that VAs: are open to defection (the free-rider problem); impose an unfair burden on the larger firms that are more likely to sign them; and are potentially unworkable given the limited number of trade associations in some sectors [*ENDS, 224, 3–4*].

Traditional voluntary agreements: Most of the early, indigenous VAs were little more than informal 'gentleman's agreements' or non-justiciable codes of good conduct. Two examples give a flavour of how they operated (Figure 1): pesticides and ozone depleting chemicals. Established in 1957, the Pesticides Safety Precautions Scheme (PSPS) was probably the first example of a VA in the UK. The main aim of the PSPS, which was non-statutory, was to safeguard human health and the environment. The scheme was criticised by the RCEP [*1979*] for not doing enough to limit the use of pesticides. More forceful critics denounced it as a:

> gentleman's agreement' between the agrochemical industry and government ... Under the [scheme] key committees [were] ... bound by the Official Secrets Act. Experts who were invited... to discuss the impact of a new insecticide ... were muzzled ... the industry was well represented on the PSPS (indeed it was a source of almost all the data) ... whereas workers' organisations were relegated to relatively powerless advisory panels. It was hardly surprising that if industry got the benefit of the doubt, and it took longer to restrict or ban a pesticide in the UK than in more openly governed countries [*Rose, 1990: 236*].

The PSBS remained in force until 1986 when, following a legal challenge from the European Commission (on the grounds that it breached free trade rules), it was replaced by a statutory registration scheme.

In 1980, the EU placed a cap on CFC production and called for a reduction in their use in aerosols. The British government achieved these with plenty of room to spare, praising an unwritten VA with users and producers. In fact, the production cap was set well above existing levels of production – thereby leaving ample room for expansion – and aerosol use was already in decline. In the 1980s, consumption rocketed as new uses were found for CFCs. Binding controls on production were only applied in 1988 after the EU signed the Montreal Protocol. A series of more formal VAs were adopted by the EU to reduce consumption [*Jordan, 1998b*].

FIGURE 1
UK NEGOTIATED AGREEMENTS

Name	Period of operation	Topic
Pesticides Safety Precautions Scheme	1957–86	Health and safety
APEs (domestic fabric washing products)	1972–78	Water pollution
NTA (domestic fabric washing products	1975–	Water pollution
'BASIS' (pesticides handling)	1978–	Health and safety
Recycled content of newsprint	1991–	Waste management
Farm Films Recovery Scheme (FFSR)	1995–97	Waste management
APEs (industrial washing products)	1995–	Water pollution
HFCs (aerosol industry)	1996–	Climate change
HFCs and PFCs (fire industry)	1996–	Climate change
HFCs (foams industry)	1996–	Climate change
Energy efficiency (chemical industry)	1997–	Climate change

Source: Jordan and Salmons [*2000*].

FIGURE 2
OTHER UK VOLUNTARY AGREEMENTS

Unilateral Commitments	Public Voluntary Schemes
TOVALOP and CRISTAL Responsible Care CFCs and HCFCs "Green Fee" scheme for used tyres Environment Business Forum 1995 Plus Group	EMAS / ISO 14001 'Making a Corporate Commitment'

Source: Jordan and Salmons [*2000*]

Contemporary voluntary agreements: There are around 20 VAs in the UK. Of these, around half are negotiated agreements [*CEC, 1997*] (Figure 1), which is relatively low compared to The Netherlands and Germany. The rest are either unilateral commitments or public voluntary schemes (see Figure 2). These tend to be unofficial, largely self-assessed and have little or no legal force. Many are more like codes of best practice than what continental Europeans would classify as negotiated agreements.

Most of these agreements have some official status (that is, they have been negotiated in partnership with or deposited with a government body). However only very few have some formal legislative status (for example, BASIS). Some of the schemes have been moderately successful but others have failed miserably (for example, that governing newsprint) and at least one (the FFSR) has completely collapsed, triggering demands for statutory intervention [*Salmons, 2000*]. In other areas (for example, washing products), industry associations have requested the government to intervene to overcome potential free-rider problems by prohibiting the use of some pollutants. Finally, some of the agreements (for example, those relating to HFCs and PFCs) have been heavily criticised for doing little more than codifying business as usual. The first modern, negotiated agreement was the energy efficiency agreement (EEA). This agreement, which was brokered between the DETR and the Chemical Industries Association (CIA) in 1997, aims to reduce the chemical industries' specific energy consumption as a part of the UK's climate change strategy. It is externally verified but it is not legally binding on either party. It is hard not to gain the impression that it was little more than a ploy to resist a carbon-energy tax [*Salmons, 2001*].

The only other clear-cut example of a negotiated agreement is the Climate Change Levy Agreement (CCLA), which superseded that EEA. CCLAs allow firms within certain economic sectors to obtain an 80 per cent reduction on the CCL (see above). At the time of writing, the DETR has signed 42 CCLAs with trade associations representing over 5,000 businesses, primarily in the supermarket and farming sectors. Each CCLA will run for ten years and be reviewed every second year. The CCLAs proved to be far more difficult to negotiate than the DETR expected, as reliable baseline data on energy use simply did not exist at the beginning of the process [*Smith, 2002*]. The administrative cost was also enormous for a supposedly 'light touch' instrument; it involved a total of 31 civil servants and consumed 17 person years of their time (House of Commons Written Answers, 4 Feb. 2002, col. 751–2W).

Eco-labels

The UK only started actively to explore the merits of eco-labels in the late 1980s. The environment and trade ministries published a joint discussion paper in 1989. Although they favoured the establishment of an EU-wide scheme, their Lordships suggested that there should be two parallel schemes – one national and one EU driven. However, plans for a UK scheme were quickly overtaken by the development (largely DETR-driven) of an EU scheme. Whitehall's enthusiasm for the EU scheme cooled in the 1990s when the take-up from industry stalled. The Department for Environment, Food and Rural Affairs (DEFRA) now accepts that eco-labelling cannot by itself transform the environmental behaviour of industry and consumers. The DEFRA continues to offers advice to businesses and consumers, but it is now shifting its attention to other instruments such as eco-management and audit systems (EMAS) and integrated product policy. Industry tends to prefer their own in house labels to the EU's involvement. The largest retailers (for example, Sainsbury's) often argue that their brand name alone is a sufficient indication of a product's quality. It is therefore unsurprising that British companies have largely failed to promote the EU eco-label and British consumers remain are largely ignorant of its existence.

EMAS

EMAS in the UK has also co-evolved with an EU system (implemented via Regulation 93/1836), although as with eco-labelling, at crucial stages the UK did a lot to initiate interest in and shape the development of European thinking. In recent years, UK authorities have sought to combine the national system (British Standard (BS) 7750) with the EU's EMAS system to avoid administrative duplication. On paper, the UK does not appear to have implemented EMAS with much enthusiasm, having far fewer registered sites than environmental 'lead' states such as Germany, Austria, Sweden and Denmark (though far more than Ireland, Greece, Portugal and Italy). However, some of these differences arise from the manner in which national accreditation systems interpret the letter of the Regulation. In other, more practical, respects the UK is enthusiastic in its implementation of

EMAS, being the first state in the EU to extend it to the non-industrial sector and to local government.

'Old' Instruments: Regulation

Finally, regulation remains the mainstay of national environmental policy in the UK, primarily because of the EU's growing influence in all aspects of UK policy development. Around 80 per cent of British policy originates in or is negotiated with the EU [*RCEP, 1998: 1.24*]. Since most EU environmental policy is legislative in nature, British policy remains heavily reliant on regulation. The steady Europeanisation of national policy has, if anything, made British legislation more mechanical and regulatory, that is, inserting numerical standards and compliance deadlines where administrative rules of thumb and unwritten 'gentleman's agreements' used to be the norm [*Jordan, 1998a; Jordan, 2002a*].

So, somewhat paradoxically, national policy is considerably *more* regulatory in nature and style than it was 30 years ago, although there are also many more NEPIs. The EU is not, of course, the only force at work here. As the DoE pointed out over ten years ago, regulation is often required to implement and enforce NEPIs (e.g. establishing the rules of the system and compliance mechanisms) [*DoE, 1993: 24*]. Interestingly, the debate about how to develop 'policy packages' combining different types of instrument started relatively early in the UK [*ibid.: 26*]. The force at work is concerted opposition to de-regulation in sectors, such as water, that have a long history of regulation [*ENDS, 277: 20–24*]. On closer inspection, government, industry and (of course) environmental pressure groups have often realised the administrative work and financial costs required to remove legislation that is effective. Industry in particular abhors uncertainty, which deregulation followed by innovation would almost certainly increase.

Conclusions

To conclude, there are far fewer VAs in the UK than other European countries of a comparable size and environmental performance. Those that have been agreed are generally: concentrated in a much narrower range of sub-sectors (agriculture, chemicals, energy) than the EU average [*EEA, 1997*]; non-binding [*ELNI, 1998: 61*]; of relatively recent origin [*ibid.: 59*]; and unilaterally volunteered by industry rather than negotiated as part of binding, long term commitment. The UK is a centrally controlled unitary state, but one might have expected to find many more VAs in a sector like environmental protection that has such a strong historical tradition of decentralisation, consensus building and negotiation with industry [cf. *EEA, 1997: 39*].

Paradoxically, the UK's highly voluntaristic policy style may have militated against the adoption of negotiated agreements. However, the raft of new CCLAs may be the harbinger of a new phase of innovation. They are new in the sense that the impetus for deploying them is beginning to come much more strongly from within Whitehall, rather than from traditional champions in industry (see above). The DEFRA is currently exploring how to use VAs to achieve a step change in waste minimisation and resource productivity. The way in which VAs are used may also be changing. Recently, an official explained that VAs are now regarded as a tool for setting tentative targets and benchmarking best practice. These may or may or may not evolve into negotiated agreements, embodying binding commitments backed by real penalties [*ENDS, 315: 6–7*].

Until very recently, there was very little interest in and use of MBIs. The idea that MBIs might one day be designed and adopted at a central government level, jarred with the founding precepts of UK policy, which are pragmatism, legalism, secrecy, decentralism and informality. These institutional barriers could have been overcome if the political pressure to change had been there, but it was not. In the 1990s, the small amount of political and institutional space available was used by the Treasury and the DETR to implement 'implicit' taxes. These had more to do with raising revenue than protecting the environment. Genuine innovation was conspicuous by its absence. Today, the situation is in danger of flipping the other way, with several innovations (for example, the CCL, the CCLAs and emissions trading) vying with one another. Whereas before there was a dearth of NEPIs there is now, as the Environment Minister recently put it, a real 'risk of a policy glut' [*ENDS, 292: 34*].

How 'new' are they in comparison to the traditional style, structure and content of national environmental policy? New Labour's programme of tax reform may be somewhat belated compared to other EU states, but it undeniably marks a decisive break with the traditional elements of UK policy. In terms of older policy structures, a major part of the drive for MBIs is now coming from outside the environment ministry, particularly the Treasury (primarily for eco-taxes) and the Department of Trade and Industry (more so for emission trading). Industry has pioneered the use PRNs and climate change emissions trading. In effect, the detailed policy work that is required to design and implement instruments is centralising at a significant rate. It is moving from the technical/regulatory agencies that specialise in the implementation of regulation, to national ministries and business associations. In terms of the content of policy, the tools described above break with the old 'optimisation of pollution' paradigm which often excluded an assessment of externalised costs.

Finally, the style in which they have been developed is significantly more structured and transparent than the regulation of old. It is significant that the EU is now increasingly regarded as a constraint upon and not a spur to domestic change. This is nowhere more apparent than in relation to climate change. First, the DETR was kept waiting by the Commission while it cleared the incentive payments offered under the emission trading scheme. Then, a potentially more important development was the Commission's 2001 decision to publish plans for an EU-level emissions trading scheme. This scheme, which is due to start in 2005 (that is, midway through the first period of UK trading), is considerably different from that now running in the UK.[1] At the time of writing, the UK is fighting to persuade the Commission to base the EU system on the UK model in order to avoid costly misfits between the two.

However, powerful barriers continue to steer the whole process of NEPI adoption down a series of institutionally defined paths. First, it is telling that rather than try and achieve too much too quickly, the DEFRA has decided to concentrate on a small number of newly emerging pollutants (for example, greenhouse gases, fertilisers and pesticides) and sectors (for example, waste and agriculture) that were either unregulated or only lightly regulated in the past. Attempts made in the late 1980s and early 1990s to replace regulation with NEPIs did not amount to much. In fact, there is now a widespread recognition that regulation is a necessary aspect of NEPI design and use. For instance, several regulations were needed to implement the aggregates tax (for example, defining the penalties for non-payment, and so on). According to Barbara Young, the Chief Executive of the Environment Agency, '[r]egulation is the bedrock that we build other action on, and ensures minimum standards' [Green Alliance, 2001: 8].

Secondly, at the level of broader policy making, it is apparent that even in the areas where Labour has innovated, it has worked within pre-existing policy commitments and socially embedded instruments. The overall pattern is somewhat muddled and confused [Helm, 1998: 12]. It is striking that the UK government is resisting Parliamentary pressure to set up a Green Tax Commission on the same model adopted in other countries, preferring instead to 'muddle through' problems as and when they appear. Moreover, the institutional 'stickiness' of traditional patterns of policy style, content and structure means that today's instruments still bear the imprint of traditional policy repertoires. Thus, VAs in the UK tend to be looser, less legally binding and smaller in number than their continental cousins; UK MBIs have tended to be more 'implicit' rather than real, although things are now changing. In other words, the NEPIs that we find in the UK bear many of the hallmarks of traditional British policy instruments. Clear and unambiguous instances of innovation in the UK are hard to find; most of the so-called 'new' instruments are a new variant of older instruments. Where governments have innovated they have generally followed the grain of existing policy traditions or, as in the case of 'implicit taxes', left them largely untouched.

NOTE

1. The Commission's proposed scheme covers carbon dioxide only, is mandatory and includes electricity generation. The UK scheme is voluntary (in fact it provides for financial incentives), covers several greenhouse gagses, contains no mandatory penalties and excludes electricity generation.

REFERENCES

Ashby, E. and M. Anderson (1981), *The Politics of Clean Air*, Oxford: Clarendon Press.
CBI (Confederation of British Industry) (2002), *Green Taxes: Rhetoric and Reality*, May, London: CBI.
CEC (Commission of the European Communities) (1997), *Study on Voluntary Agreements Concluded Between Industry and Public Authorities in the Field of the Environment*. Brussels: DG III.
DoE (1978), *Environmental Standards in Britain: How They Work*, London: HMSO.
DoE (1993), *Making Markets Work for the Environment*, London: HMSO.
EEA (1997), *Environmental Agreements*, Copenhagen: EEA.
ELNI (The Environmental Law Network International) (1998), *Environmental Agreements*, London: Cameron May.
ENDS (Environmental Data Services Ltd) (various years) *Environmental Data Services (ENDS) Report* (various issues; see text for details).
Green Alliance (2001), *Signed, Sealed and Delivered? The Role of Negotiated Agreements in the UK*, London: Green Alliance.
Green Alliance (2002), 'Barbara Young', *Inside Track* (the Green Alliance's quarterly newsletter), Summer 2001, London: Green Alliance.
Hajer, M. (1995), *The Politics of Environmental Discourse*, Oxford: Oxford University Press.
Hanley, N. *et al.* (1990), 'Why Is More Notice Not Taken of Economists' Prescriptions For the Control of Pollution?', *Environment and Planning A*, Vol.22, pp.1421–39.
Helm, D. (1998), 'The Assessment: Environment Policy', *Oxford Review of Economic Policy*, Vol.14, No.4, pp.1–19.
H.M. Government (1992), *This Common Inheritance*, Cmnd 2068, London: HMSO.
HOLSCEC (House of Lords Select Committee on the European Communities) (1980), *EEC Environment Policy*, Fifth Report, Session 1980–1, London: HMSO.
Jordan, A.J. (1993), 'Integrated Pollution Control and The Evolving Style and Structure Of Environmental Regulation in the UK', *Environmental Politics*, Vol.2, No.3, pp.405–27.
Jordan, A.J., (1998a), 'The Impact on UK Environmental Administration', in P. Lowe and S. Ward (eds.), *British Environmental Policy and Europe*, London: Routledge.
Jordan, A.J. (1998b), 'The Ozone Endgame: The Implementation of the Montreal Protocol in the UK', *Environmental Politics*, Vol.7, No.4, pp.23–52.
Jordan, A. (2002a), *The Europeanization of British Environmental Policy*, London: Palgrave.
Jordan, A.J. (2002b), 'Decarbonising the UK: A "Radical Agenda" from the Cabinet Office?', *The Political Quarterly*, Vol.73, No.3, pp.344–52.
Jordan, A, (2003), 'The Europeanisation of British Environmental Policy: From Policy "Taking" to Policy "Shaping"', in A. Jordan and D. Liefferink (eds.), *The Europeanisation of National Environmental Policy* (in press).
Jordan, A. and R. Salmons (2000), *The Use of Voluntary Agreements in the UK*, CSERGE mimeo, Norwich and London: CSERGE, UCL and UEA.
Pearce, D. Barbier, E. and A. Markandya (1989), *Blueprint for a Green Economy*, London: Earthscan.

Pearce, D. *et al.* (2000), *Market-based Instruments in the UK*, Report for the UK Round Table on Sustainable Development. London and Norwich: EFTEC/CSERGE. Available at: http://www.uea.ac.uk/env/cserge/research/fut_governance/papers.htm

RCEP (1972), *Pollution in Some British Estuaries and Coastal Waters*, Cmnd 5054, London: HMSO.

RCEP (1979), *Agriculture and Pollution*, Cmnd 7644, London: HMSO.

RCEP (1984), *Tackling Pollution*, Cmnd 9149, London: HMSO.

RCEP (1998), *Setting Emvironmental Standards*, Cmnd 4053, London: HMSO.

Rose, C. (1990), *The Duty Man of Europe*, London: Simon & Schuster.

Salmons, R (2000), *Case Studies of Negotiated Environmental Agreements: The UK: Agreement with the Farm Films Producers Group*, London: CSERGE.

Salmons, R (2001), *Case Studies of Negotiated Environmental Agreements: The Agreement on Energy Effeciency Improvement*, London: CSERGE.

Salmons, R. (2002), *New Areas for Application of Tradable Permits: Solid Waste Management*, report for the OECD Environment Directorate, London: Department of Economics, University College London.

Seccombe-Hett, T. (2000), 'Market-Based Instruments: If They're So Good, Why Aren't They the Norm?' *World Economics*, Vol.1, No.3, pp.101–26.

Smith, A. (2002), *Policy Transfer in the Development of UK Climate Policy for Business*. SPRU Electronic Paper Working Series No. 75. Available at: http://www.sussex.ac.uk/spru/publications/imprint/sewps/index.html

Sorrell, S. (1999), 'Why Sulphur Trading Failed in the UK', in S. Sorrell and J. Skea (eds.), *Pollution For Sale*, Cheltenham: Edward Elgar.

Tindale, S. (1997), 'The Political Economy of Environmental Tax Reform', in M. Jacobs (ed.), *Greening the Millennium*, Oxford: Blackwell.

Tindale, S. and C. Hewitt (2000), *New Environmental Policy Instruments in the UK*, EUI Working Paper RSC 98/13, Florence: EUI.

Tindale, S. and G. Holtham (1996), *Green Tax Reform*, London: IPPR.

Waldegrave, W. (1985), 'The British Approach', *Environmental Policy and Law*, Vol.15, Nos.3–4, pp.106–15.

Weale, A. (1997), 'The United Kingdom', in M. Janicke and H. Weidner (eds.), *National Environmental Policies*, Berlin: Springer Verlag.

Weale, A. *et al.* (2000), *Environmental Governance in Europe*, Oxford: Oxford University Press.

COMPARATIVE CONCLUSIONS

'New' Environmental Policy Instruments: An Evolution or a Revolution in Environmental Policy?

ANDREW JORDAN, RÜDIGER K.W. WURZEL and
ANTHONY R. ZITO

Introduction

The popularity of 'New' Environmental Policy Instruments (NEPIs) appears to have grown enormously since the 1970s. This has prompted widespread claims that contemporary environmental policy is undergoing a deep-seated and long-lasting revolution, characterised by a shift from environmental government to environmental *governance* (see introduction, this collection, pp.3–4). The papers assembled in this volume demonstrate unambiguously that the use of NEPIs is most certainly not 'limited' as some have claimed [*Lafferty and Meadowcroft, 2000: 452*]. Far from it – the total number and diversity of NEPIs used in the eight countries has grown significantly, with environmental taxes, voluntary agreements (VAs) and eco-labels proving especially popular.

Other market-based instruments NEPIs (for example, tradable permits) have only recently been deployed while some 'old' policy instruments (for example, subsidies) are very much discredited as a policy tool. In some countries, the adoption of NEPIs has been stunningly fast, to the extent that NEPIs are now the preferred instrument of new environmental policies in countries as diverse as the UK, Finland, and Germany. However, there are countries where the expansion of NEPI use is either proceeding much more slowly (Australia and Austria) or barely at all (Ireland).

The broad purpose of this collection is to: (a) identify where and when NEPIs are being used, and reflect upon the main drivers of (and impediments to) their uptake; and (b) assess how 'new' they are within the

The research underpinning this contribution was undertaken for a project entitled 'Innovation in Environmental Governance: A Comparative Analysis of New Environmental Policy Instruments' which was generously funded by the Economic and Social Research Council's (ESRC) Future Governance Programme under grant number L216252013. For more details see: http://www.uea.ac.uk/env/cserge/research/fut_governance/Home.htm.

context of the traditional style, structures and content of national environmental policy. In our introductory contribution we developed these two very broad aims into four specific objectives. These were to: (1) identify the most important drivers of (and barriers to) the continuing uptake of NEPIs in particular countries; (2) describe the overall pattern of use across different countries (and sectors); (3) assess how 'new' NEPIs are in comparison to the traditional style, structures and content of national environmental policy; and (4), relate the overall pattern of use to popular theories of comparative politics and public policy-making.

The purpose of this concluding analysis is to offer answers to these four questions by drawing upon the empirical material contained in the eight country case studies. The second section examines the most important drivers (question 1), the third section assesses the overall pattern of use (question 2), the fourth section tries to assess how 'new' the NEPIs in the eight countries are (question 3), while the fifth section returns to the theoretical predictions made in our introduction. The final section offers a concluding perspective on the politics of NEPI use in the eight countries, and identifies future research needs in this important and fast-moving area of environmental policy.

Drivers of Change

The overwhelming finding that emerges from the case studies is that the eight countries are experimenting with NEPIs for very strikingly similar reasons. In the introduction, we identified general drivers of change from the published literature. These were: a dissatisfaction with regulation in general and environmental regulation in particular; a perception that NEPIs are in some respect superior to 'old' instruments; the governance 'turn' in academia and policy-making circles; instrument changes in the EU; growing international competition and economic recessions in EU member states; and growing domestic political support for change. Our analysis confirms the importance of all six.

Dissatisfaction with Regulation

Dissatisfaction with regulation is identified as an immediate or proximate causal factor in all eight countries. Concerns about the economic compliance cost for industry, the implementation deficit and diminishing margins of return with regard to traditional regulation have been an important driver in most of the eight case countries [also *Andersen and Sprenger, 2000; Golub, 1998; Knill and Lenschow, 2000*]. However, the country studies also show that the dissatisfaction emerged differently in each country and often facilitated the adoption of different types of NEPIs (for example, initially mainly VAs and eco-labels in Germany, VAs and eco-taxes in the Netherlands, and eco-taxes and eco-labels in Finland).

Perceived Superiority of NEPIs

The perception that NEPIs are 'better' than regulation is also a very common driver for change. The perceived superior efficiency of market-based instruments (MBIs) compared to traditional regulation was an important factor in their uptake. What is puzzling is the time it took for this message – which initially emanated primarily from among the ranks of environmental economists in the 1970s [e.g., *Siebert, 1976*] who drew heavily on pioneering theories put forward by welfare economists such as Pigou [*1920*] and Coase [*1960*] – to be accepted and acted upon in the eight countries. Moreover, many states became attracted to eco-taxes mainly because they offered a new source of government revenue through the less politically contentious (at least initially) use of a familiar policy tool within a newly emerging policy sector (that is, environmental policy).

From Government to Governance?

The third driver identified in the introduction was the governance 'turn' in most OECD countries. By the early 1990s, older arguments about the merits of NEPIs began to receive a more sympathetic hearing as states experimented with new forms of governance. In virtually all eight countries, the governance debate appears to have provided a more propitious context in which NEPIs can thrive. Neo-liberal ideas about deregulation were identified as important drivers which facilitated the uptake of NEPIs in countries as varied as Austria, Australia, Finland, France, Germany and the UK. However, the sustainable development paradigm, which puts equal weight on environmental, economic and social considerations, has also highlighted the limitations of traditional regulatory tools in most of the case countries and especially in Finland, Germany and the UK.

Influence of the European Union

Interestingly, the authors disagree about whether the EU is mainly a driver of, or an obstacle to, the wider uptake of NEPIs in its member states. The ambivalent role played by the EU with regard to NEPI innovation has also been pointed out by Albert Weale and colleagues [*2000: 458*] who found 'illiberal instruments and liberal foundations'. In most member states at certain points in their evolution, the EU has almost certainly prompted domestic change, although it has not actually adopted many VAs [*CEC, 1996, 2002*] and no environmental taxes of its own. In 2002, the Commission concluded that it only intended to 'recognise and make use of environmental agreements on a selective case by case basis' [*COM, 2002:*

13]. However, the EU has indirectly promoted change by forcing some member states to adopt instruments which they would probably not have adopted otherwise. For instance, Ireland has had to get to grips with eco-labels and eco-audit and management systems (EMAS). States such as Finland have also had to adopt new ways of using existing tools (for example, environmental impact assessment (EIA)) as a direct result of the EU's involvement. Austria and Germany would not have taken practical steps (or at least only at a much later stage) to set up national emission trading pilot schemes without the Commission's proposals for an EU-wide trading scheme [*CEC,2000b; CEC, 2001*].

The EU has also exerted a more indirect form of pressure on states to experiment with new tools, for instance, the packaging waste Directive encouraged Ireland to experiment with VAs, and private actors in the UK to develop tradable permit systems. In the future, the water framework Directive looks set to push member states towards full cost recovery of water prices and the increasing control of non-point sources of water pollution – a task for which certain types of NEPI (for example, pesticide or fertiliser taxes) would be ideally suited. The UK is one of a number of countries which are known to be actively exploring this option. On the other hand, when Austria joined the EU, it abandoned its national fertiliser tax because of fears that it might be judged by the European Court of Justice (ECJ) to constitute a barrier to trade within the internal market.

Our Australian case study usefully reveals that outside the EU, NEPIs also continue to be adopted. Therefore, the EU's importance as a driver should not be overestimated, although it remains a hugely influential agent of lesson drawing and policy instrument transfer within Europe [*Jordan et al., 2003*].

Growing International Competition

Growing international competition and economic recession has forced countries to look for more cost-efficient policy instruments compared to traditional regulation, which is often seen as a competitive disadvantage for industry especially during a downturn of the global economy and economic recession as was the case in the early 1990s [*Golub, 1998b*]. Particularly 'high regulatory' states [*Héritier et al., 1996*] such as Austria, Finland and Germany, which during the late 1980s moved towards the adoption of the ecological modernisation paradigm (which assumes that stringent environmental regulation and economic growth are compatible), have largely abandoned this concept due to concerns about international economic competition [also *Weale et al., 2000; Wurzel, 2002*].

Growing Domestic Political Support

The case studies show that the election of centre-left political parties, in some cases with a green party presence (Finland, France and Germany), helped tip the balance towards NEPIs in a number of countries. The adoption of eco-taxes in Germany and the UK in the mid-to late 1990s were associated with so-called Third Way political philosophies while in Finland, Germany and France green parties championed eco-tax reforms. However, it is somewhat of a puzzle that so far the centre-left governments have much more enthusiastically deployed MBIs (especially eco-taxes and to a more limited degree also tradable permits), than the free market/centre-right governments that dominated politics in the 1980s and early 1990s. The former have traditionally supported 'big government' and its corollary regulation, whereas the latter advocated the very liberal economic ideas that economists often draw upon to advocate MBIs. Most free market/centre-right governments (for example, in Austria, Germany and the Netherlands) have pushed the adoption of VAs. However, it would be a mistake to assume that centre-left governments have abstained from making use of this policy instrument.

Domestic political support has also grown because environmental groups have started to give up their safe preference for traditional regulation. Environmental groups have remained critical about VAs in most of the countries and still largely oppose tradable permit schemes (particularly in Austria and Finland) although there are a few exceptions as can be seen from the German Nature Circle's (DNR) endorsement of tradable permit in principle [*DNR, 2000*]. Some businesses and especially the banking sector have also endorsed tradable permit schemes which could lead to great economic benefits, for example, for the City of London [*Jordan et al., 2003c*].

Additional Drivers

The cases themselves point to two other important drivers of change. The first is the interaction between different types of NEPI. In both France and the UK the use (or even the threat of using) environmental taxes has helped to popularise other instruments such as VAs and (in the case of the UK) tradable permits. In Germany tradable permits have been resisted by the chemical industry in particular, which has demanded the continued and expanded use of VAs instead. In this way, NEPI use can almost become self-perpetuating. The Netherlands and the UK have moved furthest towards examining the benefits of policy instrument mixes that seek to maximise the comparative advantages of the full instrument repertoire. Other countries (such as Austria and Germany) have so far relied on more narrow policy instrument mixes which have drawn only on a limited number of NEPIs (mainly VAs, eco-taxes and eco-labels) in combination with 'old' instruments (that is, regulation).

The second, much more specific factor is climate change. As a pressing global policy issue being negotiated on the international (and EU) level, climate change has greatly facilitated the use of (certain types of) NEPIs in most of the case countries. In Australia (a country with an otherwise conservative attitude to NEPIs), it has culminated in a national Greenhouse Strategy which draws on a range of different policy instruments. In Austria, Germany, France, The Netherlands and the UK, climate change has pushed governments – although to varying degrees – actively to explore MBIs (including highly complicated but innovative new tools such as tradable permits) and VAs.

Barriers to NEPI Innovation

The barriers identified in our introduction to this collection also resonate with the empirical findings of the case studies. Importantly, some of the drivers may under certain circumstances actually act as barriers to NEPI innovation.

Lack of Expertise and Familiarity

A lack of strong support for NEPIs from within Environmental Ministries used to be a significant constraint in countries such as Austria, Finland, France, Germany and the UK although it has declined significantly since the early 1990s. In some countries (for example, Austria and Germany as well as the UK) the antipathy to NEPIs was a reflection of the legal and/or scientific background of most civil servants. NEPIs were regarded as alien and unproven, whereas, for all its faults, regulation was a tried and tested tool. In Ireland, a lack of strong political support from within the Environment Ministry coupled to opposition from the Treasury and sections of industry, is continuing to throttle attempts to expand NEPI use.

Opposition from Environmental Policy Actors

Opposition from environmental pressure groups to MBIs waned significantly in the early 1990s, and is now almost fully reversed as regards eco-taxes although there is still considerable suspicion about tradable permit schemes. As was mentioned above (under 'drivers'), opposition to tradable permits has waned amongst environmental groups. In some countries environmental groups (for example, in Germany) have now even endorsed tradable permis. However, this is not the case in all countries as can be seen particularly in the Finnish case.

In 2001, the EEB announced an 18 month environmental tax reform campaign to 'get the prices right' in the EU, the chief aim being to force the EU to adopt some form of carbon dioxide/energy tax [*ENDS Daily, 27 Nov. 2001*]. At the same time, environmentalists in a number of countries including Austria, Finland, Germany and the UK, remain deeply suspicious of VAs. The Commission is reluctant to adopt VAs that are entirely free of a legislative superstructure as can be seen from various proposals which all recommend the wider use on the EU level but largely in combination with traditional regulation [*CEC, 1996, 2002*]. The Commission is aware of transparency and legitimacy problems associated with VAs [*Friedrich et al., 2000; Mol et al., 2000*] and some officials (especially in the Directorate General responsible for environmental policy) are not entirely convinced about their long-term enforceability and effectiveness (interviews, 2001).

Opposition from Vested Interests
Energy intensive industries most especially are strongly opposed to the adoption of eco-taxes and tradable permits. All countries which adopted eco-taxes granted generous exemptions to high energy users. This is despite the fact that, at least from a purely environmental economics perspective, efficiency gains would be particularly significant from taxing high energy users which constitute high polluters in terms of carbon dioxide emissions.

There has been considerable industry resistance to tradable permits in Austria, Finland, France, Germany and Ireland. Due to strong opposition from especially the German chemical industry, this industrial sector has been excluded from the Commission's proposal for an EU-wide tradable permits scheme [*CEC, 2001*]. Some industrial actors actually favour traditional regulation above NEPIs because it is a policy tool with which they are familiar and because it establishes a level playing field for all targeted actors.

Fears about Competitiveness
Fears about a loss in economic competitiveness have hampered attempts to make use of eco-taxes in most of the countries assessed in this collection. For much of the 1990s, a Centre-Right German government abstained from unilaterally adopting an ecological tax reform due to concerns about its impact on German industry. It was only when a Left–Green coalition government came to power in 1999 that an ecological tax reform was adopted. Developments in France were similar. Austria has not yet adopted a major ecological tax reform although it had been considered on the highest political level in the mid-1990s. The cultural dislike of tax measures and Treasury opposition have been a retarding element for the introduction of eco-taxes in Ireland, although it has adopted some eco-taxes (such as the tax on plastic carrier bags). However, concerns about a potential negative

impact of eco-taxes on the 'Celtic Tiger' economy are also an important factor behind the slow uptake of this NEPI type in Ireland.

Distributional Impacts

Finally, public opposition to new taxes looks set to be an emerging constraint in a number of countries. Massive public protests against rising fuel prices in particular in France and the UK as well as, though to a lesser degree, in Austria and Germany in the Summer of 2000 have made governments more reluctant to adopt new eco-taxes. In the UK, public opposition to consumer taxes has meant that recent NEPIs have tended to target industry instead while innovative plans for a household waste levy are on hold as the government seeks to second-guess public opinion.

Additional Barriers

Another specific barrier to change has emerged from the case studies: the EU. The EU is often regarded as a force for higher environmental standards in Europe [*Jordan, 2002; Sbragia, 1996; Vogel, 1995*]. However, there are many examples in our seven cases (Australia is not an EU member state) of the EU limiting the ability of its member states to innovate with NEPIs. The Commission has, for example, announced that only certain types of VA can be employed by states to implement EU legislation [*CEC, 1996: 59–61*]. Thus, they should take the form of a legal contract (that is, be negotiated agreements – see introduction), that is enforceable either under civil or under public law, specifies clear objectives and is accessible to the public. There have also been several examples where EU legislation has overwritten VAs in member states. This was the case concerning VAs on scrapped cars in Austria, Germany and the Netherlands.

The EU can constrain the ability of states to adopt NEPIs in other ways too, as national instruments must not disrupt the functioning of the internal market. For example, in the UK, the national greenhouse gas tradable permitting system has had to satisfy the EU's state aid rules. The German ecological tax reform had to be postponed by several months because of objections from the Commission mainly about exemptions for high energy users and subsidies for renewable energy. Austria abandoned its fertiliser tax shortly before it joined the EU. In the UK, the threat of a significant misfit between the national tradable permitting system and the Commission's own plans for an EU tradable permitting system is making firms wary of signing up to the national scheme. Finland, meanwhile, was forced to amend its national carbon tax proposals to any conflict with EU trade rules. Finally, EU regulations requiring the best available technology principle (BAT) to be applied may also limit the scope for national experimentation with NEPIs such as MBIs and VAs. Clearly, conflicts with

EU rules, may undermine the credibility of nationally adopted NEPIs. The examples above show the difficulties associated with using any new instrument in a complex, multi-level system of environmental governance.

Patterns of NEPI Use

The drivers discussed may be common to most or, in some respects, all states, but the resulting pattern of NEPI use is anything but homogenous. Rather, individual states appear to be adopting different NEPIs, in different sectors and at different times. The overall pattern is highly differentiated by instrument and also by country. Instead of a wholesale adoption of NEPIs right across all eight countries, pre-existing repertoires of instruments appear to have survived. In many respects the diversity of instrument used appears to have increased – not decreased – in the last 30 years.

Figure 1 provides a very simple indication of the relative popularity of the main NEPI types across the eight countries assessed in this collection. Two things are immediately apparent. The first is that the diversity of instruments used has grown significantly since 1970. Thirty years ago only a small number of countries had adopted what are now classified as NEPIs. Today, even the least innovative and environmentally ambitious countries (in our sample – Ireland and Australia) have a number of fully functioning NEPIs in place.

Secondly, although NEPIs in general are more popular and much more widely used, they are much more popular in some countries (for example, The Netherlands, Germany and Finland) than others (for example, Austria, Australia and Ireland). Significantly, even the most enthusiastic adopters have so far chosen to shun certain types of instrument (for example, VAs in Finland and tradable permits in Germany while the Netherlands was late in

FIGURE 1
THE DISTRIBUTION OF NEPIS BY COUNTRY FOR THE LATE 1990S

	Ecotaxes	Tradable permits	Voluntary agreements	Eco-labels	Regulation
Australia	Low	Low	Low	Low	Still dominant
Austria	Medium	Low	Low/ medium	Medium	Still dominant
Finland	High	Low	Medium	High	Still significant
France	Medium	Low	Low	High	Still dominant
Germany	Medium	Low	High	High	Still dominant
Ireland	Low	Low	Low/ medium	Low	Still dominant
Netherlands	High	Medium/ high	High	Low	Still significant
UK	Medium	High	Medium	Low/medium	Still significant

adopting a national eco-label scheme), whereas some countries are enthusiastic about particular NEPIs (for example, tradable permits in the UK) but fairly ambivalent about the rest. Just as there were enduring differences in the way regulation was applied in the past, there are differences in the way NEPIs are utilised today. Figure 1 gives a summary sketch of the country distribution of the NEPIs studied in this volume. Note that the descriptors only offer a general assessment of each country in relation to the others in the study, rather than to some absolute baseline.

Market-Based Instruments

Japan adopted one of the very first MBIs (an environmental tax on sulphur dioxide emissions) in 1974. The Nordic countries (such as Finland), The Netherlands and France followed soon after with charges on water and air pollution. Germany adopted a wastewater levy in the mid-1970s, but this was not fully implemented until the early 1980s. The UK did not initiate national environmental taxes until the early to mid-1990s [*OECD, 1995*]. In a 1996 survey, the EEA [*1996*] portrayed the UK as a fairly circumspect observer of events in other countries [also *OECD, 1994: 110–12*]. More recently the UK has begun to pioneer the use of various highly innovative MBIs including waste taxes and (drawing upon US experience) tradable permits. Australia is a much more recent adopter of MBIs and Ireland has barely started.

In general, though, the 'followers' are now beginning to catch up with the initial pioneers as MBIs are more widely applied across Europe [*EEA, 2000*]. However, as was pointed out in the introduction, the gap between the wealthier Northern and poorer Southern/peripheral European countries persists and on some criteria, may even be growing [*CEC, 2000; Weale et al., 2000*]. Thus the pioneers have now moved on to more sophisticated ecological tax reforms, whereas the followers have still not made much progress with first generation MBIs such as simple effluent taxes and user charges.

The array of MBIs used has also evolved. In the 1970s, cost recovery charges dominated, but there are environmentally beneficial subsidies in countries such as Austria, Australia (The Greenhouse Challenge), Germany, Finland, France and the Netherlands [*OECD, 1999: 5*]. There are very few or no environmental subsidies in the UK and Ireland. Throughout the 1980s, they were joined by user charges and incentive taxes [*EEA, 1996: 22*]. Incentive taxes (such as lower tax rates for car with catalytic converters and unleaded petrol) are particularly widely used in Austria, Finland, Germany and the Netherlands.

In the 1990s, policy-makers began to experiment with 'second generation' approaches involving hypothecation (that is, earmarking a certain portion of the revenue stream for particular (often environmentally beneficial) forms of spending) [*CEC, 2000: 16*]. In our sample of eight countries, Austria (landfill taxes), Finland (for example, the oil waste levy), Germany (for example, duty on mineral oils) and the UK (for example, the landfill tax) formally 'earmark' the revenue from environmental taxes to environmental or other 'good' causes.

Environmental tax reform is the most advanced form of MBI currently deployed among the eight countries. Here again, there are clear leaders (the Netherlands, Finland, France, Germany and the UK all adopted significant programmes in the late 1990s) and followers (Australia, Austria and especially Ireland). Very recently, countries like the UK have innovated with policy packages involving MBIs and VAs which to tackle a particular problem [*CEC, 2000: 18*]. The Netherlands has also moved towards a sophisticated mix of a wide range of policy instruments while Germany has relied mainly on a narrower mix (made up mainly of eco-taxes, VAs and traditional regulation) for the energy sector in particular.

Finally, tradable permits were originally developed by the US, but they are still relatively uncommon in the EU. In our sample, only the UK and the Netherlands have successfully explored this particular option. Germany is now seeking to respond to the European Commission proposals for an EU-wide scheme to combat climate change by setting up a tradable permits working group in 2000. However, because of resistance by the chemical industry in particular pilot projects have been limited to the regional *(Länder)* level in Germany. Austria has recently also edged towards the adoption of a national tradable permit pilot scheme. However, France and Ireland have remained reluctant to move towards national tradable permit schemes.

Finally, the overall pattern is also highly differentiated across sectors. Some sectors, such as (motor) fuels, vehicle related activities and energy consumption are relatively well covered. Other than in Scandinavia, the Netherlands and Belgium, the agricultural sector is hardly touched at all, although Austria at one point, also had fertiliser tax [*CEC, 2000: 12*].

Voluntary Agreements

The overall popularity of VAs has also grown significantly in all eight countries since the 1970s. Most VAs are non-binding and voluntary, but some states are now experimenting with more formal and binding approaches (that is, negotiated agreements) A survey undertaken by the European Commission in 1996 reported over 300 VAs in the EU. Every member state has now adopted some form of VA but the majority are to be found in the Netherlands and Germany, which together account for well over two thirds of the VAs surveyed [*CEC, 1996; EEA, 1997*]. By 2002, the Netherlands and Germany alone had together more than 230 VAs in place (interviews, 2002). Overall, the most popular type of VA within the EU 15 is the negotiated agreement [*OECD, 1999*].

As with the MBIs, the overall pattern of use is highly differentiated. In 1996, the European Commission [*CEC, 1996*] reported the following distribution of VAs: Austria (25); Belgium (14), Denmark (16), Germany (80); Spain (6); Greece (0); Ireland (1); Italy (8); Luxembourg (5); Netherlands (>100); Portugal (10); Sweden (13); the UK (c.10). The same pattern of leaders and followers is also apparent with respect to VAs: Germany, France and the Netherlands pioneered their use but nowadays they are a common feature of most national environmental policy systems in Europe [*ELNI, 1998; CEC, 1996; UBA, 1999; Öko-Institut, 1998; UNEP, 1998*].

The nature of VAs also varies quite significantly across the eight countries. In the Netherlands, VAs supplement regulation rather than being an alternative to it; they are legal contracts or 'covenants' [*Mol et al., 2000*]. In Germany, VAs are non-binding, but they are often negotiated 'in the shadow of the law' and put forward by industry which wants to pre-empt government regulation. Austria has a relatively lower number of VAs which are all non-binding for constitutional reasons. In France and Ireland, about half the VAs are binding. In the UK, VAs are not very common [*OECD, 1994: 113*] and those that do exist tend to be non-binding and very flexible in their form [*Jordan and Salmons, 2000*]. Finally, the sectoral focus of VAs is also very uneven. Most are to be found in the energy, climate change, chemical and waste management sectors [*OECD, 1999: 15; Mol et al., 2000: 4; UBA, 2000*]; VAs are much less common in the agricultural, transport and tourism sectors.

Eco-labels

Germany acted as a pioneer when it adopted the world's first national eco-label scheme in 1977. Austria (1991), Australia (1992), France (1992), and the Netherlands (1992) have all adopted national eco-label schemes. Finland has been actively participating in the Nordic Swan which is a multi-national eco-label scheme that was adopted by the Nordic Council countries in 1989. Ireland and the UK are the only case countries which have relied solely on the EU eco-label scheme despite considerable domestic demands for a national eco-label scheme. However, the EU eco-label scheme suffered from a cumbersome and non-transparent decision-making process and competition with member state eco-label schemes. It has achieved only a very low degree of producer acceptability and consumer recognition. By 2000, only 41 EU eco-labels had been awarded (for 15 EU member states) compared to almost 4,000 national eco-labels under the German Blue Angel scheme. By 2001, there was only one Germany company which had been awarded the EU eco-label while there had still not been a single application from Austria for the EU eco-label [*Jordan et al., 2002*]. However, in 2002 the number of EU eco-labels rose significantly.

During the early 1990s, a rapid diffusion of (national, multinational and supranational) eco-label schemes took place around the globe [*Kern et al., 2000; Jordan et al., 2002*]. However, not all of them turned into successful eco-label schemes as can be seen from the Australian Environmental Choice scheme which was abandoned after only two years in 1994. The Austrian, French and Dutch national eco-labels all suffer from a low take up. Even the German Blue Angel, which for long constituted the world's most successful eco-label scheme in terms of the number of labelled products and services – although it has been overtaken by the Nordic Swan in recent years, – was given a face lift in 2002 because it was losing some of its popularity.

The German Blue Angel eco-label influenced many of the schemes which were set up at a later stage. However, the followers did not simply copy the pioneer. The Austrian, Dutch, French and the Nordic White Swan label put significantly more emphasis on life-cycle analysis than the German Blue Angel scheme. Importantly, certain national and/or regional environmental *and* economic preferences are clearly reflected in the design of the various national eco-label schemes. For example, Austria pioneered an eco-label for tourism, the Netherlands were first to extend the national eco-label scheme to the food sector and flours, Finland regards forest certification as an important issue and Australia puts a lot of emphasis on energy labelling.

Eco-labels are now a very commonly used NEPI. However, their impact on producer and consumer behaviour is limited [*Jordan et al., 2002*]. Eco-labels are a relatively soft policy instrument when compared both to traditional regulation and MBIs. Moreover, the proliferation of national, multi-national and supranational as well as numerous private company eco-label schemes seems to have caused considerable confusion amongst consumers and may even endanger the continued success of relatively well-known schemes such as the German Blue Angel [*Jordan et al., 2002*].

Regulation

Judging by the material presented in our eight case studies, regulation has not gone away even in leader states such as the Netherlands, Germany and Finland. There has been no wholesale switch to NEPIs. In fact NEPIs tend to be reserved for quite specific uses such as 'filling in the cracks' not covered by regulation or dealing with emerging issues such as climate change. There are a number of reasons for this practice. First, regulation often serves a supporting function for NEPIs. For example regulations are often used to implement NEPIs, set the rules for their operation and penalise defectors. Second, there is still strong support for regulation in many countries (such as Austria, Finland and Germany) as a tool for dealing with point sources of pollution which have been heavily regulated in the past. Attempts made by France and the UK to introduce many NEPIs into the (generally) very well regulated water pollution sector, have so far not amounted to much.

Third, regulation remains the main instrument of EU environmental policy. Apart from transparency and legitimacy issues, VAs are difficult to negotiate across borders especially when well established and large industry associations are absent (that is, it is significant that the first EU VAs target the chemical and car industries and not farming or retailing). Several states (initially the UK and more recently Ireland, Italy and Spain) have sought consistently to block the Commission's ability to innovate with environmental taxation which requires the unanimous adoption by member states within the EU. Consequently, the Commission relies on regulation to underpin its NEPIs such as eco-label schemes and EMAS.

That said, in many countries the nature of regulation is changing. In Australia, it is much more 'light handed' and in Finland it serves a 'support function'. In the UK, the domestic integrated pollution control regime (that is, regulation) shares many similarities with what continental states usually refer to as negotiated agreements underpinned by the law (for example, the Netherlands – see above).

Summary

Contrary to the common perception that NEPIs are sweeping uniformly across different national environmental protection systems, our cases confirm that the overall pattern of use is actually very differentiated by country and by sector.

First, some have adopted NEPIs much earlier (for certain sectors) than the rest. Rather than a broadly synchronous pattern of change, for each instrument, it is possible to identify a set of leader states and a set of followers. This confirms the importance of lead states [*SRU, 2002*] which has been highlighted in the policy innovation and policy diffusion literature [e.g., *Kern et al., 2000*]. In our cases, the Netherlands, Germany and Finland stand out as being the most consistent leaders, whereas Ireland and Australia have often been content to follow. For the most part, France and the UK have adopted a median position. As regards sectoral differences, the energy and chemical sectors stand out as hosting the most NEPIs.

Second, NEPIs are often put to different tasks. To take one example, VAs in the Netherlands tend to target processes and are mostly obligatory, whereas in Germany they tend to target products and are legally non-binding.

Third, the differentiation is so great that states often use the same labels in very different ways. Often the definitions of a particular MBI or VA are very nation specific [*EEA, 1996: 21*]. For instance, the OECD [*1998: 4*] has referred to the "rich" terminology relating to different types of VA, which complicates any attempt to develop a consistent classification system. The EEA [*2000*] regularly complains that even compiling a simple database of the MBIs used is rendered problematic by the tendency for each country to adopt its own, independent classification system. Even a single instrument used in one country can differ greatly from the (apparently) same instrument used in another national context. The perception of how a particular NEPI is used in one country may also differ from another country. For example, the German Environmental Expert Council [*SRU: 234*] has argued that the UK's tradable permit scheme amounts to little more than a VA combined with eco-taxes.

How 'New' Are NEPIs?

In our editorial introduction (see Jordan *et al.*, this collection, pages 1–24), we explained that 'new' is normally defined as 'novel', 'not existing before', 'strange or unfamiliar', 'starting afresh', 'restored or renewed after decay'. To what extent, therefore, are the NEPIs described in the eight countries genuinely 'new'? In adopting NEPIs, are states doing new things or are they simply fine tuning old practices? Is the overall pattern one of a wholesale revolution or a slower, less uniform process of evolution?

In the introduction we explained that the best way to assess the novelty of a particular instrument is to relate it to the pre-existing style, structure and content of national policy. In the concluding part of the case study papers we asked the authors to assess the extent of revolution and/or evolution in national NEPI use. Figure 2 summarises their assessments. The labels are, of course, not hard and fast. Generally speaking, 'incrementalism' refers to

FIGURE 2
THE NATURE OF NEPI USE: INNOVATION OR INCREMENTALISM?

	Eco-taxes	Tradable permits	Voluntary agreements	Eco-labels
Australia	Incrementalism	Little change	Incrementalism	Incrementalism
Austria	Incrementalism	Little change	Incrementalism	Incrementalism
Finland	Innovation	No change	Incrementalism	Innovation
France	Incrementalism	Incrementalism	Incrementalism	Incrementalism
Germany	Some innovation	Little change	Innovation	Innovation
Ireland	Little change	No change	Incrementalism	Incrementalism
Netherlands	Innovation	Innovation	Some innovation	Incrementalism
UK	Recent innovation	Recent innovation	Incrementalism	Incrementalism

little change, or significant change that does not represent a significant break with the past. 'Innovation', on the other hand, refers to instances of real change, which break decisively with the past. Finally, 'no change' is used to characterise instances where a particular instrument is mostly or even entirely absent from a particular national setting.

The most striking feature of Figure 2 is how few countries are actually innovating in their use of NEPIs. In most countries, NEPIs are either not being used or they are being used, but in a relatively incremental and evolutionary manner. The country chapters offer explanations for the overall pattern of (non-)change, but it is probably worth highlighting the examples of real innovation, as they appear to be the exception rather than the rule. However, on closer inspection even these exhibit considerable degrees of continuity with what went before. For example, on paper, the UK's recent experimentation with tradable permits, ecological tax reforms, negotiated agreements and policy packages suggests that innovation is occurring. However, Jordan *et al.* (this collection, pages 179–98) reveal that they are still relatively few in number and are concentrated in a relatively small number of sectors.

Germany's adoption of about 130 VAs would also seem to imply that the government there has embarked upon a significant programme of instrument renewal, when in fact the German case study paints a different picture of conservative change. Importantly, Wurzel *et al.* (this collection, pages 115–36) report that regulation is still the mainstay of German environmental policy and that VAs are adopted in 'the shadow of the law'. The fact that regulation has mainly been supplemented (and not supplanted) by VAs is in keeping with the consensual and moderately proactive style of German policy. MBIs are much less common and as yet, there is still no emission trading on the national level.

Finland's pioneering adoption of eco-taxes in the 1980s is also another widely remarked upon example of innovation in instrument selection and use. However, look a little closer and Finland's appetite for NEPIs is not nearly so strong; for instance, the adoption of VAs has been much less impressive. In theory, VAs should have been easy to adopt as they fit neatly with that country's co-operative and corporatist policy style. Austria has also struggled to leave behind a strongly regulatory past but found it difficult to adopt a wide range of eco-taxes and has still not adopted a national emission trading pilot scheme.

Finally, our analysis of events in France shows over 75 different eco-taxes, but mostly of a very *ad hoc* and uncoordinated nature. With little progress in relation to tradable permitting, our French case study maintains that the overall pattern of NEPI use in France has been highly path dependent.

Theorising Instrument Selection and Adoption

In the introduction we outlined two broad theoretical perspectives, which claim to explain the adoption of policy instruments in different national settings. In summary, ideational theories regard shifts in ideas and interests (that is, policy learning) as the most prominent drivers of policy development and policy instrument selection. Of particular importance is the *cognitive* struggle between different groups to improve their understanding of the causes of policy problems or the suitability of particular instruments as solutions. According to this view, a broad pattern of innovation across countries is capable of occurring if and only if the ideas and the political will to use them are present. Finally, policy instruments perform an *instrumental* role in the policy process; they have no independent life of their own. In other words, actors look for instruments to implement their ideas. When certain instruments fail to work properly or if new ideas emerge and become dominant, the repertoire of instruments will be adjusted accordingly.

Institutional theories on the other hand argue that the overall pattern of instrument use will be fairly heterogeneous, reflecting the resilience and longevity of national institutional traditions. Common pressure to adopt NEPIs will be refracted by these national institutional forms, producing a very 'bounded' form of innovation [*Weir, 1992*] as countries experiment with what they know well, while shunning institutionally incompatible tools used elsewhere in the world. The structuring effect is so strong that each country develops its own 'national repertoire' of instruments [*Bennett, 1988: 439*]. Over time, policy instruments and the institutional contexts in which they are deeply embedded, adapt slowly and imperfectly to political demands. This is because the instruments are deeply rooted in national bureaucracies, national societies and national economies, and while not completely impervious to change, they do have the ability to perpetuate themselves.

Ideational Theories

It is possible to identify opposing advocacy coalitions whose core beliefs and values have changed little as regards the adoption of a particular policy instrument. At first, NEPIs were only advocated by a small number of academics, think tanks and advisory committees, but since the 1970 a shift in ideas about their usefulness has occurred. However, trade unions and environmental NGOs have remained largely sceptical about the wide use of VAs and tradable permits, while advocating eco-taxes and traditional environmental regulation. National environmental ministries have converted to NEPIs more recently. Industry representatives and Economics (and Finance) Ministry officials often take a very different perspective.

From the ideas perspective, the shift towards a wider range of policy instruments can be explained by the presence of these shifting advocacy coalitions pressing at the national level for the adoption of NEPIs. The EU, OECD and UN all have provided transnational platforms for those advocating NEPIs. A recent example is the way in which European advocates 'borrowed' the idea of tradable permits from the US and then used them to develop European pilot projects. In doing this, some member states (such as the Netherlands) have been able to draw on domestic experience in other sectors while other member states have gone through extensive consultation processes (for example, Germany) in order to take account of national peculiarities. Tradable permits schemes do not therefore constitute a copycat of the American model.

However, ideational theories struggle to explain three things in particular. First they struggle to explain the highly differential pattern of NEPI use. Our case studies demonstrate that a VA in one country is not necessarily functionally equivalent to a VA in a neighbouring country. There do appear to be fairly persistent national repertoires of instruments. Much of the innovation that has occurred has been bounded by pre-existing national policy structures, styles and contents. Our preliminary findings suggest that there are marked differences in instrument use and/or enduring rigidities, which could be explained, by institutional differences.

Second, they struggle to explain the difficulty of replacing regulation with NEPIs. What is striking about the pattern of change over time is the continuity of national approaches and traditions. Over the course of time, path dependent processes have conditioned the choice and application of tools. In many examples, the increasing returns reaped from remaining with regulation outweighed the putative benefits of alternative tools and so the overall level of innovation was low. When challenged, policy makers clung to traditional tools (competency traps) even when the ideological climate of the time was deregulatory and only very weakly environmental.

Third, the pattern of change in many countries was far more chaotic and chance-like than ideational theories might imply. At any one time there, were several debates – on governance, on subsidiarity, on the merits of NEPIs – taking place at the same time. Often NEPIs owe their existence to an intervention from outside (for example, the EU), the election of a new ruling party or the activities of an individual. So, although the clash of advocacy coalitions provides the broad content within which instruments were analysed, they do not explain why some instruments were selected while others were rejected.

Institutional Theories

Institutional theories have no trouble explaining why no two governments have used the same NEPI in exactly the same manner [cf. *Hood, 1983: 106*]. In fact, different countries do not even define the same type of NEPI in precisely the same way. Different jurisdictions have also responded to new ideas about NEPIs in hugely different ways because of national and/or supranational path dependencies. States (and the EU) usually alter the scope and form of NEPIs in order to ensure that they fit in with wider national (and supranational) institutional features and regulatory 'styles'. These adaptations may occur during the implementation phase as was shown with regard to eco-taxes following fuel protests in several countries. Innovation is therefore likely to take place only gradually. Moreover, policy convergence during the adoption process may give way to divergence during the implementation of a particular type of NEPI.

So, game, set and match to institutional theories? Well, not quite. It is indubitably the case that a widespread shift is occurring in the instruments of national environmental policy. Major changes in instrument use have occurred over time. The relatively recent move towards the adoption of different types of NEPI is also difficult to explain from the institutional perspective. Admittedly, states are not responding in precisely the same manner, but they are proceeding along broadly similar tracks. This suggests some exogenous factor at work in pushing adoption.

Secondly, institutional theories struggle to account for the convulsive shift, which has occurred in instrument usage, other than as an institutionally lagged response to some external crisis or crises. The external drivers (for example, new environmental problems such as climate change and sustainability) which challenge traditional policy paradigms have been important, but they offer an insufficient explanation for the *direction* in which the change is occurring.

Finally, are all the obstacles to – or mediators of – innovation entirely institutional? Quite clearly, they are not; in many countries, the delayed or modulated uptake of NEPIs can also be put down to 'old-fashioned' political factors, specifically the weakness of environmental political parties and pressure groups, the political power of the Treasury *vis-à-vis* the environment department and industry's suspicion of ecological modernist arguments. Institutional scholars would presumably respond that while political factors may have been important, they still do not really explain the consistency with which countries maintained their pre-existing national repertoires of instruments.

In conclusion, neither perspective offers an entirely satisfactory explanation for the pattern of NEPI use revealed by our case studies. Ideational theories are better at explaining the motives and dynamics of change, whereas institutional theories concentrate more upon the filtering effect of national institutional forms.

Comparative Conclusions

There is a widespread assumption that national governments are transforming their national policies by adopting more and more so-called 'new' instruments of environmental policy. International bodies such as the OECD and the EEA manage databases which contain rapidly lengthening lists of the most important NEPIs, and describe their distribution within and between different sectors. The assumption that is often made is that the proliferation of NEPIs is constitutive of a fundamental shift from environmental government to environmental governance. In this volume we have tried to subject these assumptions to more detailed empirical and theoretical scrutiny. Four points emerge from our analysis.

First, the processes of change in the eight countries appear to share very similar causes. That is to say, the influence of half a dozen key drivers can be identified, although of course their relative importance varies from country to country.

Second, although the countries share a common set of drivers, the resulting pattern of NEPI use is highly differentiated across and within countries and sectors. States have used different NEPIs for different reasons, in different contexts, at different times. The huge difference that sometimes exist between instruments used in national contexts, strongly suggests that we should not easily assume that instruments from the same sub-type (for example, VAs) are functionally equivalent. By looking at the comparative politics of instrument selection and adoption, we have hopefully revealed the value of going beyond simple typologies and databases and looking at how NEPIs are actually used.

Third, theories of comparative politics and public policy can account for part of the pattern of use we observe in the eight countries but not all of it. Ideational theories help to explain the growing popularity of NEPIs, but they struggle to explain the highly differentiated pattern of use. Institutional theories, which emphasise the filtering effect of national styles, structures and policy forms, provide part of the explanation, but cannot account for the instances of instrument innovation revealed in our eight case studies. There is a continuing debate about whether national policies are converging towards a common model. To the extent that states used to apply different variants of the same instrument (regulation) but now apply different variants of different instruments, national environmental policies have probably diverged in the last 30 years in spite of the EU's attempts to promote greater harmonisation and hence convergence.

Fourth, what is or is not 'new' is properly a matter for detailed empirical comparative and historical investigation, which traces current patterns of instrument use back along their historical pathways of change. By adopting such an approach, we have revealed that the overall pattern is more one of steady evolution and less of sudden, revolutionary change [cf. *Lafferty and Meadowcroft, 2000: 452*].

Does it matter if states adopt NEPIs in different forms at different times, and deploy them in often highly different ways? In one important sense, no. States adopt common policy objectives at the international level and in the EU, but by and large retain the right to determine the precise means of achieving them. In any case, a basic level of difference is probably immutable: national policies have always differed in respect of the content, structure and style of policy, so there is no reason to expect the use of NEPIs to be any different. That said, there are two circumstances in which we might consider the persistence of different approaches and instruments to be a bad thing.

First, if one country adopts a VA with its industry to reduce pollution, it could put it at a competitive disadvantage with similar industries in less heavily regulated neighbouring countries. The Commission has already pointed out that VAs should not interfere with the functioning of the single market [*CEC, 1996: 14*]. By their very nature, NEPIs which target products rather than processes are especially important to harmonise. The fear of creating uneven playing fields is often used by parts of industry to push for the EU to be involved. The irony is that current decisional rules in the EU prevent the Commission from innovating with many types of MBI.

Second, if different instruments have different environmental outcomes (that is, some are more effective at tackling problems than others), then some stakeholders will legitimately ask whether the overall effort is fairly distributed. We have not explicitly addressed the question of environmental effectiveness in this particular volume, but it is now being actively researched both by academics and international bodies [*Knill and Lenschow, 2000; OECD, 1997; EEA, 2000*]. The emerging consensus is that some instruments work better in some circumstances than others, but this is not the same thing as saying that every state should adopt the same instrument.

We close by reflecting upon what our findings reveal about the putative shift from environmental government to environmental governance. The case studies indicate that governance is becoming increasingly important, but that government remains – and will probably continue to remain – important. We argued above that regulation often provides an important support function when NEPIs are used. It provides practical authority to the agency designing and implementing a NEPI, and establishes the rules governing its operation.

As environmental protection systems become more and more crowded with instruments, more attention has to be devoted to ensuring that they do not overlap or come into conflict with one another. Indeed, as the realisation sinks in that there is no one single perfect instrument and that each has its merits and demerits, authorities are trying to design complex policy instrument packages. But the state's involvement also extends way beyond the matter of regulating, to include the day-to-day administration of NEPIs (for example, negotiating VAs, issuing tradable permits, undertaking economic valuation studies to set the initial level of a pollution tax, ensuring fair play, monitoring compliance and penalising defectors). The total administrative load involved required to develop NEPIs can be surprisingly high. In the UK, the environment ministry devoted 17 person years to negotiating just 42 climate change VAs (see Jordan *et al.*, this collection, pages 179–83). NEPIs may, therefore, involve more, not less state involvement, and certainly much more central government involvement than the days when most regulation was implemented and enforced at a fairly local level. On the basis of our close empirical analysis of how NEPIs are actually being deployed, our overall finding is that environmental governance is at best supplementing, and most certainly not comprehensively supplanting, environmental government by regulatory means.

REFERENCES

Andersen, M.S. and R.-U. Sprenger (eds.) (2000), *Market-Based Instruments for Environmental Management. Politics and Institutions*, Cheltenham: Edward Elgar.
Bennett, C.J. (1988), 'Regulating the Computer: Comparing Policy Instruments in Europe and the US', *European Journal of Political Science*, Vol.16, pp.437–66.
CEC (Commission of the European Communities) (1996), *Communication from the Commission on Environmental Agreements (COM (96) 561 final)*, Brussels: CEC.
CEC (2000a), *Database on Environmental Taxes in the EU Member States*, consultancy prepared by Forum for the Future, July 2001, Brussels: CEC.
CEC (2000b), *Green Paper on Greenhouse Gas Emission Trading Within the European Union*, COM (2000) 87,8.3.2000, Brussels: CEC.
CEC (2001), *Proposal for a Directive of the European Parliament and of the Council Establishing a Scheme for Greenhouse Gas Emission Allowance Trading Within the Community and Amending Council Directive 96/61/EC, COM (2001) 581 final, 23.10.2001*, Brussels: CEC.
CEC (2002), *Communication From the Commission to the European Parliament, the Council, the Economic and Social Committee and the Committee of the Regions. Environmental Agreements at Community Level Within the Framework of the Action Plan on the Simplification and Improvement of the Regulatory Environment, COM (2002) 412 final*, Brussels: CEC.
Coase, R.H. (1960), 'The Problem of Social Cost', *The Journal of Law and Economics*, No.3, pp. 1–44.

DNR (2000), *German NGO Comments Concerning the EU Green Paper on Greenhouse Gas Emission Trading Within the EU*, Bonn/Berlin: Deutscher Naturschutzring.

EEA (European Environment Agency), (1996), *Environmental Taxes: Implementation and Environmental Effectiveness*, Copenhagen: EEA.

EEA (1997), *Environmental Agreements: Environmental Effectiveness*, Copenhagen: EEA.

EEA (2000), *Environmental Taxes: Recent Developments in Tools for Integration and Sustainable Development*, Copenhagen: EEA.

ELNI (The Environmental Law Network International), (1998), *Environmental Agreements*, London: Cameron May.

ENDS (Environmental Data Services Ltd.) (various years), *Environmental Data Services (ENDS) Report* (various issues; see text for details).

Friedrich, A., Tappe, M. and R.K.W. Wurzel (2000), A New Approach to EU Environmental Policy-Making? The Auto-Oil I Programme', *Journal of European Public Policy*, Vol.7, No.4, pp.593–612.

Golub, J. (ed.) (1998a), *New Instruments of Environmental Policy*, London: Routledge.

Golub, J. (ed.) (1998b), *Global Competition and EU Environmental Policy*, London: Routledge.

Héritier, A., Knill, C. and S. Mingers (1996), *Ringing the Changes in Europe. Regulatory Competition and the Redefinition of the State. Britain, France and Germany*, Berlin: de Gruyter.

Hood, C. (1983), *The Tools of Government*, London: Macmillan.

Jordan, Andrew (2003), The Europeanisation of British Environmental Policy: A Departmental Perspective, Basingstoke: Palgrave.

Jordan, A., Wurzel, R., Zito, A. and L. Brückner (2002), 'Consumer Responsibility-Taking and Eco-label Schemes in Europe', in M. Micheletti *et al.* (eds.), *Politics, Products and Markets*, New Brunswick, NJ: Transaction Press.

Jordan, A., Wurzel, R. and A. Zito (2003), 'European Governance and the Transfer of 'New' Environmental Policy Instruments', *Public Administration* (in press)

Jordan, A. and R. Salmons (2000), 'The Use of Voluntary Agreements in the UK', CSERGE mimeo, Norwich and London: CSERGE, UCL and UEA.

Kern, K., H. Jörgens and M Jänicke (2000), 'Die Diffusion umweltpolitscher Innoationen. Ein Beitrag zur Globalisierung von Umweltpolitik', *Zeitschrift für Umweltpolitik*, Vol.23, pp.507–46.

Knill, C. and A. Lenschow (eds.) (2000), *Implementing EU Environmental Policy*, Manchester: Manchester University Press.

Lafferty, W. and J. Meadowcroft (2000), 'Concluding Perspectives', in W. Lafferty and J. Meadowcroft (eds.), *Implementing Sustainable Development*, Oxford: Oxford University Press.

Mol, A. *et al.* (eds.) (2000), *The Voluntary Approach to Environmental Policy*, Oxford: Oxford University Press.

OECD (1994), *Environmental Performance Reviews: The UK*, Paris: OECD.

OECD (1995), *Environmental Taxes in OECD Countries*, Paris: OECD.

OECD (1997), *Evaluating Economic Instruments for Environmental Policy*, Paris: OECD.

OECD (1998), *Voluntary Approaches for Environmental Policy*, Paris: OECD.

OECD (1999), *Implementing Domestic Tradable Permits for Environmental Protection*, Paris: OECD.

Öko-Institut (1998), *New Instruments for Sustainablility – The New Contribution of Voluntary Agreements to Environmental Policy*, Freiburg: Öko Institut e. V.

Pigou, A. C. (1920), *The Economics of Welfare*, London: Macmillan.

Sbragia, Alberta (1996), 'Environmental policy', in H. Wallace and W. Wallace (eds.), *Policy Making in the European Union, Third Editon*, Oxford: Oxford University Press, pp.235–55.

Siebert, H. (1976), *Analyse der Instrumente der Umweltpolitik*, Göttingen.

SRU (2002), *Umweltgutachten 2002. Für eine neue Vorreiterrolle*, Berlin: Der Rat von Sachverständigen für Umweltfragen.

UBA (1999), *Selbstverpflichtungen und Normersetzende Umweltverträge als Instrumente des Umweltschutzes, Berichte 5/99* (Commissioned report by Jürgen Knebel, Lutz Wicke and Gerhard Michael), Berlin: Umweltbundesamt.

UNEP (1998), 'Voluntary Initiatives', *Industry and Environment*, Vol.21, No.1–2, pp.3–69.

Vogel, David (1995), *Trading Up: Consumer and Environmental Regulation in a Global Economy*, Cambridge, MA: Harvard University Press.

Weale, A., Pridham, G., Cini, M., Konstadadkopulos, D., Porter, M. and B. Flynn (2000), *Environmental Governance in Europe: An Even Closer Ecological Union?* Oxford: Oxford University Press.

Weir, M. (1992), 'Ideas and the Politics of Bounded Innovation', in S. Steinmo *et al.* (eds.), *Structuring Politics*, Cambridge: Cambridge University Press.

Wurzel, R.K.W. (2002), *Environmental Policy-Making in Britain, Germany and the European Union. The Europeanisation of Air and Water Pollution Control*, Manchester: Manchester University Press.

Zito, A. (2000), *Creating Environmental Policy in the European Union*, London: Macmillan.

Abstracts

'New' Instruments of Environmental Governance: Patterns and Pathways of Change
ANDREW JORDAN, RÜDIGER K.W. WURZEL and ANTHONY R. ZITO

In recent years most industrialised countries have adopted 'new' environmental policy instruments (NEPIs) voluntary agreements, environmental taxes, tradable permits and eco-labels. This collection examines the current pattern of use over time (that is, 1970–2000) in eight industrialised countries. This introduction defines a NEPI and introduces the two main objectives of the whole collection, which are to: (1) identify where and when NEPIs are being used, and reflect upon the main drivers of (and barriers to) their continuing uptake, especially in Europe; and (2) assess how 'new' they actually are in comparison to the traditional style, structures and content of national environmental policy. The aim here is to assess how far NEPIs are actually replacing or simply supplementing 'old' instruments, namely regulation. By offering a fresh perspective on the comparative politics of NEPIs, this collection provides an important empirical test of whether government is giving way to a system of environmental governance, in which the level of central steering by the state is much reduced.

The Politics of 'Ligh-Handed Regulation': 'New' Environmental Policy Instruments in Australia
ELIM PAPADAKIS and RICHARD GRANT

In order to understand the potential of new policy instruments in tackling environmental problems we locate their development in the context of challenges to traditional roles of the Australian state in promoting welfare and national economic development through regulatory measures. This contextual information is crucial to understanding the mix of policy instruments adopted by policy-makers. The analysis of environmental policy highlights persistence of regulatory traditions and emergence of new ways of organising state interventions, including voluntary agreements, targeting resources to create competitive eco-efficient industries and research on economic or market-based systems like emissions trading.

Struggling to Leave Behind a Highly Regulatory Past? 'New' Environmental Policy Instruments in Austria
RÜDIGER K.W. WURZEL, LARS BRÜCKNER, ANDREW JORDAN and ANTHONY R. ZITO

Austria has long been urged to make wider use of market-based instruments by the Organisation for Economic Cooperation and Development. Despite this and the significant increase in domestic demands in recent years, the uptake of 'new' environmental policy instruments (NEPIs), namely market-based instruments (such as eco-taxes and tradable permits), voluntary agreements and informational devices (such as eco-labels and eco-audits) has been only moderate. Austria has used some eco-taxes but has refrained from adopting an ecological tax reform. Tradable permits have arrived on the domestic political agenda primarily because of the European Union's efforts to make use of this type of NEPI. Voluntary agreements have been used only very sparingly despite a consensual domestic policy style. Overall, NEPIs have mainly supplemented traditional regulatory instruments and subsidies which continue to dominate Austrian environmental policy. Austria is struggling to leave behind a strongly regulatory past. The Austrian policy structures and style as well as its formidable past environmental record have retarded NEPI innovation.

The Politics of Regulatory Reform: 'New' Environmental Policy Instruments in Finland
RAUNO SAIRINEN

This contribution analyses the adaptation of new environmental policy instruments in Finland. As an environmental forerunner country, Finland has been characteristically active in using market-based instruments and eco-labels. However, voluntary agreements have been used much less. All in all, EU membership, deregulation trend and new administrative cultures have produced a general pressure to reform the national regulatory system. The design of the NEPIs that have been adopted was heavily disputed. The different ministries and stakeholders seem to be especially vulnerable to conflict, because of their different mentality in environmental governing. At first, the national environmental ministry was strongly committed to a legalistic culture and showed very little interest in NEPIs.

The Politics of Bounded Innovation: 'New' Environmental Policy Instruments in France
JOSEPH SZARKA

French environmental policy-making has been characterised by a 'dual policy style' including both statist and meso-corporatist elements. This style translated into a multiplication of environmental institutions and a wide set of policy instruments, with hypothecated environmental charges and voluntary agreements being used as early as the 1960s and 1970s. From the late 1990s, a second phase of experimentation with 'new' instruments was conducted under the left-wing Jospin government. In particular, an innovative 'pollution tax' (the 'TGAP') sought to redefine the meso-corporatist bargain and reconfigure environmental institutions. However, the main reforms were stalemated by the opposition of economic actors and the electoral defeat of the left in 2002. Thus despite auspicious beginnings, the overall impact of 'new' environmental instruments in France has so far been limited in comparison to other OECD countries. Indeed, 'new' instruments have either been contained within long-standing policy paradigms, or excluded and largely ignored.

From High Regulatory State to Social and Ecological Market Economy? 'New' Environmental Policy Instruments in Germany
RÜDIGER K.W. WURZEL, ANDREW JORDAN, ANTHONY R. ZITO and LARS BRÜCKNER

Demands for wider use of 'new' environmental policy instruments (NEPIs), namely market-based instruments (such as eco-taxes and tradable permits), voluntary agreements and informational devices (such as eco-labels and eco-audits) have increased significantly in Germany in recent years. Germany has also been urged to make wider use of market-based instruments by external actors (such as the Organisation for Economic Cooperation and Development and the World Bank). However, the uptake of 'new' policy instruments in Germany has remained uneven despite considerable NEPI innovation. German environmental policy has shown a high uptake of VAs and eco-labels. However, it has made only moderate use of eco-taxes although they have increased significantly with the introduction of the ecological tax reform in 1999. Tradable permits have not yet been tested on the national level although some states (Länder) set up pilot projects to gain practical experience ahead of the EU's tradable permit scheme. Overall, NEPIs have been used mainly to supplement traditional regulatory instruments which still dominate German environmental policy. Germany's transformation from a 'high regulatory' state (which makes wide use of traditional regulation and VAs) towards an ecological market economy (which relies primarily on market-based instruments) has therefore been a slow one.

Much Talk But Little Action? 'New' Environmental Policy Instruments in Ireland
BRENDAN FLYNN

The Irish experience with NEPIs has been essentially tentative and disappointing. In particular, there has been a dearth of market-based instruments until very recently, whereas some voluntary instruments have emerged. It is argued that this pattern of change can be explained by reference to a variety of diffuse factors, such as a political-institutional setting which is traditionally cautious towards fiscal reforms, and wider cultural influences. The 'drivers' for what limited NEPIs have emerged, appear to be mainly external, namely the EU and policy transfer from Britain. The Irish case suggests that NEPIs do not offer an easy 'short-cut' towards agreeing a more ambitions environmental policy, and that conventional regulatory tools require careful integration with NEPIs.

Instrument Innovation in an Environmental Lead State: 'New' Environmental Policy Instruments in the Netherlands
ANTHONY R. ZITO, LARS BRÜCKNER, ANDREW JORDAN and RÜDIGER K.W. WURZEL

'New Environmental Policy Instruments' (NEPIs) have a vital role to play in the Netherlands, but should not be overemphasised. They remain part of a mix of instruments that retains a considerable role for the traditional command and control instruments. Dutch environmental innovation shows much evidence of gradual, adaptive learning stimulated by changes in governments, philosophies and external pressures, such as the Kyoto Agreement. Some instruments (that is, covenants) fit the Dutch institutional context and style, and its economic context, better than others, such as eco-labels.

Policy Innovation or 'Muddling Through'? 'New' Environmental Policy Instruments in the United Kingdom
ANDREW JORDAN, RÜDIGER K.W. WURZEL, ANTHONY R. ZITO and LARS BRÜCKNER

The UK began to experiment with voluntary agreements and market-based instruments much later than other northern, industrialised member states of the EU. This delayed start can be accounted for by the comparatively low level of environmental awareness in the UK throughout much of the 1980s, and the belief that domestic regulation, when suitably fine-tuned, was more than capable of addressing most domestic environmental problems. The deployment of 'new' environmental policy instruments grew significantly in the 1990s, although the UK still has comparatively few voluntary agreements. The aim of this contribution is to assess how far these tools are genuinely 'new' or not as compared to pre-existing institutional forms and policy instrument types. The findings suggest that the UK's institutional setting has restricted and strongly conditioned the development and functioning of voluntary agreements. Until recently, the same could be said of economic instruments, but the arrival of tradable permits, complex policy packages and various other eco-taxes is indicative of genuine innovation, which breaks decisively with the past.

'New' Environmental Policy Instruments: An Evolution or a Revolution in Environmental Policy?
ANDREW JORDAN, RÜDIGER K.W. WURZEL and ANTHONY R. ZITO

The popularity of 'New' Environmental Policy Instruments (NEPIs) has prompted widespread claims that contemporary environmental policy is undergoing a deep seated and long lasting revolution, characterised by a shift from environmental government to environmental governance. This study compares the adoption of NEPIs in the eight case study countries. It reveals that there are common drivers of change, but that the resulting pattern of use is highly differentiated across instrument types and countries. Very few countries are actually innovating in the way they use NEPIs; in most countries, certain types of NEPIs are either not being used or are being used but in a relatively incremental and evolutionary manner. These patterns of change are related to popular theories of comparative politics and public policy. It is concluded that a close empirical analysis of how NEPIs are actually being deployed in different national contexts, suggests that environmental governance is at best supplementing environmental government, not comprehensively supplanting it.

Notes on Contributors

Lars Brückner was a research associate in the Department of Politics and International Studies at the University of Hull, UK. He currently works as an environmental adviser in Brussels. Email: Larsbruckner @yahoo.com

Brendan Flynn is a lecturer in the Department of Political Science and Sociology, NUI, Galway. His research interests include EU environmental policy and comparative environmental policy developments. Email: brendan.flynn@ nuigalway.ie

Richard Grant is Research Officer in the School of Social Sciences and the National Europe Centre at The Australian National University. Email: Richard.Grant@anu. edu.au

Andrew Jordan manages the £2.2m ESRC Programme on Environmental Decision Making based at the CSERGE, UEA, Norwich, UK. His most recent book is *The Europeanisation of British Environmental Policy* (Palgrave, 2002). Email: a.jordan@uea.ac.uk

Elim Papadakis is Professor of Modern European Studies in the School of Social Sciences and Director of the National Europe Centre at The Australian National University. Email: Elim.Papadakis@anu.edu.au

Rauno Sairinen is a research director in the Centre for Urban and Regional Studies at the Helsinki University of Technology in Finland. Email: rauno.sairinen@hut.fi

Joseph Szarka is Senior Lecturer in the Department of European Studies, Bath University, England. His research interests cover political behaviour, environmental politics and policy-making, especially in France and the EU. He has published extensively in academic journals such as *West European Politics, Political Science* and *Espaces et sociétés*. His most recent book is *The Shaping of Environmental Policy in France* (Oxford: Berghahn, 2002). Email: J.P.Szarka@bath.ac.uk.

Rüdiger K.W. Wurzel is a lecturer in the Department of Politics and International Studies at the University of Hull, UK. His latest book is *Environmental Policy-Making in Britain, Germany and the European Union: The Europeanisation of Air and Water Pollution Control* (Manchester University Press, 2002). He is principal investigator for an ESRC funded project on 'Innovation in Environmental Governance: A Comparative Analysis of New Environmental Policy Instruments'. Email: R.K.Wurzel@hull.ac.uk

Anthony R. Zito is a lecturer in the Department of Politics, University of Newcastle, UK. He is the author of *Creating Environmental Policy in the European Union* (Macmillan). E-mail: A.R.Zito@ncl.ac.uk

Index